T0146783

IN THE MIDST OF THE STORM THERE IS PURPOSE

DESIGN INTENT UNVEILED

Yeshua Ha-Mashiach

Ambassadors4Christ

EVANGELIST DELMELODIA TIPTON

REVISED EDITION

authorHOUSE®

AuthorHouse™
1663 Liberty Drive
Bloomington, IN 47403
www.authorhouse.com
Phone: 1 (800) 839-8640

Published by AuthorHouse 08/09/2017

ISBN: 978-1-5049-7849-1 (sc)
ISBN: 978-1-5049-7847-7 (hc)
ISBN: 978-1-5049-7848-4 (e)

Library of Congress Control Number: 2016902366

Editor: Rhonda Wilson
Logo Artist: Rasheda Davis
Website: www.bvpllc.biz

Print information available on the last page.

In the Midst Of the Storm There Is Purpose

AMBASSADORS 4CHRIST APOSTOLIC TELECAST MINISTRY
Elder Delmelodia Tipton
Website: www.ambassaduer4christ.net

KJV
Scripture quotations marked KJV are from the Holy Bible, King James Version
(Authorized Version). First published in 1611. Quoted from the KJV Classic
Reference Bible, Copyright © 1983 by The Zondervan Corporation.
NIV
Scripture quotations marked NIV are taken from the Holy Bible, New International
Version®. NIV®. Copyright © 1973, 1978, 1984 by International Bible Society.
Used by permission of Zondervan. All rights reserved. [Biblica]

Strong Concordance
Vine's Concordance
Nelson's Bible dictionary
Holman's Bible Dictionary

DEDICATION

Dedicated to my Lord and Savior for His Demonstrative
Power of Love Shown In My Life Now For The
Purpose of Gathering In the Harvest; Releasing The
Impartation of the Apostolic and Prophetic Supernatural
Transfer of Healing, Counsel, Insight, Knowledge,
Grace, Truth and the Wisdom of the Demonstrated
Power of Yeshua HaMashiach (Jesus Christ).

CONTENTS

ACKNOWLEDGEMENTS

I give honor, praise, and glory unto the Lord Jesus Christ, for such a time as this, placing in my heart, a burden a passion at this appointed time to write, release and self publish my first book by the wisdom of God. I know it is God because the passion the urgency the time to birth this baby (1st book) is leaping in my spiritual womb. Holy Spirit is confirming even as I type, that it is by His leading. It has been 18 years since the premature death of my firstborn. Hallelujah, in saying that I can testify, "I know God is my strength, my refuge, my fortress and my deliverer; to Him alone I bow my heart and lay my life prostrate as a living sacrifice.

Thanks to my husband David Tipton (24yrs.) to my daughters Melissa and Aleccia Tipton for their love, patience and support during this endeavor and much gratitude and unconditional love to my mother, Lizzie Hamilton.

I give honor to Apostle Larry and Iliana Pratcher Jr., I certainly have learned and gleaned a lot from you spiritually. I would like to say thanks to you both with deep sincerity, great appreciation and honor. You have nurtured me as the Holy Spirit birth forward his gifts in me. We can see now the manifestations of what God is doing. Thank you for being a man and woman of intercession and warfare prayer. Thanks for all the corrections, pushing, encouragement, training and for preaching Holiness and Truth. You have equipped me for ministry by the leading of the Spirit of God. I am grateful that God used you to prophetically speak His destiny over me. You are a devout man and woman of God. You both are true to the calling of Yahweh (LORD). I see what God has shown you in the spirit realm. I say thank you ABBA for placing you in my path at His appointed time. You have been a trailblazer and you are passing the torch to other torch carriers.

I also give special thanks to all the Spirit filled, Spirit lead men and women of God not mentioned, to whom God has used and placed in the my path when I did not know God in the magnitude of grace that He has revealed Himself unto to me as of now; especially, as an infant in the Lord. God had me in His plan and on His mind, Glory! Yahweh (LORD) used other Spirit-filled, Spirit-lead vessels to speak a word into my spirit, shaping divine destiny, speaking forth the will of God, that I will walk in my God-given calling and office fulfilling divine assignments and not be destroyed in the wilderness. I cooperatively say a special "thank you" because you are not forgotten.

Lastly, thank you for investing in this manual in the form of a book; may more insight, revelation, strength, wisdom, counsel, understanding, knowledge, patience, hope, virtue be poured into your thirsty souls, that your reservoir might be filled with faith of expectancy that God will move on your behalf as he promised in His Word In Jesus Name.

FOREWORD

I t is with great honor and respect that I offer you this
foreword for this great resource. This is more than just
a book for good reading, but it is a great resource for
reflection and activation of faith through the storms of life. I
have had the privilege and honor to witness the growth and
spiritual maturity of Evangelist Delmelodia Tipton first-hand.
Over the past 12 years it has been so apparent of the working
of Ruach HaKodesh in this woman of God's life. This epistle
is evidence of a person that has weathered the storms that life
brings, and how one can overcome the storms of life with the
help of Yeshua. This epistle will serve as a valuable resource
for anyone that finds themselves battling the storms of life.
Many times, we do not fully understand why we have to go
through hard times, trials, and tribulations. And this drives
us to ask the ancient old question to God, "Why me?" This
epistle will answer many of your questions of why me and
more importantly, how do we navigate through these storms
and enter into the rest of Yahweh. Evangelist Tipton has been
well trained by Ruach HaKodesh in trusting in the Lord to
walk with you in the hardest times of life. It is my belief that

after reading this epistle, you will have more understanding of the process of maturation and sanctification as the Ruach of God teaches us how to stop going through storms and start growing through them. This epistle will bless your life. I declare that you will be blessed from the many tears, prayers and dedication it took to write an end-time epistle. Enjoy & Receive!

Apostle Larry Pratcher, Jr.
TBOC (The Body of Christ) MINISTRIES

PREFACE

I greet and welcome each of you personally to a life changing experience that I encountered not by will or by force, but by chance. Life happens to everyone without consent. Every crisis is an opportunity to experience the Presence of Yahweh in your life and receive divine impartations through the Power of Divine Persuasion, Waiting on the Lord, Pressing in the prayer chamber and A.S.K. I believe as you read this teaching epistle, you will find that divine purpose avails supernaturally beyond our human facilities, understanding, knowledge, wisdom, imagination, mind or strength when a leap of faith is put into action, LEAP! "Let Go and Let God." I am no better than the next person. I've realized I can do nothing without the Lord being on my side and me being in the Lord Jesus. God is no respect of persons, in Him there isn't any contradiction, favoritism or partiality. What He did for me; He will do for anyone who turns to Him in faith. We can't pick or choose which trials and tribulations we want or when they can start or finish. Many things can happen in a person's life unexpectantly that can be horrific or even of great disturbance. The unveiling of crisis in life comes with no heads up, no preparation, no warning to brace your heart, your mind, your emotions, your stability, your finances or your well-being. No! Chance Happens To Us All At Any Given Time Or Moment! It Warns Us Not! Like A Pregnant Woman's Labor Pains…It's Suddenly Upon You At Once eating away at your soul and possibly all that you have worked so hard to build and secure yourself in this life. However, in that season I remind you in all that comes take hold of GOD unswerving Hand that pours fresh oil into new skin for His anointing and divine purpose to come forth out of your pain and suffering. Faith comes by hearing and hearing by the Word of God. Divine revelation comes through the tunnel of experience with the Lord.

Ecclesiastes 9:11-12a
The race is not to the swift, nor the battle to the strong, neither bread to the wise, nor wealth to the smart, nor recognition to the skilled or men of understanding. Instead time and circumstances meet them (us) all. For man know not his time (season appointed)…

During the grievous moment of the passing of our baby boy, Isaac DeShaun Tipton, I had begun to write letters (1997) to God about Isaac. This was part of releasing and healing. After writing a few, I heard in my spirit "write a book". I had no idea what that consisted of totally, no knowledge of how to write a book. So I took the thought no further than just a thought. Little did I know Holy Spirit was going to use my story for The Lord's Glory to usher within measure mysteries of the Kingdom of Yahweh into my spirit for external and internal purposes. Holy Spirit was birthing forth ministry out from me toward others with urgency of the power of deliverance within Him to break chains and to set the captives free after He dealt severely with me. No matter what type of winds have blown your way, pain and agony, it has no lines of demarcation. Each storm may be different in event, but the common factor for souls that suffer is the aftermath of the pain that can rise and destroy a person emotionally, socially, economically, as well as, spiritually. I've tasted through some of my life's experiences things that will call for the very Hand of GOD to rescue any person from the after effects or duration of overwhelming emotions as though I had been to hell and back. That is the very reason this teaching deliverance manual was birth in order to unveil the mystery to others the way of Supernatural spiritual triumph over tragedies residue that overflows in the soul to bring total healing…and because what the Spirit of God has done for me, through me, in me and to me through this experience. It is His wisdom on display before the eyes of many others through the fire of purification; yet, it is ordained that I (you) would come out with a revelatory knowing of who God really is in the power of His grace. The Father's dealing with those that suffer in the faith as a son (no gender, covenant boundaries in grace) to directs us on a path that brings about perpetual spiritual awareness, transformation, divine wisdom, divine strength, purpose driven power and a true awakening in Him. We all want the experience and closeness to ABBA, which involves suffering a little while.

1 Peter 5:6-7

Humble yourselves therefore under the mighty hand of God, that He may exalt you in due time: Casting all your cares upon Him, for He cares for you.

WOW! That's the part we do not see, want or comprehend when we are in the storm fires that are permitted by sovereignty of Yahweh to come. Yes, it may sound way off; even harsh, I thought so too, until ABBA delivered my soul; better yet, snatched me out of deep sorrows, hopelessness and grief and begin to give me pieces of divine revelation over time not just about my storm fires, but a glimpse in the realm of the spirit about the residue of powers behind that the storms that desire sift your life. I had no knowledge of the power of spiritual discernment or soaking in His Presence. Many, like my self at the time, don't know or really realize how the storms are the spiritual thermostat energy pressures in the spirit realm allowed into the physical realm of life are so powerful. Those undetected forces behind the scene will break down an individual emotionally, spiritually, mentally and physically. They will to live, kill dreams, relationships even desires to be productive or move forward. Since I've been in such a place and have came out through the power of God, with much slobbering, much crying, groaning and moaning, some prayer, some faith; I've gained revelation about who the One True Living God is. It is He who empowers and visits by His Holy Spirit those that rely on Him and seek Him through Christ Jesus. I am obligated, honored and privileged to use my story and testimony for the Glory of God for the advancement of others and the manifestation of the power of deliverance. The process is not easy, glamorous, friendly, smooth nor instant, but GOD will do it and His bound by His Word. My testimony today is the LORD removed my ashes and gave me beauty. He will deliver you out of the pit and set you in a place filled with royal beneficiary wealth that your spiritual well may be filled with Living Water from the Spring Fountain that gives abundant life. No matter what comes this wealth carries the believer victoriously throughout life hidden in Christ.

In the Midst of the Storm There is Purpose- for that cause- all of the things He revealed- I will share abroad in chapter seven the valley: high risk pregnancy, prenatal tests to determine abnormities, fear of the unknown, sleepless nights, high income to extreme low income, not being able to fully work, husband's job relocation, business took a turn; Isaac's birth, death, and burial. Amazingly, God's Hand of deliverance, protection, grace, truth and love was at work through all these different windstorms. And the LORD is still working deliverance miracles today. You are one; even if you don't realize it or see it yet. It's not a matter of if, but a matter of when the soul suffering makes the decision to take a giant leap of faith in the face of any opposition, tragedy, bitterness, set backs, hopelessness, lack of courage, embarrassment, deep hurt, pity and agony that GOD will show up with His heavenly host to engage in the unseen destroying demonic forces that seek to destroy us in the wilderness and to bring that soul into a wealthy place of peace in supernatural knowledge of Him.

Psalms 34:19
Many are the afflictions of the righteous, but the Lord delivers them out of them all.

John 16:33
Jesus said these things I have spoken unto you, that in me ye might have peace. In the world ye shall have tribulation: but be of good cheer; I have overcome the world.

CHAPTER ONE

FAITH SPHERE

The storm is there for the initiation of the faith sphere governance and your spiritual probation period. This is the period of testing allowed for substance approval and testing. When a soul is genuinely governed by faith, faith will take us to places that were not on our map. GOD will use the disqualified, cruel, lifeless and hopeless situations to unveil His nature, influence, supremacy and atmosphere. The LORD has a way of using the storms of life to unveil His mystery to souls that will cleave to Him from that place of interruption {**Deuteronomy 4:4**}. Suffering like desperation will call for a SHIFT which starts with us. Although the storm is seemingly gloomy and bares no light God's divine intent is to bring increase with fruitfulness to the totality of your being and to stir an unquenchable fire seeded by Him from within our soul. *As you begin your study through this*

manual, you will learn to exercise God's ordained power in the midst of storms and how to rise up in your God given authority in times of current or prolonged pain and suffering in the sphere of faith You will learn how to recognize and overcome the pitfalls which targets the mind and emotions. You will learn how to draw nearer to dwell in His Presence obtaining healing. You will learn in desperate seasons the call for the bowing of your heart, will and mind; and how to really let go and let JESUS. You will learn Kingdom strategies mandated by Holy Spirit to counteract what the evil one means for your bad. You will learn the spiritual blessings that are titled deed and sealed in the Blood of Yeshua (JESUS) the Christ for every believer to demonstrate in any wilderness season. Open your hearts and minds to receive the Ruach Hakodesh (Hebrew ROO-akh ha-KOH-desh, Holy Spirit) impartations. Transformation is bound to take place, divine paradigms will shift you, new depths will be accelerated in you, word of knowledge and understanding is being sown by the Holy Spirit as you partake. Healing of the mind, heart, spirit and deliverance is coming forth from the rule of Yahweh to your atmosphere. The storm is the season and atmosphere that the LORD will use to teach, cultivate, develop personal integrity, to clear the mind and demonstrate His divine authority, dominion, purpose, plan and thought toward and through us about Him. He ordained it before time existed that the Ecclesia *(Church, called out ones)* is "to be" used for His Glory, filled with His Glory and that the called out ones' steps are "to be" ordered by Him who endorsed the call. It's the King's release of increase. Fret not; the Lion of Judah *(Hebraic title for JESUS)* is our Victor, who will lead us through every valley and over every mountain victoriously.

GOD withholds no good thing from souls that trust and obey Him through bearable or unbearable times…when hope seems lost {**Psalm 84:11**}. GOD searches for hungry hearts and minds to enter His atmosphere for total healing and restoration. As you indulge whole heartedly in your quiet time with the LORD, you will feel God's Presence visit you. Some will feel His Presence in tears, urgency, a spiritual awakening, and a thirst to draw closer to ABBA or a holy conviction from His Spirit. While many will ponder on the divine revelations; take to heart the prophetic declarations, pray the prophetic prayers and others will be drawn back in repentance to the household of faith faithfully and empowered. Faith mixed with the ingredients of submission, commitment and prayer will lead you into the place of divine favor and rest for the soul. The faith dominion and faith sphere call for a supernatural shift to accept the reality of what one cannot fully comprehend naturally or see physically.

Habakkuk 2:4

Behold the proud, his soul is not upright in him; but the just shall live by his faith.

First, the Kingdom of Yahweh must be a faith reality to you in order to lay claim of the inheritance that activates the Kingdom Heavenly Courts in the atmosphere. If you are born of Christ, filled with His Spirit, then He has qualified you for his inheritance and placed the inheritance of His Kingdom within you for the purpose of flowing out of you. There is nothing stale, foul, stagnated, still-born or at a stand-still operating in the Kingdom of Yahweh. That's how real it needs to be in your heart. Just as trees are supernaturally uprooted in windstorms…blessings are released supernaturally on account of faith that overcomes windstorms. The Kingdom is Righteousness, Demonstration, Light, Power, Electricity and Energy in constant mobility by the Ruach Hakodesh *(Holy Spirit)*. The Spirit of Christ lives on the inside of each believer to will the kingdom of Yahweh's Government by the Power of Holy Spirit through you into the midst. A believer's paradigm must shift from the physical dimension to the faith dimension in Christ Jesus to execute the Kingdom into our situations. The Kingdom paradigm will lead believers to react the opposite of what any windstorm may mentally or visually demand while blowing; putting faith into motion.

Hebrew word for English term Kingdom
Mamlakah: royal dominion, sovereignty, reign

Greek word for English term Kingdom
Basileia: Kingship, territory of a King, authority, rule of Christ in the hearts of believers

Faith, the **supernatural access substance**, is the target when we face afflictions. It is the substance and evidence that authorizes a soul to shift out of any sphere- territory that works to overrule the Rule of Heaven. Nothing remains inactive when faith deposit is employed. One thing I can assure you of in the journey of life, when abnormal measures of suffering come upon us and we don't know what to do, how to handle them, which way to go or who to confide; in that matter, God-kind of faith is required. Faith supernaturally reverses the odd's powers to control and releases His created order designed for success. Faith domain and power is based on the laws of the universal sphere of Yahweh's thought, purpose and covenant in JESUS. The sphere of faith relates to the supernatural, spiritual domain, territory and monarchy unified by the Supreme-Being attributes and nature.

The only power that will conquer emotional after effects, help us to overcome all the sorrow and all the grief is the Power of GOD! The faith sphere is the atmosphere where the impossibilities are *Already* made possible. It starts in the mind and heart of an individual first. Our minds and hearts are key components in the midst of any storm that rages in one's life. God's plan for the sphere of the mind is to become a one cell unit in hard times with His thought- mind. What enters the mind- soul and remains contributes to your course in life. The *mind* like the arena of battles functions like the reins on a horse *(to control, direct, guide)* and like the function of kidneys *(to filter, cleanse, detoxify and eliminate all chemical impurities, filth and carnal-minded pollution)*. Spiritual blockage will cause the mind and heart to become faint or inactive in faith substance power. In the midst of storms that come and go in life, a *soul* can be left in an emotional uproar in mind and body if the blockage *(which is spiritual first, then natural)* remains spiritually untreated. The faith sphere reality of God's thought must become our reality in this physical sphere during valley experiences. Bondage and freedom cannot coexist in the God-faith sphere. Therefore, meet Him from where you are, not to remain in that same state, but in order to enlarge, be elevated and advance in Him. This is a prize reward of suffering. Although it looks bad, even emotionally disturbing, the storm is there to direct you into the faith sphere; out from your thoughts- mind. The **nous** must connect; become one with the LORD.

Greek word for the English term Mind
Nous: seat of thought, perception, reasoning, will, feeling, conscious
Dianoia: sub-conscious, spirit, faulty renewed by the Spirit
Phronema: to think, imagination

It takes the Supernatural Power of Yahweh to interrupt; manifesting divine deliverance and healing to the **nous, nephesh** and physical body. When the **psuche** is restored to health, then deliverance of the **nephesh** and body can shift into divine order. Yet, with Yahweh-kind of faith things that may seem "to be" bleak to the visual are made possible with Yahweh faith-power…YESHUA.

Greek word for the English term Soul
Psuche *(psyche)*: mind, heart, being, personhood

Hebrew word for the term Soul
Nephesh: breath, spirit, living being

The Bible speaks of faith in dimensional levels. Dimensions which are spiritual spheres encountered during difficult experiences. A believer must engage forcefully in those seasons into the Divine Kingdom Jurisdiction Faith Dimension and elevate to the realm of expectation that moves GOD to intervene on the believer's behalf.

Dimensional Functions of Faith
• Saving faith
• Common faith
• Human faith
• Weak/ Wavering faith
• Strong/ Unwavering faith
• Abundant/ Increasing faith
• Gift of faith
• Great faith
• Little faith
• Dead faith

Yahweh *(divine)* faith is the supernatural **Gift of Faith** supplied by Ruach HaKodesh *(Holy Spirit)* that impacts the soul to take the step, to do, move, act and respond regardless of the odds you may face in order to overcome a prolonged delivery of the unraveling of a situation. Depending on what you are facing to overcome will demand a higher level of faith capacity to impact the supply for release. Believers who experience an increasing measure have been conditioned in what I call the spiritual incubator process: stretching, to trust the Ruach *(Spirit)* and not flesh, follow GOD, wait, bear the consequences in hope, reflection, change, growth and produce by active faith. My husband and I experienced the physical incubator procedure when our baby boy was not only born prematurely, but was actually smaller than He should have been the day he was born. Isaac's condition *(chapter 6)* took him beyond the normal premature baby care. The incubator served to help prepare him inwardly and outwardly in order to live and respond to the elements outside of the incubator by functioning properly inwardly. The method causes changes to take place that we cannot see with the natural eye, but we can observe the thriving of the one who has been under such conditions. There are changes that take place from within to empower you to prevail against that which may attempt to arrest you from the inside and outside. The spiritual incubator process serves in maturing the believer and causing our inner-man to rise to the occasion set before us in Christ. The carnal-mind comprehends this as blind faith, useless, since the progress is without one's own ability and intellectuality; the physical capability of not seeing the next move or going through without learning. However, through scripture study and divine wisdom, I disagree with the blind faith theory. Faith is Spiritual and Supernatural. Therefore, faith sees spiritually and afar off for those who believe. It's our new sight. This sphere breathes divine wisdom, revelation and activations. As the LORD brought me out, although, He was carrying me all along in my storm, this is what Ruach Hakodesh *(Holy Spirit)* reveals to open hearts: First, you follow because your inner ear is responsive to hearing *(present tense)* **I AM** summons you. Second, because my voice and Presence *(the Lord)* is not like an imaginary friend to you. And thirdly, because when I *(Spirit)* gave you me *(Spirit)*, it is also me *(the Lord)* who gives you sight beyond your natural sight. I *(the Lord)* created in you a mind *(will)* to step out of the sphere of human limitations and to step into the faith dimension not blindly, but in assurance by responding to the leading of Holy Spirit from a deep reverence- awe of the **Sovereignty of I AM** revelation. Now, you may not understand this revelation at this moment, but when our spiritual eyes and ears become open we recognize and discern our weakness of not being capable of rescuing ourselves out of the trenches of what seems like the jaws of hell. We readily recognize and understand we need to be empowered by the higher divine reality, Almighty GOD, for change to exist in matters of long or short term residue. The faith sphere releases Yahweh's kingdom reality, promises, glory, revelation, knowledge, boldness, dominance, order, access, guidance, protection, wisdom, favor, vision, strength, peace and destiny.

The Ruach Hakodesh unfolds the revelation of the mystery of the Kingdom of Yahweh which is at hand through the sphere of faith divine. The Kingdom is a royal territory ruled by KING JESUS with unlimited Power of restoration for the royal priesthood. In order for us, the royal priesthood, to perceive divine revelation and divine counsel we must comply by the principles that our Heavenly Father expressed through Yeshua HaMashiach in faith...offering up spiritual sacrifices at all times. **The Bible tells us {Colossians 3:23} and whatsoever you do, do it heartily, as to the LORD, and not unto man.** The LORD faithfulness is guaranteed to meet the demand His children face with a multifold supply.

The storm holds no power in the heart of an active believer; Yahweh divine purpose prevails.

When the Ruach of Yahweh speaks into your spirit that is His supernatural breathe, breathing divine power and knowledge into your inward parts for the strengthening of the inner-man. And what He speaks is His divine covenant purpose concerning believers. The breath of the Ruach *(Spirit)* is like medicine to our souls; as marrow is to the bones. And when you partake of that prescribed prescription spoken that is wisdom's deposit into your spiritual account for a prosperity withdrawal. Empowered-faith releases Kingdom benefits of healing to believers from their heavenly account. GOD, who is Wisdom, is able to give revelatory understanding of a believer's course at the proper time for their spiritual wellbeing and territory expansion. Whatever you're suffering keep your eye single on the Author and the Finisher of your faith, KING JESUS. This sphere of faith leads us to soberness and discipline, both spiritually and physically. The believer's course is started by and with faith. The believer's course must remain in faith. And the believer's course in Christ must end in faith no matter what happens. **The Bible tells us {Proverbs 3:13} blessed is the soul who finds wisdom and gets understanding.**

Hebraic Personal Proper Name of GOD of Israel: Yahweh
(yeh-ho-vaw)
YHWH (Y-H-V-H): transcendence, self Existent,
Eternal, source and foundation of all being,
infinite, Covenant LORD God_YHVH
Yod-Hey-Vav-Hey
"to be" to cause to become or come to pass, exist
God of Abraham, God of Isaac and God of Jacob

Greek word for the English term Saint
Hagios: set apart (by or for God, distinguished,
distinct) special to the Lord, holy, sacred, blameless;
likeness of the nature, character with the Lord,
different from the world, like the Lord

Study Review:

1.) What does the phrase "faith sphere" means? Explain.

_____

_____

_____

2.) How do you gain access into the faith sphere? Explain.

_____

_____

_____

3.) Will that sphere move God? _____. If yes, does the answer move you to change in order to transition? _____. How? Why? Explain.

_____

_____

_____

4.) By you answering the questions honestly, what did you receive from Holy Spirit? _____.

5.) Write your insight below for your record. Anytime Holy Spirit reveals something to you, write it down; don't take it for granted. This is something that will become useable directly and indirectly in your present future.

_____

_____

_____

6.) Write John 10:10…recognize the function of the adversary, satan.

_____

_____

_____

7.) Write, learn, memorize and dissect Ephesians 2:6-7. It's the Ecclesia's reality at all times in all seasons.

_____

_____

_____

8.) Write, learn, memorize and dissect Ephesians 1:19-21. It's the Ecclesia's reality at all times in all seasons.

_____

_____

_____

9.) How does faith come? Write the scripture and verse and rehearse the revelation daily.

_____

_____

_____

CHAPTER TWO

EMPOWERED BY FAITH

Empowerment and faith acts as one unit of force working for the common cause within the children of Yahweh in Messiah *(Christ)* to bring us to an expected end of victory. No human storm experience can be battled and won effectively without these components working effectively. **Empowered** *(endunamoo like dynamoo)* faith is an authorized strength or force that we don't see or can fully explain or describe which is greater than our common strength. It is the only power that will supersede any other influence that is of threat to an heir of Yeshua *(Hebraic **Yeshua**: Salvation, to rescue, deliverer, Jesus)* in distressful seasons of chaos in life. Believe it; it is the **Authority of the Spirit** *(Hebraic **Ruach/ Neshamah**: Air, Wind, Mind)* of the Living GOD activation. Again, It's Supernatural! It is one thing to say you believe, yet do nothing. But it is certainly another thing for what you say you believe "to be" active in your life and manifest before your very eyes. These are two totally different reality spheres with consequences depending on your response. Ruach Hakodesh will impart to believers seeking him an intensified measure of the gift in the midst of windstorms. It is a filling of the Supernatural invasion that is above and beyond the natural know how, perception, thought or scope of the human mind. When we experience and attempt to handle trials in our natural ability, they will often expose our weakness, our nature, our outlook, temper, attitudes, qualities and behavior, our leaks; letting us know that we will not make it to the other side if we don't completely put our trust in GOD. It is better to have the Lord with you going through anything on this side than not to have him when facing hell fires and windstorms in your life. When He is with us and working from within us, greater and greatness will abound, because He's great. **The Bible tells us {Romans 8:31} if GOD be for us, the believer, who or what can be against us.** Remember, this is manifested as you surrender to attract His attention to act. You must yield your right in order for His right of way to come into your heart matter and situation. **The Bible tells us {Isaiah 40:29 NIV} he gives strength to the weary and increases the power of the weak. {Isaiah 40:31 NIV} But those who hope in the LORD will renew their strength. They will soar on wings like eagles; they will run and not grow weary, they will walk and not faint.** Circumstances we face may appear equipped to take us under; on the other hand, with the Lord GOD on our side He will work in our favor a good return if the soul faints not. **Jesus declares in John 15:5 apart from Him we can do nothing.** Faith keeps the believer connected and grounded in the True Vine with evidence…**Evidence.**

Storms function as a tool for the Fire of Yahweh to begin perfecting His work through us by pruning away, curing us, making us spiritually aware, focus, making the path of mixed up priorities straight and tightening the loose screws and hinges. Loose screws can be defined as anything that is unbalanced in your life that attempts to offset itself in your future-present state to render you faint…wobbling, feeble, unsteady or immovable in your spirit and not secure to stand, move or conquer in the physical realm. This is a work and trap of the evil one; to render any soul paralyzed in capacity or to make one impaired in thought-mind so that soul will not perform as it was created to do. Therefore, when something else comes your way you must be more closely entwined in Holy Spirit than before, mounting increasingly in the Grace of Yahweh provided through Christ and saturated by Ruach HaKodesh. Empowered faith positions believers **"to be"** *(to exist in the reality of the Spirit)* supernaturally powerful, holds the soul together, alert and make us fit to stand in resistance against opposition and to usher in the Kingdom of GOD.

As long as we exist in this physical sphere troubles, storms and hardship will locate any person's address regardless of age, creed, belief, race, statue and neighborhood, rich or poor. I am persuaded through experience and Holy Ghost revelation that earth has no sorrows, no pains and no distresses or burdens that heaven cannot heal. What is in us and what we are made of, good or bad, will be exposed under pressure and by the supernatural chastening rod of sweet Holy Spirit. Beloved of Yahweh in Christ Jesus, anyone may have speech that sounds of faith or sound apart, but faith must be activated from within flowing without by divine persuasion of Yahweh through the Spirit of Christ. We cannot proclaim that we have divine-faith and have no fruit of it. Fruit produced is the evidence of the seed that is planted. Empowered by faith is the Kingdom Governmental demonstration by the Ruach *(Spirit, Mind, Breath of God)* to position a believer forward in spite of current distresses to the next dimension that Yahweh, the Father, has designed for that set time. When the carnal nature, fleshly mindset, wants you to freeze up, it is Yahweh's faith...pointing to the Cross...that stands firm like concrete and is able to penetrate through difficulties for the assurance of a come back; directing you in your GOD ordained destiny. An appointed time can be missed by us if we are not in tuned to the move of the Holy Spirit. Sometimes when believers miss GOD and remain in an out of time- *season (set or appointed time)* it can be due to several factors: 1.) we did not know- recognize the voice of the Lord 2.) fear or not recognizing the timing of Yahweh 3.) simple disobedience. As we **walk** with the Lord Jesus and learn obedience and put into practice discipline we become more sensitive to the spiritual riches of the Master *(ADONAI)*. Yahweh *(GOD)* has awesome purposes for trials. Another purpose GOD allows windstorms is to sharpen the child of GOD in the spiritual blessings pertaining to life, godliness and His **Royal Ruling Governmental Power** in the earth. These things are to be exhibited through the believer's spirit, mind, relationships, conversation and lifestyle.

Empowered by faith is another level of divine-faith that puts a demand from your inner man upon the Kingdom of Yahweh *(Jehovah, LORD)* to respond during a crisis; and sends a judgment call to the kingdom of darkness by declaring what YHWH has *Already* declared to be established on your behalf because the faith- power is Yahweh. The empowerment of faith is an aggressive delegated response of action that a believer is called to from their resurrected position in Yeshua HaMashiach *(Jesus, Messiah) in* the third heaven as warriors against oppositional turmoil from the second heaven while in the earth realm. Our battle isn't against the doctors, co-workers, boss, teachers, police, family, friends, parents, children or spouse. The struggle or battle is not flesh and blood. It is spiritual {**Ephesians 6:12**}. Even though our storms are natural, there is a commotion stirring behind the scene. The divine empowerment is the **expression** of Holy Spirit's Governing **Rule of Dominion** working in your favor.

If you are breathing that's a sure sign letting you know you need faith and faith is present. How many people do you know who can cause breath to enter and exit through their lungs at their own will? Faith operates similar to breathing it cannot be taken for granted. We cannot see the vapor of **breath** *(Greek **Pneuma**: Wind, Spirit, spirit)* within its function, but we certainly know there is a mystery behind it. Nothing that exists can exist without the Eternal Self-Existing One. Faith existence exists in Him, without God-faith we can't do anything of ourselves at anytime. We will have many experiences in life that will have to be dealt with in faith and only faith. Life will present to you situations that will tear you to pieces if they are not handled by divine faith. You don't necessarily have to be looking for something to happen; as long as you live something unexpected might show up out of nowhere in your space. I can testify that trouble can trace you, but I also testify that when troubles show up there should be a faith-power residue, a spiritual uproar that is stirred within you, that is superior to the trouble. That divine power is connected to the lawyer in the heavenly courtroom. Faith empowerment is the logic, thought, vision, arrangement and purpose of the Eternal One concerning those of faith. Faith is established to manifest the Rule of Christ for covenant believers. In seasons of suffering, as well as, up time, I want to encourage you to be connected and remain connected to the source that will supply every need. He is the great **I Am That I Am** *(I will be)*. The LORD will be all things to you in any given burden if you step out of you and step into him. I feel the anointing, I'll say it again, **"If You Step Out of Self Awareness and Step Into Him Awareness."** That's A New Day! Hallelujah! Somebody is receiving that activation. ABBA in JESUS is always willing and ready to disclose, mantle and clothe His character- nature upon and within His chosen people.

If we say we have faith and trust in the Lord the opportunity for the evidence to be proven will appear. The **Law of Faith** says you have endowed *(invested, favor, grace)* power in you to stand firm against the pressures that stare you in the face during episodes of pain, hardship or suffering. The **Law of Faith** charged me to stand against every neonatal test that pointed me to abortion, disappointment, shame, pain and grief. Faith, which is an ingredient of Yahweh, is the unseen substance that breaks through the hardest crisis. Just as concrete is solid like a crisis, pure faith breaks through that which came to crush with benefits to preserve, fulfill and bless you and others through you. The strength and power and source are not of this world sphere, but of ABBA, authorized faith. The empowerment of faith is what qualifies believers to press and push through all storms and distress in a lifetime, but it must be recognized and displayed in the life of the one who believes and trusts the Lord when all else says otherwise. Others prayers are wonderful and needed, but there will come a time when ***The LORD Says, "I Want to Hear from You, From Your Heart to My Throne. I Want You To Touch Me And In Return I Will Touch You."*** Faith is the lifestyle and the life-line of the covenant believer. Beloved, there is a word in your womb to announce openly to the heavens. You are commissioned, entitled, delegated, ordered and empowered by faith to act on the Word of faith in action in all circumstances; **knowing that all *(the bad and good)* things work together for the good to them that love the Lord and are called according to his purpose {Romans 8:28}.** GOD is not a liar what He promises He will perform. Yet, the promises of Yahweh are conditional. All things working together is the promise, but the condition stated above is to them that love the Lord and are called according to His purpose, not the purpose of the world or our own fleshly purposes. The condition and the promise and the heart must be in alignment. Love is rooted in Yahweh's holiness shown through Yeshua; and our obedience is rooted in love. Time will pass, but purpose will keep on living.

In 1996-1997 before the purpose was ever revealed, I experienced a heavy trial going through what is called "a high risk pregnancy, Isaac's birth and death." Faith authorized me not only to face each ordeal through the process, but upheld me through all the hurt, pain, agony and suffering. I clutched, pressed and held on to all I knew, which was faith and hope. I was in training to learn how to hold on beyond what I saw, what I heard, felt and thought. GOD wants you, the **Church** *(Greek: **Ecclesia**, the Body of Christ)* to become one with faith and hope; holding on faithfully regardless of the disappointments, pain and suffering. The Lord had to show himself mightily to me during this crisis. No season of distress feels good in the present stages of it; yet, the LORD in the storms will teach all His children how to hold up under weights of pressures, because tribulation will come to America in which we live. We must know personally how to faithfully hold-on and how to position the mind under suffering in the Power of His Might. He will bring justice. Yeshua's question is "Will He Find Faith in the Earth *(your heart)* When He Return?" The Holy Spirit through suffering teaches and equips the believer to become sons of GOD; an intense growth spurt of being lead consciously by the Spirit. When experiencing extreme trials and tribulations in your life with divine-faith and perseverance, you will be empowered to leap over mountains that were impossible to clear in your natural state of mind. It is the Holy Spirit who imparts the soul supernaturally to see light_ the supplying_ in the darkest valley. **The Bible tells us {Psalm 23:4} Even though I walk through the valley of the shadow of death I will fear no evil: for thy art with me, Your rod and Your staff they**

comfort me. The measure is supernatural, Rise! The things that are trying to destroy your judgment and peace will be conquered through perseverance in divine-faith. Before you emerge in the power of the Gift of faith you must experience the baptism of being **submerged** in the power of the Gift of faith. This gift is given of the Spirit; not self originated or willed. Everyone experiences a degree of some type of faith. Remember, there are different measures, levels, functions and heights of faith *(view chart few pages back)*. Grace virtues which are planted as grace and truth will take on the process called spiritual germicide in the heart- soul of man. The planting of what will come forth must first go into the pit of the heart like heat or radiation as fertilizer to stimulate the inner man. It is the fertilizing spiritual seed incubator transitioning awakening for a spiritual increase to avail for the maturing and duration of going in or coming through a crisis. Afterwards, a birthing or manifestation takes place. Over a period of time, the Lord began to make known to me in fragments of His perfect work that He had begun to work in me by the touch of His outstretched arm during the process of my trial under great pressure. Holy Spirit put pieces of the puzzle together on my behalf that pointed me in more precise steps into the depths of ministry and holiness.

In the life cycle, many of us will experience winds of change. These winds will come in different forms that can cause exceedingly mild to great damage financially, mentally, emotionally or physically. Storms will challenge any person level of security; money, wealth, jobs, earthly riches, bank accounts, social security or welfare checks. Which are all temporal things; here today, gone tomorrow. How safe really are you? How secure do you think you have it made? What happens when all we have turns out not to be enough at all? What happens when all the savings or credit accounts are maxed out and other resource doors are closed? I have been in that sinking wrecked ship with holes in the bottom of it on several occasions. And I have come to realize faith is the soul's security source not material things or people or spouses or jobs. Faith supernaturally releases blessings; and unlocks what is locked or held up. **Faith Is Your Wealth Currency and Security In This World of Uncertainties and the Time to Come Like A Passport.** As the Church truly walks the path of the LORD and embraces it, many of us will not be so easily entangled in the distresses of not having enough, but will engage in the truth that all my needs are met according to the riches in Christ Jesus. Yeshua sees the need, but He also sees the condition of the heart. How to be content {**Philippians 4:11**} in whatever circumstance one may find himself is learned and taught by the Ruach Hakodesh *(Holy Spirit)*. After while, abased through the garment of humility and supernatural revelation recognizing that FAITH will see the fervent believer through all cases. The spiritual alignment for Kingdom manifestation is waiting for your posture to shift. The shifting is dual, in your mind- **nous** and in your actions. The dual shift works together by the knitting of the WORD. It's natural, as well as, spiritual. The Spirit is subject to you; therefore, make your mind, body and *soul (psuche, appetite)* subject to the Spirit of Christ {**1 Thessalonians 5:19**}. The believer must reverse the order. Yeshua is Head of the Ecclesia; not the church *(you)* head of Yeshua *(Jesus)*

HaMashiach *(Hebrew Messiah-Anointed One: Greek Christos).* You are the tabernacle of the Lord; His Spirit dwells in the believer to fill you with Himself. And because we leak due to the flesh we need the infilling of Holy Spirit continually on a kinship level {**Ephesians 5:18; Acts 13:52**}.

1 Corinthians 6:19

Do you not know that your bodies are the temples of the Holy Spirit, who is in you, whom you have received from God? You are not your own.

1 Corinthians 3:16

Don't you know that you yourselves are God's temple and that the Spirit dwells in your midst?

We never know where our faith thermostat is until windstorms or fire storms of life come raging against us directly or indirectly. Mild or great storms reveal all types of impurities of the heart that surface during an environmental climate shift *(change that effects your livelihood),* as well as, our frailties. These climate shifts take us out of our so called normal or comfort zones. A major purpose when the winds of change come is to bring change. Another major change is to uproot the soul of the outer-man's *(soulish)* behavior, insecurities and thoughts springing forth the character of the inner-man or the new creature in Christ. Our faith level is constantly being challenged to produce in us abundance of faith and faith that is effective. The grain of a mustard seed produces beyond measure. It never stops increasing because the divine substance is a life giving form. That is the kingdom illustration of how the mustard seed of faith is to function within our heart in any type of trial in which believers face today. Now, we would be at fault if the process did not work. We are the soil and the divine-faith seed is liken unto a mustard seed grain. We can request a lot of things in prayer, yet for some reason never receive the answers to the petitions. And sometimes when the Lord is silent to your prayer petitions that don't necessarily mean He did not hear your plea, but maybe a caution that you need to seek Him, wait, bathe and marinade the request in prayer, meditation and/ or the studying of His WORD. The Ruach *(Spirit)* of Yahweh will reveal.

Several Reasons Prayers Go Unanswered
• Praying out of the spirit of fear
• Not Praying According to the Will of GOD
• Unbelief, Backslidden
• Anxious, Impatient
• Inconsistency in prayer
• Think God will not hear to answer
• Unforgiving heart
• Double mindedness
• Double tongue
• Sinful- Compromising lifestyle
• Pride, Unrepentant

Faith works to turn our will in a great way to the wheel in the middle of a wheel which turns and attracts supernaturally… melting to become one with the knowledge and Will of God that gives direction. Faith authorizes the soul to approach the Faithful One with acceptances. **Christ is the object of faith**, not material things or people. **The Bible tells us {Matthew 17:20} truly I tell you, if you have faith as small as a mustard seed, you can say to this mountain, Move from here to there, and it will move. Nothing will be impossible to you.** You have an alternative to let your faith fade away by going with the flow of the world or choose to be prepared by faith acting on that foundation which securely holds you up no matter what comes your way. You may not physically see it yet, but divine help is *already* available with covenant blessings for you. Let that be your charge to shift in thought and in action leading from your heart. Even in the storm, we have a vital role to participate in order to move Yahweh. The LORD is always moving. However, it is impossible to please Him without faith *(divine)* being present **{Hebrew 11:6}**. When you ask, seek and knock with consistency and persistence that is enacting diligence upward to the LORD not outwardly toward man. The Supernatural gift- Yahweh's faith, like a key, it accesses doors. Therefore, we must search by engaging in the Will to see according to birthright what belongs to us in Christ. What is blocked in the heavens that belong to you as a child of Yahweh through the Royal Bloodline of Yeshua? Now that you recognize you have blessings blocked that belong to you for your deliverance and to be restored better than before, you will have to walk in this capacity of power for that level of release. We have no control over the performance of deliverance; when or how the answers to our prayers manifest themselves. This is where practicing trust, leaning on JESUS and learning to persevere comes into action. Wow, serious business! It's up to us personally to come into agreement with the **Law of Faith**. And that's a victory lap of praise. Faith Equals Victory!

Divine-faith is a jurisdictional rule of the government of Yahweh *(LORD)*. **The Bible tells us {Romans 10:17} so then faith comes by hearing and hearing by the Word of God.** This lets you know you must hear Truth **repetitiously** and receive Truth for yourself. Remember, faith is an inherent lifestyle. You must listen, hear and apply faith that comes by hearing to your problem upon arrival. This is activation of developing a spiritual ear to hear what the Spirit of the Lord is saying to the believer. If you fail the test, dust yourself off, learn and start over again from a pure heart and clean hands. 1.) First, listen with your natural ear 2.) Second, hear with your spiritual ear and receive it into your spirit as the Truth making it applicable when you face crisis, hardship, trials and tribulations *(all things)* 3.) Thirdly, practice and obey the wisdom heard 4.) Create an atmosphere of worship unto the LORD for who He is 5.) Practice the process continuously. The *WORD of TRUTH* is your Sword to combat-stand against other words or idle talk spoken in your ear that you may hear during any season from the spiritually immature, spiritually blind, the ignorant or the unsaved.

Your physical ear is a gateway- road into your soul. Words you speak or hear can be sown or planted in your mind. Words are like electricity, energy, thoughts and persuasions that forms to create or shape your reality. Whether you hear in the natural or hear something from the spirit realm it enters the ear gate. **The Bible tells us {Proverbs 23:7} so as a man thinks *(phronema)* in his heart *(leb- psuche),* so is he.** Your actions are a creation of the way you think or from the persuasion received. Thoughts that are not seen yet they are powerful; your action is the fruit of the seed of that thought. We must change our thinking, our mind to match the mind of the Word of GOD. When the mind/ heart change, the words and actions change. People have opinions and love to give them whether you ask for them or not. Opinions can work against you or in your favor. If opinions are not faith-based advice, why accept them as being valid ideas? Check the source or motive from which it came. You should never take to heart any spoken words that aren't of faith. When you are in seasons of grieving or suffering you must turn a deaf ear to every voice that works consistently to drown out your faith and to convert you. Those darts are targeted to weaken and strip your spiritual muscles. **The Bible tells us {Proverbs 18:21} the tongue has the power of life and death; those who love it will eat its fruit by reaping the consequences.** Satan has an agenda in the time of difficulties too, as well as, in any other season. Sometimes people are sent on assignments by the enemy and are not conscious of the unclean spirit that is working through them. Remember, just as faith comes by hearing, doubt also enter by hearing doubtful or negative conversations. All trash and unwanted waste goes into a trash container so don't allow others to empty garbage into your mind. You are not a dumpster, but a priceless jewel in the LORD. **The Bible tells us {Proverbs 4:23} to guard our heart from it flows the issues of life.** Several years ago as the youth director and youth minister I taught the youth, **"Be Careful Little Ears What You Hear, Yours Ears *(hear)* And Eyes *(see- vision)* Are Gateways Into Your Soul."** Words are spirit and they travel in the realm of the spirit, in the atmosphere ready to enter through an open door of a persons mind or spirit to create and manifest *(negatively or positively)*. Take Heed! Be watchful, as well as, prayerful…and not condemning.

Faith operates like an armor shield to protect the ***Seed of Righteousness*** that lives in each born again blood redeemed believer and the believer is the righteousness of Yahweh in Christ. Since faith operates as a shield this informs believers of their position as sons of Yahweh that there will be attacks from opposing demonic forces that are not seen with the naked eye. Disembodied unclean spirits will manifest themselves through people minds and bodies. Because we are emotional beings, when a crisis arise and prolongs itself the worst can come out of a person. Things that were lying inactive will rise up and rule to protect its domain. Heavy burdens can bring out that which is not clean or pure, the ugly; whatever it might be. Faith, hope and prayer is our posture to take at all times and reinforcement in hard times. When you recognize the rising, engage the faith-power within to breakdown the barriers that rise to build its fortress. It is not something you think about, but it's something that has to be set in motion. Faith authority is needed so when things try to attach itself to you through association, as you're being taught and trained by Holy Spirit how to spiritually discern; then, you are employed by faith to cast out and cast off what does not belong to you as a citizen of the Kingdom of Yahweh in Messiah JESUS. Therefore, disconnect with any associations that bring on a shake in your faith walk. Remember, to tighten up loose bolts in your life in order to stand determined in **authorized** faith. The WORD of GOD will ambush and defeat our spiritual foes.

Foes that will Setup Ambush Against your Faith
• Faintheartedness
• Pride, Greed
• Idle, Unwholesome Speech
• Ungodly Soul-ties
• Vagabond Spirit
• Ungodly movies, music, entertainment
• Compromise/ False teaching
• Stubbornness
• A Lying Tongue
• Unbelief
• Competitiveness
• Worldly Appetite
• Unteachable Spirit
• Spirit of Character Assassination
• Spirit of Conspiracy
• Spirit of Jezebel / Ahab Spirit
• Spirit of Sabotage

When you **recognize**, **acknowledge** and **denounce** the influence that desires to control your behavior you will sever, cut the cords *(soul-ties)* with that which entices you, by operating in faith and obedience to shut it down. Faith develops powerfully with intimate time, so don't beat yourself up if you trip along the way. As Holy Spirit exposes the flaws do not continue to walk in them for your sake and freedom is in Christ. See your errors, flaws, sins, **repent** and **seek** the Lord for strength and the authority of His Spirit's influence. Do not allow the offenses to become consistent; break the pattern in Jesus Name. This works for all of us who love the Lord and are called according to His purpose. When negative or positive things are consistent they grow and spread. Snares can be like weeds; they will eventually entangle you, get you off track and choke the WORD of GOD out of you rendering a person powerless to overcome and the WORD of GOD of no effect. Now you should have a clear understanding of the activity of *hearing* or *to hear* (*Hebrew* **Shema**: *to listen, to heed, hearken, obey; being obedient*) the Word of GOD is the key component for the planting of the seed of faith, its development and for your welfare. Now you're held accountable to respond in receiving from the Ruach *(Spirit)* of Yahweh. What good news that is to understanding. Now be sure to apply the good news when crossroads call for you to be empowered by acting faith out. You are **hearing** the Spirit of Knowledge and Revelation speak to you now, meditate on it, digest, activate and repeat it. Remember, JESUS is perfecting His work in the soul of true believers.

Faith is like electricity, it is powerful when it is charged in the Word of GOD, which is the Source. On the flip side of that coin, if faith has no power then it's disconnected from the Source and is dead faith. Make sure you stay connected… plugged into the one true Source, JESUS the Anointed One. Your faith connection will impact your life actions and others;

because it is supernatural favor from Jehovah GOD. Whatever comes to take you out, will get taken out when you stand in the Strength of the Lord. We overcome every time, not sometimes, but every time in the Power of His Might. **The Bible tells us {1 John 4:4} greater is he that is in you than he that is in the world.** Do you trust that judgment? You are strengthened, built up; empowered inwardly to take your stand. You are not standing alone because you are joint-heir with Christ {1 Corinthians 6:17}. The new creature in Christ is spiritually raised with Him. David conquered Goliath at battle, not with King Saul's armor or by his will, but by the matchless undefeated Name and Strength of the LORD. When a crisis happens, the impact can knock us back to regress, but we are not to stay in that dying suffocating place of danger. That is where the devil wants you to remain, in a state of pity, deterioration, humiliation or a place of torment. A believer has been given divine power, divine favor and divine promise; not the giant, not the storms, not the dysfunctions, not setbacks, not despair, not depression or loneliness, but the CHRIST in you. The anointing takes faith, not your natural eye sight. Empowered by faith is aggressive in action, because it functions like a seed. It has vision and purpose. It visualizes and carries out what it was planted to do as long as the soil- heart is pliable. It has No fear or thought of defeat. As we live and pray by faith, this is the mandate thought for the believer to take to heart through faith…No fear! No defeat! Receive the prophetic revelation of the Ruach Hakodesh *(Holy Spirit)*. This is the Kingdom of Yahweh Supernatural Power Task Force in your spirit through His Spirit. I am saying this repetitiously throughout this chapter purposefully as a foundation. You must grab hold of this spiritual divine revelation. Where there is divine revelation there will also be transformation, illumination and elevation which come with great responsibility. Our crisis is packaged with revelation that the LORD wants to bring to the light as we go through the fire of deliverance. Do you trust Holy Spirit to reveal? Confess: Yes, LORD, I will trust you.

During my teenage years, I experienced situations that worked for my good in causing my faith to grow. I am sure you're able to recall experiences in your early life where faith began to take root and increase. The experience, as I look back was purposeful used as an object lesson to increase God's faith inwardly. When the divine gift of faith is stirred inwardly it causes our response of action of trust in the Lord to **intensify** to His dimension of timelessness regardless of what time/ season it may be in time. The situations will always speak opposite of the timing of Yahweh. Yahweh is not bound by time or circumstances. He exists in a timeless sphere. Intensified faith is what is needed to approach oncoming windstorms; although we have to grow to get to His set time for release; remember it's *already* done. Let the capacity of your faith become more intense. Let It Rise!

At the age of sixteen, filled with the Holy Ghost with the evidence of speaking in tongues, a babe in Christ, I was attacked by a demonic spirit(s) while I slept. As I lay asleep positioned on my back, I awake consciously to move, but I could not move. There was a power that had arrested the mobility of my body completely. I was unable to move my arms, legs, lift up or turn over. I could not open my eyes or even mouth to scream. My body was locked down by what could not be seen with the natural eye or touched with the physical hand. I could hear myself talking to myself, like a body corpse with life still inside. Yes, this brought the spirit of fear over me. The spirit of fear tried to steer me into a panic. I was not aware at that time in my walk with the Lord that He, Holy Spirit, was sustaining and keeping me from having a panic attack from the spirit of fear and terror. As I lay there beyond scared tears begin to roll down the sides of my face as I lay on my back with my hands across my chest area. I don't remember how long this attack lasted, but I remembered being taught about the Power in *the Name of Jesus (Yeshua)*; with tears running downside my face, I heard something say call on *the Name of JESUS* in a declared tone. Circumstances don't wait on anyone to prepare or be ready to tackle them with readiness. But as you walk with the LORD JESUS, Holy Spirit will teach and equip you to be ready in season and out of season for approaching attacks that may come with consequences for accepting JESUS CHRIST as Savior and Lord. You may not be ready or feeling it in your emotions, but small steps enlarges quickly in the faith dimension. It's not in the emotions or feelings. IT'S SPIRITUAL! Remember, the union is by His Spirit abiding in your spirit and you in Him. The winds of change don't appear with the intention for us to approve them, but for us to shift- move in the realm of the Spirit as sons of Yahweh GOD IN CHRIST… to declare the atmospheric wind to shift and manifest change according to ABBA's Will in YESHUA. Meanwhile, as a babe or seasoned saint in the Lord, embrace each step in learning for the possession of continual supernatural persuasion and insight. The steps will supernaturally expand. Hallelujah…I feel the Presence of the Lord. That something that I heard was the voice of the Holy Ghost empowering me to battle within Him with His armor. I heard, I obeyed and I begin to call on that great powerful name **JESUS**. This was an act of taking dominion and authority empowered by faith that belongs to every blood-redeemed Spirited-filled believer in the Kingdom of Yahweh in Christ…***DOMINION, POWER AND AUTHORITY IN THE REALM OF THE SPIRIT BY THE POWER OF GOD IN CHRIST.*** Are you hearing me in the Spirit? What the LORD has *already* released unto each believer: the right to rule, the right to act and to reign in Jesus Name will not work independent of the other. The role is unified…one power cell. The King's decree is sanctioned by Himself and is governed by His Ruach in the physical realm within His faithful covenant people. This experience was part of the constructing of the mustard seed forming faith increase in GOD. He was shifting my faith to another level, grounding me in Him with experiential evidence of His wonder working power *(dunamis, miraculous)*. And this is what the Lord wills, that you be grounded securely in His Word. That you know Him foundationally, personally and dependently for yourself…so you will not be shaken from your faith in Him or converted to falsehood. The Holy Spirit spoke into my spirit the formula to counteract this spiritual demonic attack for my defense. This ammunition of the Spoken Eternal Word defeated that diabolic attack. For those that do not believe the Lord is speaking by His Spirit in today's time are in for a spiritual awakening in their spirit from Ruach Hakodesh

(Holy Spirit). All that Biblically deals and surrounds faith is supernatural…not common or religious. When believers are in dreadful or desperate situations and cry out to JESUS, there will be a response whether it come directly in the form of an audible voice or indirectly. We cannot determine what methods Yahweh God will use to speak to us or how, when or where He chose to speak to us. Just be open to a radical moving of His Spirit in the consistency of your walk of faith as sons- heirs of the King; or the one who approaches the Lord to obtain His Grace- salvation code. As I obeyed, I cried out from my spirit into the atmosphere of the unseen spirit realm the **Name of JESUS!** Keep in mind my mouth was as if something had muzzled it shut, but my spirit at liberty; free by the Spirit to soar and ascend. This revelation impartation to you is to speak, declare into the atmosphere life substance when you're in need of a breakthrough. The isn't labeled under tradition or religion, but apostolic…the Power of GOD today to Authorize, Delegate, Heal, Deliverance, Miracles, Witness, Prophesy, Break Chains and Yokes By Demonstrating Himself through pure souls that have removed the old wine skin in exchange for the new wine skin…the Supernatural.

The provision power source of Yahweh was working on my behalf supernaturally and demonstratively. The third time when my spirit cried out the Name of JESUS, that demonic presence which had arrested my body's mobility, as if I was lying there dead, suddenly loosed me. Glory Hallelujah! When you are confused, bound up, locked up, don't know what to say, "I implore you to invoke the **Name of JESUS** into the atmosphere in holy boldness, **'The Power-line!'** "Say and

Believe on the NAME that causes chains to break into pieces so that you can freely move forward into destiny." Beloved this is far fetch from crazy; the manifestations of the Power of GOD are to be demonstrated through us and by us, the Ecclesia-Church of GOD in Jesus Christ in the age in which we live. People around us are in need to see the move of the Ruach Hakodesh through you through witnessing, prayer or even giving a testimony of His greatness. You never know how these truth factors may silence attacks from the evil one and release blessings. You never know when someone may be in a desperate plea for the move of the LORD in their life; you just never know. That is why believers should testify openly in conversations when a door open's about the demonstrative manifesting glory of the Kingdom of Yahweh in your life. Make your boast in the things of the Lord. People are battling everywhere in different ways. Know that a Word from heaven will shift the atmosphere. That was the first time, but not the last I ever dealt with evil spirits directly concerning my physical body. The Kingdom of GOD was at hand in the midst. **The Bible tells us {Matthew 11:12} the kingdom of GOD suffers violence and the violent take it by force.** The **Church** *(Greek **Ecclesia**: believers-called out of darkness, belonging to the Lord)* has been given a silver spoon with the upper hand of royal power to move like a chess player; to take all by divine strategy and divine confidence. If you miss it, get back up and start afresh. It is work and that work calls for persistent of your spirit in the Holy Spirit, not aggression of the flesh or carnal perception. Remember, cultivation and growth is the process of Holy Spirit plowing, uprooting and planting. The Church has been given the Identity, Power,

Dominion and Authority to counteract against the kingdom of darkness that will confront the believer in this foreign land by the wisdom of GOD in the Name of Jesus; lifting up the banner to war in the spirit by the Ruach *(Spirit)* that the gates of hell shall not prevail against the believer. In the midst of any crisis, storms, emotional distress or faint heartedness call on the Name of JESUS out a ***genuine*** heart of faith.

As a teen, I had many intriguing experiences. Once I laid hands on the dog that belonged to my brother and me. A car had hit the dog and I prayed for healing. I was taking GOD at His Word. We had no money for vet care, but I was empowered to move in faith. Pets are like family and friends; we can become closely attached to them. We did not know if the injured area was severe or not, all we knew was that the dog would groan and couldn't walk or stand. I laid hands on the dog throughout that day and evening along with a healing prayer, by morning he was healed. That is active faith in action. We must start gravitating in appointed dimensions of faith. Start in your present circumstance*(s)*. When faced with challenges that can produce great suffering and discouragement and weigh us down like a ton of bricks, we must be pinned in battle to divine faith which is superior. You have to move out of that place of shock or denial and move into the faith dimension. Distress will cause spiritual paralysis, immobility and numbness. That leads to a non responsive heart toward the things of Yahweh promised in Christ that frees us from being in a bound state of mind under limited conditions. Beloved of YHVH it is not an emotional feeling. Divine faith is faith that exceeds what your feelings, your mind and body speaks; it rules out the faintness of only talking about I have faith. **Faith supersedes the law of gravity, space.** Yahweh's faith have authorized you to advance against the devices that the enemy of our souls will use in challenging times; unseen strikes to execute defeat little by little contributing to its evil goal. The **Law of Faith** says we are *already* prepared, not getting prepared, to fight the good fight of faith. Faith sees the believer in the future tense stage. You must Move! GOD-Faith Transcends Dimensions! Yes, you will have to do some things in the natural to align your thoughts and words: like practicing confessing the Word, shifting wrong behavior patterns, practicing not conforming to the pattern of this world and practice conforming to Him. Preparation with readiness is to be the believer's life practice. What you are to understand is what is already spiritually done in heaven by ABBA with a physical reflection through Christ is to be implemented in your faith life for expression. Pray and decree the promises of GOD pertaining to your situation over your situation. Yahweh and the devil which are unseen with the natural eye have the mind *(male or female)* in common; the immaterial substance which is a tool of weaponry connecting man's spirit to spiritual blessedness. Our minds are powerful fields of battle. **Destroying the mind** will destroy the person or others by such chemical energies of wickedness. **Empowering the mind** -nous- will empower the person for a lifetime of victory through any season that may come. The **mind of Christ** is law, royalty, illumination, kingdom and governmental. It transcends physical laws and nature and knows no defeat.

The Bible tells us {Philippians 2:5} to let the mindset of Christ be in you, the higher refined quality of mind.

Faith, hope, love and **prayer** in the finished work of the Lord Jesus Christ play tremendous roles in our natural and spiritual relationships. Even in our daily course our expression of faith that exhibits our spiritual condition *(sphere of the soul-psuche)* and character will be evident by how we respond or conduct ourselves among people and by ourselves. For this cause faith is a fragrance fruit of the Spirit of Yahweh through Christ Jesus, a sweet smelling aroma. There is an aroma that rises from the impartation of this gift and it's noticeable when it is present. When we have a clear revelation of knowledge of what faith is and what faith is not, only then can a faulty intellectual foundation about faith be expunged. Faith is not abracadabra or magical. It's not clicking yours heels together or closing eyes for wishful thinking or throwing money in a wishing well or the crossing of the fingers. Faith, the supernatural gift from GOD, is activated in the heart, obeyed and expressed in thought, act and deed. Faith is doing not talking. As we believe on the knowledge of what we understand about GOD we are to respond. A few forms of GOD-faith is divine persuasion, moral conviction of truth and conviction to sinfulness, divine confidence, trust, reliance, obedience, expression and dependence upon the LORD GOD Almighty; whom we should mirror in our new nature in spite of what is in clear view or what the facts may be. All these forms will be needed actively working in the heart/mind to wipe out any unstable emotions leading to the overthrow of your faith in the Lord Jesus during trying times.

This is foundational teaching to bring simplicity, firmness and increase.

⸻

Hebrew word for the English term Faith
Aman: to nourish, make firm and
strong, faithfulness, loyalty
Emunah: perseverance, fidelity and steadfast;
to securely trust upon, obedience

Greek word for English term Faith
Pistis: believing, confidence, persuasion

⸻

Many have a belief that GOD exists or that there is a GOD, that he has provided redemption for the sins of mankind, that he died and even the creation being formed by Him, but amazingly many do not believe in the Savior's resurrection, do not trust GOD to perform His promises, manifest miracles or work through them by His Supernatural source of Power which is Holy Spirit…His divine Presence. It is inadequate to have head knowledge, be a church member somewhere or practice the religious ritual of church attendance. Faith *(Emunah)* must be expressed toward Yahweh and lived outwardly in the course of our lives through loyalty followed by obedience. He wills to demonstrate through you; soul and body. When you live by faith, you are exemplifying trust toward GOD about what he has promised you that He will do. Because there is no lying, nor failure in GOD, you must make a heart decision to believe, trust, obey Him and have a heart and mind that is fully persuaded. Now, at this point, in the face of oppositions you must come to an end of self and don't try to figure out how the Lord will do what He said He will do.

Facts are real as with the testimony of Sarah's womb was shut up. She was not able to bear children because her womb was barren. Even though the facts seemed to be convincing; nonetheless, the facts were not the Truth. The facts brought in the spirit of fear and the spirit of fear brought in the spirits of doubt, shame, confusion, frustration, contention and unbelief. The facts that were evident were seen by the visible eye and in their aged bodies. The promise seed Isaac still yet had to be born. Isn't this how many of us today are targeted and trapped by intellectuality and the deceit of the enemy and find it easier to come into agreement with what the view of the storm is speaking? What is seen as being normal conditions is thought to be normal, but not new to society, it's normal. That perception is more easily acceptable than that which is of faith, the unseen. That is the standard for the way of the world and its fallen system. Can I tell you something? That is not God's faith, but a spirit of fear and a spirit of deception. It is easier for many to go alone rather than express what is out of sight or unseen…that takes muscle endurance. The **Law of Faith** had *already* declared that the promise from the government of Yahweh will be established...***AND THIS TO SHALL COME TO PASS...*** because it is *already* done it must and will come forth. That is the mystery of faith that the LORD desires to unveil to the Ecclesia. It takes GOD-faith ability to stand on the counsel of GOD and Act on the Promises!

Now is the time to make the sound, concrete decisions, not later, to trust the Lord no matter what the winds of change are saying loudly. Abraham and Sarah faith had to rise to where GOD had already declared the result of the promise. Sarah female organs were restored by the Supernatural Power of Yahweh, her womb was open miraculously to carry a baby full term, give birth, enjoy pleasure and live afterwards. When windstorms come your way that seems impossible to get through or get over or get beyond, there is a spiritual womb within your spirit that Holy Spirit is activating to produce the impossibilities through you. Miracles are still happening. The storm disturbance is there to awaken you spiritually. I testify of that. The empowered faith of GOD desires to stimulate divine substance in you to bring you out and to break off the yokes of strain that seek to hold us captive during difficulties. I have learned by experiential revelation that if you speak forth what GOD is saying about the adversities that are in your midst, the WORD of GOD you are speaking forth along with faith and endurance will begin to shape, dress and manifest those things right before you in God's set time. But the Lord through His Holy Spirit first will have to work on you to get your faith up to the next level. Pass the test that is arranged by the vehicle called the storm to get you to that high point. **The Bible tells us {Ephesians 3:20}**

He who is able to do immeasurable…and it is according to the power that works in you. Feed your power source. God's Word is the final Authority of Truth. Faith is bound to respond. Some of the greatest developing factors that faith is elevated through are troubles, hardships, calamities and tragedies. Nevertheless, faith endures to the end; So Hold On, giving up is not a choice to go backwards. **The Bible tells us {Philippians 2:13} for it is the Lord GOD who works in you to will and act in order to fulfill His purpose.** GOD Is Awesome! Try him for yourself.

• Faith's origin is GOD not man
• Faith is a Kingdom principle
• Faith is the hope of substance
• Faith is obedience, endurance and love at work
• Faith shows us how to see as GOD sees
• Faith has difference levels
• Faith leads and grow
• Faith opens our spiritual ears, eyes and heart to the unseen dimensions
• Faith manifests the impossible or the unthinkable

Therefore, with hope and faith being the foundation, we will certainly overcome the distress that surfaces along life's way. Living in faith and hope with prayer is an intimate ongoing covenant between you and the Lord. When people say they have faith, but they are not living it, it is not faith. **The Bible tells us {Romans 14:23} whatever is not of faith is sin.** If we locate ourselves in this place through moral conviction of truth, **we must repent**. Unbelief and doubt can destroy the bond and the will to act. Remember, faith will produce growth, obedience and maturity in the things pertaining to life and godliness {**2Peter 1:3**}. Therefore, faith must be worked out in your life and demonstrated {**James 2:8**}. Faith that is not being worked is little faith, dead faith, blind and lazy or no faith all results in zero power of evidence. Faith is power that transforms; moves and shifts things in the realm of the spirit for right now blessings, miracles and answers. As you hold on to the **Hand of GOD** by faith through any trial, tribulation, disappointment, agony or suffering that you may encounter, Yahweh is bounded to Himself to lead you step by step as He did with Abraham and Sarah; and as he did in my distress into success which equals triumph. But will you **humble** yourself? **The Bible tells us {Hebrew 13:8} GOD is the same yesterday, today and forevermore. He changes not.** What awesome reassuring good news that is to souls who choose to turn, submit, humble, believe and trust Him at all cost. For GOD in Christ who promises is faithful to perform just what He said with conditions. You will never go bankrupt at anytime.

At the age of forty-six, through experiential knowledge, time and divine wisdom, I have come to realize that the storms of life that are permitted will usher in GOD through us *(reflectors of divine light)*. The **Refiner's Fire** builds **godly character** on the inward parts of man, singleness of heart and mind, to develop and increase our faith level, purge our conscience, holiness, build endurance and call us to respond to GOD re-creative divine purpose by His design. Sometimes we respond to life as if we are in control of where, how, when and what will happen at our discretion. Sometimes we can take things for granted, people for granted, jobs for granted, health for granted, family for granted or choices for granted as if we are untouchable. We may say I got it all under control. Surely, I can handle anything that may come. This is how some of us may think and have viewed things in life. When negative, generational or weak character traits are present most of the time they're not visible in the eyes of that person. When such ways are visible, it may be viewed as being normal or a personality trait. Then it seems like that's the way it is meant to be. Some examples would be: Oh, that is the way they have always been they won't change or that's just them being them. But that is not completely true, it's a false perception. Our true image was marred in the fall of in the garden *(Adam/ Eve)* which was germicide to the human race as a whole taking us into total depravity. Our life molecule, DNA, spiritual-being was deadened to a state of unresponsive and our soul's became influenced by deception by the accuser of the brethren, the devil, making accusations with a plan to assassinated divine character and covenant with Yahweh Elohim. This was the very act of satan robbing our spiritual birthright so we would not have access to the Yahweh's Presence- Glory Encounter- vision or revelation of our true identity. *(Purchase second book: <u>Bloodline Spiritual DNA</u>)*. The sins of trespass, iniquity, unbelief, doubt and disobedience seeks to rob anyone of truth, the saved or the lost. Now through the free gift of salvation the believer's sight is restored, immediately in the spirit by His Ruach. The Kingdom of Yahweh's manifestations and evidence is received by faith to retrieve what is rightfully ours from the spirit realm into the physical realm. That manifestation will be evident through our own increasing lifestyle of faith with the Lord. Listen, Beloved of GOD, our true identity in Christ Jesus is unveiled through character as we overcome by faith. Ruach Hakodesh *(Holy Spirit)* elevates us from glory to glory, faith to faith. The treasure is there, but it has to be exposed, not remain hidden. Holy Spirit cuts out and Holy Spirit deposits and Holy Spirit seals the nature of ABBA through JESUS. We'll achieve greatness by completely trusting in what GOD promised will come. When you open your mouth to speak life, the Word of Truth grabs a hold to your faith and swells; Yes, The Word will take on flesh and become visible to the eye. Samson didn't fail, but for a season due to disobedience. He was entrapped and caught in a net of deception. Yet, who and what Samson possessed was hidden deep within him and his purpose as a victorious deliverer was exposed in front of all those who sought to destroy him and bring GOD to shame. But the Lord said not so.

As we learn to lean not to our frail limited understanding, but begin to acknowledge GOD in all our ways, He promises to direct the path of those that will put their confidence, trust in Him. He promised to be the guide who will guide you through all seasons in your life; not man, not self, not your spouse, not your job, not positions, not titles, not money, but the quickening Power of the Ruach of Yahweh. He chooses at His will any avenue to maneuver in blessings. Jehovah Jireh *(God will provide)* is the source of the supply, not the other way around, He has *Already* provided emotionally, physically, naturally and personally. The world's silent sales pitch image to society is that the resources are the source; get over by any means necessary. However, you have to survive in this world, do what it takes, you're in control; this is a lie and a strategy the devil wants people to buy. The truth is when the resources become a god to a soul and confidence is put in the resource and not in the Source and when the resource runs out, the question is, "What are you left with?" Resources and conditions are temporary, but Yeshua is forever a present help in troublesome times….forever. You don't have to watch over your shoulders. Resources can become a god to anyone that is not fully aware of the danger of idolatry, lack knowledge and not fully persuaded by faith. **The Bible tells us {Hosea 4:6} My people are destroyed for the lack of knowledge; because thou hast rejected knowledge, I will also reject thee, that thou shall not be a priest to me, seeing thou hast forgotten the law of thy GOD. I will also forget thy children.** Anything or any person someone sets above or worship in the place of Yahweh-Yeshua *(one)* in heart becomes an idol that includes material things, objects, jobs, spouse, pastor or children, etc. Another form of idolatry is to know the Truth and don't walk in it or obey it. God desires to sit on the throne of your heart. The Lord Jesus will be to you whatever you need Him to be. He is your present help in the time of troubles: your defense lawyer, refuge, your strength and all else. That's my testimony.

FAITH DECLARATION

Open Your Mouth And Speak Life...

I DECLARE THE EMPOWERMENT OF FAITH INFUSE MY HUMAN SPIRIT WITH INCREASING SUBSTANCE TO PUSH BACK WEAKNESS, CARNALITY, DOUBT, GRIEF, LOW SELF ESTEEM, DOUBLEMINDEDNESS, SELF PITY AND TO SEVER THE HEAD OF INTIMIDATING GIANTS IN MY LAND IN JESUS NAME. I WILL NOT BOW OR GIVE IN OR GIVE UP TO DEFEAT OR THE WEAKNESS OF MY FLESH IN JESUS NAME. I WILL HOLD ON AND HOLD OUT BECAUSE YOU LORD ARE FIGHTING MY BATTLE AND IN THE WAIT LORD I SEEK YOUR FACE AND INQUIRE OF YOU FOR SUPERNATURAL STRENGTH AND SUPERNATURAL STABILITY. I AM MORE THAN A CONQUERER IN CHRIST JESUS. I DECLARE AGAIN, I AM MORE THAN A CONQUERER IN CHRIST JESUS. I COMMAND MY SPIRIT TO ARISE TO THE VOICE OF FAITH AND ACT BY THE AUTHORITY AND POWER OF HOLY SPIRIT. I BIND AND COMMAND THE SPIRIT OF INTIMIDATION, SLOTHFULNESS AND PASSIVITY TO BREAK OFF OF ME NOW IN JESUS NAME. I AM VICTORIOUS IN JESUS, THE NAME THAT CONQUERS MY FOES ON EVERY SIDE AND BRING ME INTO MY DESTINY THROUGH LIFE TRIALS.

Glory Be To God.

AMEN.

Memorize and Pray It:

Write Romans 8:28

Write John 14:6

Hebrew 10:38-39

The righteous one [those hidden in Christ] shall live by faith; and if he shrinks back, my soul has no pleasure in him. But we are not of those who shrink back to destruction, but of those who have faith to the preserving of the soul.

James 1:2-4

Consider it nothing but joy, my brothers and sisters, whenever you fall into various trials. Be assured that the testing of your faith [through experience] produces endurance [leading to spiritual maturity and inner peace]. And let endurance have its perfect result and do a thorough work, so that you may be perfect and completely developed [in your faith], lacking in nothing.

Weigh Your Heart Self Examination:

1. What is God faith? Scripture.

   _____

   _____

   _____

2. How many times have you <u>magnified</u> the outlook of a circumstance instead trusting what God has <u>already</u> promised you? _____. What will you do to change your mind and heart to reflect the heavenly Father's design for you according to his will?

   _____

   _____

   _____

3. What are you willing to do <u>differently</u> to move into your place of success (victory) according to His divine will?

   _____

   _____

   _____

4. No matter how long it takes for what God has promised and revealed to you through His Spoken Eternal Word <u>will you wait on the Lord</u>? Give two steps forward of you waiting on the Lord.

   _____

   _____

   _____

5. What <u>strategy</u> has Holy Spirit revealed unto through this teaching to overcome your challenges?

_____

_____

_____

6. What are you <u>doing</u> to usher in the manifestation Presence of God in your situation? In your atmosphere? Are you being persistent in the Word regarding your faith walk?

_____

_____

_____

7. Are you back and forth, forth and back? What will you do to correct the seesaw confusion?

_____

_____

_____

8. Explain what it means to be spiritually empowered by faith and the natural response to it.

_____

_____

_____

9. What are the three <u>elements</u> that are to be displayed actively in your walk of faith?

- _____
- _____
- _____

10. Because of active faith what weapon will be used out of your mouth? _____

11. Because you have an adversary who targets to silence you what caution signs are part of your plea? Hint: Sentence above the reasons prayers go unanswered.

    • _____
    • _____
    • _____
    • _____
    • _____

NOTES:

CHAPTER THREE

FAITH ENDURANCE AT WORK

Endurance conditions us not to be easily swayed from our intentional purpose; unmovable, abounding, unswerving, loyal in our faith and devoted to GOD in seasons of testing. Endurance supernaturally builds from the inside out. This is another measure of grace. We are to be patient in the waiting of the manifestation of our deliverance. But most of us will have to be pruned for the supernatural fruit of divine patience to begin its perfect work within our being. I believe that there are different levels in patience; therefore, patience must grow continually. We need the fruit of patience with our daily activities, such as, with our children, grandchildren, relationships, spouses, in traffic, co-workers, relatives, job conditions, and ministry or for life transition stages. These areas can be used as instruments of testing for building and increasing your spiritual muscle endurance ability. This patience differs from your natural measure of patience, no comparison. No matter what adversities you may encounter, endurance will always direct you to aim further to oppose the odds that are against your victory. This supernatural strength is linked with longsuffering. Endurance does not inactively stand still or coward down it comes in agreement with what heaven has decreed about your case on trial in the heavenly court of justice. *The Heavenly Court Declares That It Doesn't Matter What We Face, Small or Huge, It Doesn't Matter The Weight Of The Pressure, It Doesn't Matter Who It May or May Not Be or How Long It Has Been, God's Justice To All That Look Upon Him With A Pure Heart In Trust Will Be Delivered, Rewarded In This Life And The Life To Come.* In the midst of any storm that seems to rise with a threat to shut you down, in the heavenly court our Judge has *already* declared that threat itself to be shut down against you. Remember, Holy Spirit -**SUPERNATURAL SPHERE**- is the reality of faith walkers. We are cautioned to endure in patience for the manifestations. Nevertheless, we must go through the process of being processed. **The Bible tells us {Hebrew 4:15-16} for we do not have a high priest who is unable to empathize with our weaknesses, but we have one who has been tempted in every way, just has we are, yet he did not sin. Let us come boldly to the throne of our gracious GOD. There we will receive his mercy, and we find will grace to help us in the time of need.** The Ecclesia's benefits never run out. Things may come quickly, but they don't leave or resolve themselves as quick as they come. This is a good reason for us to initiate patience during the storms probation that blow in our zones. Faith endurance is not setting quietly and accepting whatever is going to happen will happen. That most certainly is not faith that endures, that is a spirit of passivity; bondage. Jesus nailed that bondage to the Cross. He was not passive. Therefore, by the authority and power of the Ruach Hakodesh, we rebuke and dismiss that character trait in Jesus Name. The Holy Spirit in the Spirit-filled believer carries a push back resistance DNA Spirit trait called **"Staying Power."** That Supernatural trait will compel us to push back, to resist the devil, resist giving-up, resist throwing in the towel, resist willful sin, resist appearances of evil, temptation and to remain in the race of endurance in the boundaries of faith. We do not need faith endurance when everything is going well on the job, on the college campus, in the home, in the marriage, in the single's life or when the bank account is flowing gracefully. Endurance positions itself to fight against disorder; like David's situation before becoming King. **Endurance** *(Staying Power)* is faith remaining under pressure with a flint heart standing on the promises of JESUS, the mark that is set before you despising all the disappointments that may appear to be in the form of closed doors. This level is an awakening of the soul. The Spirit of Endurance reality authorizes staying power while prompting the supernatural ability to withstand when the physical reality speaks otherwise. The test for endurance will surface when there is a tremendous need that will require much pressing, much pushing, much travailing in prayer and your stance to become unshakable in the spirit of your mind. **The Bible tells us {James 1:3} when your faith is tested it has a chance to produce endurance. Allow perseverance to finish its work so that you may mature** *(be perfect)* **and**

complete, lacking nothing. The word perfect is a maturing of the soul and training of the body.

During the time of my pregnancy with Isaac, born 6-17-97, I learned in time what it meant to be shaken, to endure… what it meant to remain in faith…what it meant to plead my case before the Lord…what it meant to pour out of a desperate soul. In time, I learned what it meant to be patient…what it meant to wait in hope as the Lord gave me strength from moment to moment, night and day; even throughout the days that were to come. The drought season had appeared, but GOD SHIFTED the atmosphere and the sphere of my faith transitioned. I experienced emotionally what it felt like to be mad at the Lover of your life *(referring to the Lord)*. It is not easy to wait on hope to show up when the condition tells you to give it up and turn your back on your GOD. And another voice- mind gives you the reason: because He does not hear your cry or feel the pain of your infirmity. It takes a made up, desperate heart that pushes to stay, to endure and to stand faithfully while under pressure, facing maybe a dying case. That spiritual muscle that was cramping began flexing and building up when all else was shattering me. Meanwhile, in the midst of holding on, wrecked in emotions, I said, "GOD for you I'll live and for you I'll die, whatever you decide is well with me. When you get to this spiritual state of mind, a dying to your thoughts and feelings, opening yourself; then, ABBA is released by you to lift up His banner like a canopy to spread deeper into the soul for protection. Glory to GOD! Do you sense the Presence of GOD right here? Bathe in that revelation until it registers in the spirit of your mind what is taking place for the soul that reaches this peak. But!!! The pains and prayers may come with a **"but"** *clause* when you never traveled the path before or been in the storm that seems to have no ending.

I remember my husband and me sitting in Applebee's restaurant after leaving the doctor visit receiving disturbing news. The doctor gave us the results from the amniocentesis testing and relating all the bad news that no expecting parents want to hear regarding their unborn baby. The doctor shows us different pictures in a book of what he did not really understand himself due to the rareness of the birth defect of our unborn baby. And because I had a made up heart that GOD would have to make this call, I refused to have an abortion early or late in my pregnancy knowing that it was high risk. However, at this moment in the pregnancy it was considerably late which would have put me, as well as, our unborn baby in the death bracket. I was more crushed than anything. As we sat talking, with no appetite, not knowing how to respond to each other about what had just transpired with a little fear trying to raise its head by replaying the disturbing, mind boggling pictures we saw along with the doctor's report we heard in our heads, *"I Bluntly Told My Husband With Tears In My Eyes I Am Believing GOD! If GOD Wants This Baby He Will Have To Take Isaac Himself, I Will Not Kill My Baby, I Would Rather Die With Him."* This stage is the beginning of the very act of enduring, the fruit of patience, the fruit of longsuffering and the gift of faith being infused working to perfect the greater good out of a bad situation...because GOD is good. This is also a sacrificial, selfless sacrifice, on behalf for the life of another. A portion of your endurance consists of becoming a living sacrifice, willing to give up yourself at the cost of trusting the Lord. The condition involved here is **"If In The Wait,"** will you allow the fruit of patience, longsuffering, unconditional sacrificial love have its perfect work within you. A sowing of the Lord to produce fruitfulness for reaping a future harvest. There are many in the Church who are not awaken to the revelation knowledge of bearing the **Fruit of the Spirit**. The Fruit of the Spirit is a one cell unit with many factors; a vital Power of the essences of Christ that are to show forth in each believer's behavior in their regenerated life. It is not a choice to pick or choose what you want or how to obtain the Supernatural Fruit of GOD at your discretion.

When GOD is for you He is more and He is greater than that which stands against you. He gives the weak His strength to stand and stand and when it's all over to remain faithfully under His shadow. And the poor in spirit who realize our need for **The Great I Am That I Am** totally in our inadequacy is rewarded the Kingdom of Heaven eternal realities and riches in now time. Heed the promise here, to them is the Kingdom of Heaven {**Matthew 5:3**}. The promise attached is to those realizing the spiritual poverty condition of their stricken souls, the conscious awareness of the need of dependence on the KING, JESUS, who is the divine legislator and intercessor of Heaven. KING JESUS is He who has All Dominion and Authority to overstep the boundaries of time to bring things into alignment for the humble and pure in heart. My emotional outlook placed me in a place of recognizing that all I am and all I have gain is nothing, worthless; showing me my spiritual poverty state. You can have everything you think in order or going on for yourself, but it only takes one wrong wind that can blow that out of range. Be aware when going through deep waters how the imagination can throw you into a catastrophic state of mind if you don't hold on to the unchanging **Hand of the LORD** *(Spirit of GOD)* for hope and resuscitation to breathe and not crash. Yes, Breathe…Inhale and Exhale JESUS! A crisis can take the wind out of your breathing. The imagination under pressure can throw anyone…anyone into a devastatingly state if JESUS is not real or become real in your heart and life. The test doesn't get easier because believers are saved. It will take the divine power of endurance by faith to shift the mindset to a higher mind which is the mind of Christ. Christ's mind is the replicate of ABBA Father and supernatural minds create, establish, governs and accomplish supernatural things in now time *(chronos)*… transferring from one location into another location.

Lay Your Hands On Your Head And Decree By Faith

- *I HAVE THE MIND OF CHRIST RESIDING IN ME!*

- *I AM CREATED IN THE IMAGE OF GOD!*

- *I AM ENDURING!*

- *I AM PERSEVERING!*

- *I AM AN OVERCOMER!*

- *I AM STRONG IN THE LORD!*

- *I AM ESTABLISHING!*

- *I AM ACCOMPLISHING!*

- *I AM HEALED!*

- *I AM DELIVERED!*

- *I AM TRANSFORMING!*

- *I AM LIBERATED IN MIND, SOUL, BODY AND SPIRIT!*

- *I AM FREE!*

- *I AM A REFLECTION OF MY HEAVENLY FATHER!*

- *I AM LIGHT!*

- *I AM THE HEAD NOT THE TAIL, ABOVE NOT BENEATH!*

- *I AM WALKING BY FAITH, NOT BY SIGHT!*

- *I AM CREATED TO CREATE!*

- *I AM HOLY!*

- *I AM HIDDEN IN CHRIST!*

- *I AM CREATED TO WORSHIP!*

Even through the release of my uttered words a page back in the second paragraph didn't become real until death knocked on the door before my very eyes and the mind went into distress shock. These types of needs will call for crying out- empting yourself, petitioning the throne of Grace, perseverance and devotion toward the Lord while waiting. The wait in the midst is there to summon you to humble yourself, rethink things over, to dine with the Lord, to lay your heavy loads or burdens down, consider your actions, your heart, thoughts to the Lord, unloading your cares, bowing down and seeking Him; that is worship *(intimacy)* at the next level in the secret place of the Most High. This reality is the act of entering into the reality of the faith sphere from the testing experience. Endurance is to be exercised away from your intelligence, emotions and self-will; areas of the soul that are carnal *(fleshly)* in need of being made whole, sanctified and holy. Yes, set apart by the Fire of Yahweh. The Ruach endurance work will cause the shift to override our thinking and will empowering the soul to do exceedingly and above its own will power. When divine endurance has its perfect work within the soul during a severe storm, the grace work deposits other virtues through the suffering over time into your spirit that are more valuable than anything money can buy. Endurance is a divine grace that sprouts and bud other like seed from its source to bring that soul into a wealthy place by the Glory of the Lord. The gift of faith linked to walking by faith is the anointing of Holy Spirit breathing life forth sustaining believers as they endure. Endurance by Faith is not of flesh and blood, but it is supernatural strength that causes the mind of the flesh to submit. The **Spirit of Endurance**, even during suffering, unction's and gives the supernatural ability to endure time after time after time. However, knowing deep in my knower that I just could not give up because something some way some how had to happen; something good must come out of this devastating situation. The end is not the end as we may know the end to be, when we trust in the Lord with all our heart, mind and soul.

When we hurt it is common to have intervals of breakdowns, crying spell or even isolated moments, but as we reach to the mountain of GOD stepping out of the boat into the deep water, GOD will fight and add grace to us as we push to endure in faith and call peace to come forth. GOD will make away on your behalf to come out of that dark place. He will supernaturally shift the atmosphere and reposition you. The believer will overcome the emotional exhaustion from the fight of suffering. The eyes of your heart must stay on JESUS during the course of what looks like or seems like failure or a hopeless case. The end may be the very beginning of greatness that will swell in your spirit like a baby growing in the spiritual womb to be born forth for such a time as time. Divine patience births endurance, longsuffering, trust, humility, vision, contentment, submission, the ability to be taught, self-control, steadiness, gentleness and compassion out of being crushed under weighs of hurt.

THE WORD OF FAITH IS THE POWER THAT DELIVERS SALVATION (Greek Sozo: to preserve, deliverance from penalties, rescue from danger) FROM

JUDGMENT TO THE BODY, MIND, SPIRIT AND SOUL TO THOSE WHO BELIEVE. This is faith recovering like fine gold under the Hand of GOD. Staying Power spiritually prepares, teaches and equips us with graces listed above that in whatever state in life you may find yourself, good or bad, you're empowered to handle what may come in a state of humility, grace, power and assurance. GOD has securely unveiled by His Ruach divine revelation and manifestation that He will not leave nor forsake anyone that put their faith, trust and allegiance in Him. This is a dual spiritual transaction of impartation by the Ruach Hakodesh, a supernatural invasion in a soul that has humbled at heart by throwing off its self independence.

Hebrew word for the English term Wait
Qavah: strength, remain, tension of enduring,
to look for with anticipation,
tarry, stretch, to expect, twist, bind together

Money is declared to answer to all things. Even in that there are still limitations; money is not the answer to many things. Many attempt to buy love, but love isn't a commodity. Have you ever faced a conflict with any person for any length of time and you come to the conclusion that you are always being misunderstood or not liked? Well, money can't answer or fix that conflict. Maybe you received a wrong diagnosis from a blood test at the doctor's office which resulted in receiving the wrong medication or the wrong diagnosis or the medicine received didn't relieve the symptoms; well, money will buys the medicine, but may not cure the pains. Let's take it a step further, look at the testimony of how the woman with the issue of blood for twelve years struggled in her crisis of bleeding **{Matthew 9:20}**. She spent much money with some of the best physicians seeking for the right solution to cure her dying problem. And although these doctors were educated, highly trained, skillful doctors they could not heal her of her ailment. She was desperate and when a person is desperate they will take desperate measures. This means pushing all of what you've been told about GOD not healing or doing miracles today out of your system completely. This desperation was not negative; it set her in motion to move out of the nature/carnal mindset. She did not take her frustration out on any one else. She didn't seek to end her life even though her life possibly would have been prematurely shortened because of losing extreme amounts of blood. Yet, no remedy, no cure for the issue of blood was extended from man hands. The pressure of her situation called for her to go deeper. The woman with the issue of blood realized she needed not only a physical healing, but an inner healing as well from a true doctor…one who operates by His nature…Supernatural. She needed a touch from the Presence of a King. She decided not to visit another doctor, not be probed, tested, or poked any longer, but to put her hope in YESHUA HAMASHIACH, the deliverer and Messiah. She pushed her way with intensity through the crowd to get to King Jesus; the greatest physician of all times. This is also a demonstration of faith capacity. She knew without a doubt and without hesitation, if I could just touch the hem of His garment; just only a touch…I will be made whole. She had a divine encounter which gave her first hand revelation of the Power from the effect of the Glory Encounter of being in His Presence that would rest upon her for the rest her life affecting her whole mentality.

The Spirit of Christ is resident in the believer's spirit, and when we humbly seek, tarry and call out in our secret place, forming a conducive atmosphere for the Spirit of the Living GOD to meet with us face to face; that means being in His Presence. And when His Glory Presence is in the atmosphere deliverance, healing, peace and transformation concerning the need takes place because the Kingdom dwells where He is. The Kingdom of GOD manifests where His Presence is. Glory Hallelujah!!! All that He is and all that He has can be received in His Presence when the heart is turn diligently toward Him ready to receive the materialization of a supernatural miracle. The heart condition and state of mind is so vital to the move of the Power of Christ. Many want to experience and see Him face to face…the heart must change. The pushing and pressing work is done in the labor and delivery room before the birth is manifested. In my turbulence, the Spirit of the Lord met me when I poured out of my soul for help, out of a state of distress and anguish, a desperate call unto Him. That place was also part of my spiritual labor and delivery before the spiritual birthing. I recall several accounts where the atmosphere was conducive *(favorable)* for His Presence.

Miracles are still happening in the Presence of the LORD. When the atmosphere is favorable, virtue is released out of the spirit realm toward you, in you and upon you. The Church's *(Christ)* adversary, the devil, sends attacks against what is being released in the realm of the spirit to block blessings from materializing.

The virtue Christ Jesus felt drawn from the touch from the edge of His garment, the tassel on the tallit which symbolized obedience to the 613 commandments in Tanakh *(1st five books of the Bible)*, filled with the anointing, a point of contact; was a reliance of dependency upon the promises of ABBA. We can learn a lot from the woman with the issue of blood. The answer was not with money, not with the doctors, not with boyfriends, girlfriends, marital issues or losses, but a matter of reaching beyond limitations to the one who is able to take all disease and sickness away by one touch; through an extreme matter of sincerity of the heart displaying genuine faith at all cost. All limitations were deleted by the power shown through faithfulness manifesting the reality of truth; the truth revealed about the Governmental Power of the Kingdom of Yahweh. Every barrier which existed with her was removed. Her determination to push and push and press, press and push for a miraculous birthing from Glory was made evident. She had traveled in the Spirit through dimensions by faith, where expectation was granted, where time was not bound and limitations did not exist for the true worshiper. What about your push? What about your press? Woman, man, boy or girl don't abort that spiritual baby…anointing…out of your spiritual womb. The push and press in prayer is a spiritual thing resulting in a natural birth of miracles from your prayers. You must live in expectation in the faith dimension where faith urgency shifts us to rise above dimensions of defeat, deceit, sickness, intimidation, ignorance, lack, doubt, despair, fear, tradition and spiritual poverty. The woman with the issue of blood thoughts gravitated to the inconceivable which reflected her outward reaction. She died in the process of the supernatural transition, not physically, but spiritually to old laws and her old concept. She went down in order to come up and out of her natural mindset to obtain the impossible. She experienced a supernatural paradigm shift. She could now see a vision, a picture of herself healed; in her imagination, mind; she saw herself librated in soul, mind and body.

We have to see ourselves the way Yahweh God foresees us by what He has promised those that believe. Are you willing to go deep as the woman with the issue of blood pressed her way in the midst although she knew she was lawfully unclean? You need to see your situation as GOD sees it. GOD sees the potential in the situation change to active force. She saw herself whole, complete, healed, restored and not lacking for nothing. **Shout I Am Living In Expectation!** Say it until it registers in your spirit. *"I AM LIVING IN EXPECTATION!"* That's Faith Talk! Faith Is Delivering the Shift, the Transfer, You've Been Waiting For! Who is like our GOD? No One is like Great Jehovah *(Yahweh, LORD)*! He's A Healer! He's the Deliverer for you today in this hour. The pressures of suffering from the woman with the issue of blood gave her a never-ending experience exposing the very nature, identity and revelation of JESUS, the Incarnate Christ *(GOD* *in the flesh, Son of Yahweh God)* and Emmanuel with us. GOD revealed in the likeness of mankind, The GOD-man; yet, without defilement, without sin. This experience changed the rest of her natural born life. The weight of her storm escorted her right into seeking truth verses the traditions of men or Old Testament law. Truth not only healed her, but revealed her divine purpose. She was equipped *one on one* with divine revelation, divine knowledge, divine counsel, and divine strength, the Spirit of the Lord and the wisdom of Yahweh. Church…money cannot and will not give this to you. It comes by way of the storm. Man had nothing to with the spheres she entered and man had nothing to do with the Glory release. Man had nothing to do with the Glory that elevated her from the bowels of hell into the royalties and realities of the Kingdom of GOD. Now she had the testimony of New Wine *(Oil)* saturating her, which deputized her to go restore others that maybe suffering, chained in their minds and bound by lies of philosophy through the Grace and the Power of GOD which has been revealed unto her on that appointed day. The storm has come for you to know GOD through experience in a greater dimension. I believe this lady lost her natural mind, because I lost my natural mind and took on the mind of Christ. The manifestation and divine revelations might not have come together all at once, but it happened in Yahweh's set time. She got just what she needed from the LORD with Kingdom benefits. There old wine skin couldn't hold what had to come forth as a result of being in JESUS Glory presence.

Don't allow a negative situation to speak volumes into your mind, your thought faculty. If that unseen *(spiritual)* door is open, diabolical activity can enter in, join itself to the circumstance, your emotions and intensify the pressure. Demonic spirits, that's what the bible say they are. **They will to dictate to your future from the present about the past, and if you are not sensitive to or filled with the Spirit of Truth, you will think the thoughts are yours alone.** Silence the demonic voices of torment with the WORD of GOD in JESUS Name. Be patient, believe, pray and trust GOD to make the crooked paths straight, while He is working on and conditioning you at the same time. Anytime a person may be in a season of going through does not mean throw in the towel or you're defeated. Defeat shows up when a believer doesn't initiate the WORD of GOD and/ or living a compromising lifestyle before GOD without truly repenting. Most times the crookedness is within us; the man in the mirror.

⌒

2 Corinthians 10:5
Casting down (overthrow) every speculation, argument, high minded thing that exalts (raise) itself against the knowledge of God and bring into captivity every thought into the obedience in Christ.

⌒

Every thought, deed or word that stands against the knowledge of GOD is of the devil and comes out of a rebellious antichrist spirit. We destroy these arguments by personally taking those thoughts captive with the Power of the Spoken Eternal Word of God and teach those that will heed to **repent** and **obey**. When you are persuaded you will speak to your marriage, health, single life, disappointments, hang ups and regrets or troubles about your GOD. Yes, ABBA, Father, daddy GOD is bigger than any extreme crisis. No one can approach the Lord on their on terms using self gratifying ways; there is a wrong and right method. Approaching GOD is only done by His method, which is in sincere, genuine faith and repentance. I encourage you, as well as, myself to work your spiritual muscles of perseverance, faith, hope, prayer and unconditional love and build yourselves up in your most holy faith. Our reward is beyond measure that we cannot even imagine until Ruach Hakodesh *(Holy Spirit)* reveals it to us. There is a forceful power beyond our natural strength to be reckoned with in the realm of the spirit. Remember, there is a spirit world which is not seen with natural eyes that enter acts with this earthly realm **{Ephesians 6:12}**. The Spirit of GOD, another title for the Holy Spirit, has to open your eyes and ears to the spiritual world. Because GOD is Spirit, He deals with the spirit of man and His angels and expose and conquers evil spirits. Because GOD is GOD of war, as His heirs in the earth we are a people of spiritual warfare. This is not sorcery, not spiritual occult or witchcraft **{Deuteronomy 18:10-12}**. But all the wickedness the devil works against the born again, blood bought, Spirit-filled Christian and in this world is witchcraft. The Bible tells us **{1 Samuel**

15:23} rebellion is as the sin of witchcraft. I pray that GOD will take the spirit of fear from many in the Body of Christ who fear the mysteries and Kingdom principles and wealth of Yahweh GOD and experience Him face to face; in His Presence. **I DECREE THE SPIRIT OF HOLY GHOST BOLDNESS AND HOLY GHOST FIRE SATURATE THE CHURCH THROUGH HIS HOLY HABITATION AND HOLY CONVICTION!** The purpose of GOD in time passed was to conceal His mystery from the world and generations, but through the Wisdom of GOD, those hidden things, predestinated before time existed has been revealed in Christ by the Ruach of Yahweh for His people **{Colossians 1:26}** advancement. The storm that was permitted is for the purpose of the Kingdom of GOD seeded within you to increase in elevation. GOD in you wants to increase gradually without limitations. The storm processes us for the next **encounter** with GOD if we let go our way.

None of us at anytime know for sure what the next day, the next hour, the next year or any act of GOD will bring our way or the duration of that wind when it blows. Most of the time, we as a people tend not to think about the uncertainty that could possibly happen in our personal zone. We see other people struggles around us, in different places or on television, without thinking we take no further thought into consideration that the same struggles could easily knock at our front door. However, some of us have been guilty of thinking silently, saying or expressing those thoughts openly, that will never happen to me or I would not take that or do such a thing or what were they thinking; in others words we should not be dogmatic or critical. Remember we can't pick the storm and its damage, but we can intercede on behalf of others that are suffering by standing in the gap.

When the windstorms blow in your direction, the weight of it will cause the things in ones heart such as: secret sins, unforgiveness, vain imaginations, self centeredness, lack of compassion, lack of mercy for others, cold heartedness, spirit of retaliation, mean spirit, spirit of pride, spirit of hatred, spirit of greed, spirit of intimidation, lust, spirit of bitterness, spirit of greed, stubbornness, faultfinding spirit, an unteachable spirit, domineering, strong willed spirit, phony spirit, defeat, insecure, low self esteem, bad character, weaknesses, double-mindedness: all the impurities and defections of the heart to rise to the surface to be dealt with by the Fire of GOD. This action is defined as purging for reasons of heart purification. Sometimes the anguish and the agony that floats up in different forms will show us the man in the mirror. Purging is like a laxative which gets rid of unwanted waste out of our system. If there is a blockage in this phrase it will cause inward spiritual discomfort and pain. Little by little, the spiritual laxative washes, cleanses and expels conditions of the soul that are unfit and not tolerable for the new creature in Christ. Therefore, your trials and tribulations first of all will be used as an instrument to get your attention and second to turn your attention toward pleasing the Lord. Those who say they are children of GOD through the finished work of the Cross, GOD will discipline with His rod to bring order, fruitfulness, holiness and wholeness to our inward parts. I can testify to ABBA disciplinary actions; a father's love. You are not to simply exist, but your life should have an impact because of the Light of Christ that is shining from Him through you.

FAITH DECREE

In Jesus Name I Decree That Every Unfruitful Weed, Branch or Twig Be Pruned, Cut That Does Not Belong In You. I Decree That Your Life Be Fruitful, Springing Forth Of Divine Life From This Moment Forward!

Yahweh is Spirit, Yahweh is Just, Yahweh is Holy and His children who are spiritual are to reflect the essence of their Heavenly Father's heritage. The divine purpose of GOD establishes you as being priestly and kingly *(royalties)* as a child of King Jesus. All that He does is done without the permission of another. The Blood, the Cross, the Spirit and the Spoken Eternal Word have sealed your destiny as a believer remaining in Him. Royalties are not manifested without your faith being proven for the riches of the Kingdom. You have salvation, but you want to receive the manifestations of the benefits of the inheritance. It's as if you inherit $40,000.00. The deposit in full is in your bank account, but you neglect to claim it. So it sits there day after day, month after month, and you have needs to be met and some desires. Well, what's your thought on that? Exactly! You have received salvation with an inheritance. You are rich and wealthy, but don't want to pay what it may cost spiritually and naturally. Jesus said, take up your cross and follow me to possess the true wealth of my

Father's Kingdom {**Matthew 16:24-26**}. The tribulations or trials in life will be the ugly instrument to get you and me to that place of consistently moving forward, but it will be your choice how you respond in the heat of existing situations. A hard heart is not fit to receive discipline, instructions or healing. Windstorms will show up as judgment toward a person with a hard dark heart to bring rebuke, correction and a godly sorrow on this side of the heavens, but on the other side a lost soul or someone with a drawback spirit will suffer eternal condemnation. I caution and admonished any such heart to acknowledge its nakedness, repent and begin to live a life of faith and obedience watered in love. Is there anything to hard for JESUS? No, there is nothing to hard or No sin to great that GOD cannot forgive or heal. Let the healing process start immediately. Don't forfeit your soul.

There may be times through neglect, lack of experience or knowledge that we simply may just not do what is necessary or within our power if possible to prevent certain issues from happening or spreading unnecessarily; prolonged lengths of time. Sometime setbacks or failures may be in our control to correct or rearrange, while others are beyond the human control of correcting or erasing. There are also hearts that have just given up or lost hope. Even though this condition is a result from an unfruitful seed of hopelessness, **"By the Power And Authority of Holy Spirit I Decree the Root Is Being Up-Rooted As the Impartation of Knowledge, Revelation, Counsel and Insight Is Received Into Your Heart In JESUS Name."** Then there are times that in life, you're on the right track, things seem to be great, life is wonderful, good to you and the outcome is a good report. Then a different wind blows without any warning signals, life throws a curve ball that could knock you off the foundation of your feet, but your hope is still alive and the recover was suddenly…in the making. I am sure you have experienced such places before directly or indirectly. You were affected, but you pressed and pushed your way through by faith until victory showed up. Your faith may have been or wasn't shaken to the point of breaking; yet, tested to increase trust, endurance and stability in the Lord no matter what comes. Long as we live something is bound to come. When we learn to hear what GOD is saying in the rough uncomfortable seasons and heed what is said I believe our going through may not be as deadly to our life or our faith walk as the devil paints the outcome. I believe without a shadow of doubt your faith endurance will be deadly in and toward those windstorms that rise up to reflect harm and defeat toward you. The devil is not more powerful than GOD. I don't care what it looks like. Repeat it out loud in your atmosphere, **"DEVIL YOU ARE NOT MORE POWERFUL THAN GOD IN ME!"** What GOD promised will come to pass. Another one of satan's tactics is to pervert your thoughts to magnify issues or take out of content what Yeshua *(Jesus)* has *Already* conquered and redeemed through His blood sacrifice as victorious. The enemy will plant images in your mind or dream that are lies. Don't allow the trials of life toss you back and forth like a wet dish towel. Stand your ground by faith, with faith and in faith. Faith endurance is going to bring you into your next season of victory with divine benefits and blessings attached to it. GOD will not take you out of the trial of testing, but He will actually be in it with you to carry you through it. I am a witness. I have no doubt about that. Those footprints are not yours carrying you through the storm. As you learn to lean not to your own understanding and to acknowledge him in all that you do, not some, but all, He will carry you. Defeat and pity is nailed to the Cross. You warfare from a place of victory and after you have done all stand.

Faith with endurance builds character and strength from above within you. Before an athlete is placed to perform in his arena he must train, undergo extreme exercise and be consistent in building muscle, definition, hardness and character. This is how **endurance and faith** works behind the scene when we face windstorms that do not blow over smoothly; with consistency they build spiritual strength, alertness, soundness, sharpness, sensitivity and power. The problem with many of us is that we start looking with our physical eyes at the problem. Then, we'll let the problem dictate to us what the outcome will be. Faith is not what you see or even feel, but trusting GOD to bring you out because He promised in spite of what opposition is facing you. **Remember, He Promised!** He who Promised is Faithful to Perform that which He Promised to His faithful ones. God is not a man that He shall lie; that which He speaks, He will also act to demonstrate His power {**Numbers 23:19**}. Stand Your Ground In Faith Firmly! At the moment you might be crumbling inside, emotionally distressed, in pain, agony of soul, can't see or think clear, weak in your faith…you may be saying, you don't know what they did to me or what I went through or what happen or it's all my fault…I was raped, I prostituted or I was battered or verbally or mentally abused…I was falsely accused…I lost almost everything…I am rejected…I am torn down by people that suppose to love me. I declare this to your spirit, "I Know That GOD Will Heal It As He Promised!" Trust in the Lord with all your heart, mind and soul; by His power He will restore your breach.

Of course, we are human-beings with feelings expressed through physical reactions-emotions; however, GOD sees, GOD knows and has answered that need in the Blood of JESUS on the Cross. In suffering we must engage in taking up our cross and follow Him. Holy Spirit says each believer should be filled with His Holy Spirit. Believers have been given supernatural power beyond our natural strength to rise out of that soulish or carnal mindset *(the old nature)*. The power to combat the kingdom of darkness with the keys that give access to lock and unlock *(bind and loosen)* in the Kingdom of GOD which is infused in your spirit by the Spirit of GOD; deliverance and demonstration as the Holy Spirit leads. Your mass may consist of broken relationships, the police force, the sick, youth, spouse, self, job, finances, prostitutes, addicts or salvation for your family or health; to determine that the gates of hell shall not prevail. The Church, believer, have been given the keys. Use Your Ordained Spiritual Authority! Receive It…heed the instructions from heaven. Shout, HALLELUJAH! Keys that give access, the legal right to open and close and to approach are beneficial to your inheritance through commitment to GOD. The Lord GOD Almighty is greater than the devil or any demon. **Believers have been**

given keys to the Kingdom of God, such as, the key of faith, keys of authority, prayer, knowledge, wisdom, the key to bind and loose, the key to open and shut, to lock and unlock in the realm of the spirit. Those who respond in faith, repentance and live by faith are granted access *(keys)* to the Kingdom of Heaven abiding by His protocol. The devil wants to keep you in the dark about who you are and whose you are. Satan is a liar and the truth is not in him. He is the Father of lies, deception, and falsehood.

The Spirit of GOD deals with the spirit of mankind not our flesh. What is born of the flesh is flesh and that which is born of the spirit is spirit. The Spirit gives birth to the spirit **{John 3:6}**. The flesh lusted against the Spirit and the Spirit against the flesh **{Galatians 5:17}**. Because Yeshua *(Jesus)* is able to touch the infirmities and weakness of humanity by being man and GOD, conquering the power of the **law** of sin and death, He showed believers through the Power of the Spirit the Kingdom method to overcoming human frailties… through the Kingdom of GOD administrations which are now available to access under the direction of Holy Spirit. The Holy Spirit reveals to us, as the sons of GOD the power of speaking forth- declaring and commanding our storms to be at peace according to His Holy Word. No matter how many more windstorms, chains of testing come active faith, prayer, perseverance, steadfastness and hope will see us through it. **The Bible tells in us {Galatians 5:18} to as many be led of the Spirit are the sons of God.**

Now I must inform the elect of GOD, born again believers, because of the hidden treasure that is in you, before formed in the womb of your mother is equipped for divine creative purposes. ABBA Father has appointed a season, a set time, to birth the purpose forward of His anointing calling upon your life for the masses. However, the testing first is always tailored personally for the person going through. Nobody is cut for your testing except you, even though we may have similar trials. The inward parts must be placed through the fire. The fire is what consumes the corrupt nature of the heart mind and soul and replace it with the characteristics, heart and mind of GOD in a measurable way as you humble and yield. The Fire of GOD can establish His judgment and His favor. Remember, God is creating the manifestation of the real new you to be a representation or reflection of Him. You have to pass your own test. ABBA approves and justifies the calling, the gifts and the mantles, not mere men. When we go through the trials of suffering, it's for us first, and then after its work is complete in that area. The Hand of GOD which you experienced in the storm will be for others to receive healing virtue from you through your testimony and the power of the inner witness *(Holy Spirit)*. Listen now, that only applies if a person truly was touched by the Hand of GOD. When someone has been delivered and touched by the LORD, the fragrance of His Oil will become evident on the person's life. Transformation *(inward/ outward change)* is evident by the witness of others, whether they say it or not. A butterfly does not continue to look like or behave like or have the same characteristics of a caterpillar after the metaphoric cycle is completed.

There is a blood cost for the anointing, which includes **pain** and **suffering**, two processes that are divinely effective for the Potter to remold the clay for the benefit of Kingdom promotions to be occupied in this land and the eternal life reward at the second coming of the Lord on the clouds *(Greek Parousia: arrival, visible presence)*. I understand clearly, no one with common sense picks or have desires to go through any type of suffering, windstorm or fire for no reason. However, this is the process for processing which the LORD has chosen. And certainly we all want what GOD has for us, but who would ever think or expect that the Anointing of GOD was given to a degree which consisted of pain and suffering. None of us thought or comprehended that thought; yet it's biblical.

As you study the WORD of GOD, you'll find the way of son-ship *(heir)* involves not only favor, but suffering, a spiritual whip used just has our Savior was fogged and scourged for the sins of humanity. It's not a pretty, fun, delightful, desirable or attractive road to travel, but afterwards there are spiritual blessings, if we are trained by it and proven by GOD. The Lord's discipline is an act of His love and holiness.

FAITH DECLARATON

OPEN YOUR MOUTH! SPEAK GOD'S WORD BY FAITH!

IN JESUS NAME, I DECREE THAT I BE LOOSEN FROM MY WORRIES, GRIEFS, PAINS AND DISAPPOINTMENTS BY THE AUHORITY AND POWER OF HOLY SPIRIT. I ARREST AND TAKE CAPTIVE EVERY VAIN THOUGHT. I COMMAND THOSE CHAINS OF DEFEAT, PRAYERLESSNESS AND HOPELESSNESS TO LOOSE ME IN JESUS NAME. I DECREE THE ENEMY THAT WAS CHASING ME BE CUT DOWN BROKEN INTO PIECES BY THE WORD OF GOD IN JESUS NAME. I COMMAND EVERY SYMPTOM OF THE ISSUE TO BE DESOLVED IN JESUS NAME BY THE FIRE OF THE HOLY GHOST AND THAT LOFTY MOUNTAIN BOUGHT LOW. I COMMAND EVERY TORMENTING SPIRIT BE BROKEN IN JESUS NAME. I COMMAND THE FORCE AGAINST ME TO BOW AT THE NAME OF JESUS AND EVERY WEAPON FORMED TO BE BROKEN NOW IN JESUS NAME. I DECREE IT TO BE SO IN JESUS NAME. I THANK YOU LORD FOR VICTORY NOW! FOR HEALING NOW! FOR THE MANIFESTATION NOW IN JESUS NOW!

The answer is in the making. You keep praying by faith and abide in alignment with Truth until it is revealed in Jesus name. The Presence of the Lord is here. Expectation! Receive It!
It's Already…Done.

I DECREE THAT THE POWER OF GOD STIR MY SPIRIT. BREATHE HOLY SPIRIT, OH, BREATH BREATHE. I DECREE MY MIND AND HEART BE HEALED, RESTORED NOW! LORD I PRAY YOU MANIFEST YOUR PRESENCE IN MY ATMOSPHERE IN JESUS NAME! IN JESUS NAME! I COMMAND MY SPIRIT TO RESPOND IN OBEDIENCE TO THE VOICE OF THE SPIRIT OF THE LIVING GOD. BE AWAKENED!

The Spirit of GOD is meeting the need now. Hallelujah! Hallelujah! Receive it by Faith and tell the Lord I Thank You. Hallelujah! Let Praise Continually Flow from Your Heart Off Your Lips In Spite Of. GOD Is Turning It Around For Your Good. Hallelujah! Receive It By Faith! Bless the Lord.

AMEN.

Self Examination between you and the Lord:

1. Am I in alignment with the Word of GOD? How does <u>endurance</u> apply to you personally? Why?

_____

_____

_____

2. How would I respond if I was clothed in the pain, frustration, agony or grief that I may see another clothed with? Are my actions pleasing or displeasing in the sight of the Lord?

_____

_____

_____

3. Is there any hope in me praying? And How? I'm I praying according to the will? Do I need to change the way I am seeking GOD?

_____

_____

_____

4. Write strategies: How does God command me to respond in distressful seasons?

_____

_____

_____

5. What should I be doing in the wait, while waiting for God to manifest my answer?

_____

_____

_____

6. Am I showing fruitful acts of mercy, compassion, patience, meekness or love toward others whole heartily?

_____

_____

_____

7. Am I reflecting the Yahweh Supernatural Fruit of Patience? _____.

8. What is the grace virtue for obtaining <u>endurance</u> growth? _____.

9. How are you seeing your self?

_____

_____

_____

10. Do what you see and think line up with the Word of God? _____.

11. Create three goals to change your vision to God's vision about who you are in Christ.

     • _____

     • _____

     • _____

b) And create three goals to change your thinking to match Christ's thinking.

     • _____

     • _____

     • _____

Write, Memorize & Pray the Sword of the Spirit:

1. Psalm 130:5

_____

_____

_____

2. Psalm 33:20

_____

_____

_____

3. Psalm 27:14

_____

_____

_____

4. Galatians 2:20

_____

_____

_____

5. Romans 10:13

_____

_____

_____

6. Lamentations 3:24-26

_____

_____

_____

NOTES:

CHAPTER FOUR

HUMAN SUFFERING WITH
A SUPERNATURAL GAIN

As we watch the world news we see many horrific incidents and injustice. Incidents such as forest fires, destruction of homes, neighborhoods, hunger, Christians being martyred for their faith in Jesus Christ, people loosing their lives in senseless crimes, healthcare downfall, diseases claiming the lives, mother's loosing babies to deadly diseases, children killed by drive by shootings, premature deaths, marital difficulties, dysfunctional family patterns and generational curses rehearsed in every day life. Sufferings come in many forms as you see. The point is that suffering in some form of another is bound to happen in this world in which we live due to spiritual immorality of humanity. All will eventually experience some type of suffering: mild, light, heavy or severe. **The Bible tells us {Ecclesiastes 1:9} even**

from the times of old, there is nothing new under the sun. However, those that truly believe and are desperate for change can experience the Glory encounter. The LORD has given the believer His **Holy Spirit** *(Greek **Parakletos**, Comforter)* who will comfort us, guide and teach us all things {**John 14:16-17, 26; 16:13**}. Even though suffering can be sad, difficult or devastating to a person's emotional well being, you must believe that GOD cares for you. And the promises He made to guide you also are qualified for the wilderness experiences; those dry, weary, shadowy and empty places where no one can rescue you from the fangs of agony, but Almighty GOD. And in knowing because He cares, He is obligated to perform His TRUTH for those who will confidently seek and rely on Him. He is waiting to intervene on your behalf, but you must invite Him into your conflict arena of confusion, sadness, pain or deep hurt. The Kingdom mandate now is to tear the wall down which blocks you and GOD and open up your mouth- heart to communicate. Declare the justice of the LORD be established from the front door to the back door of your atmosphere; that means all that is connected to or concerns you. In order to declare the justice of the Lord you must partake of the WORD of God daily…study the WORD.

Suffering in many cases is ordained for the purpose of the sufferer and for GOD to meet *one on one* without any direct intervention from other people. There are some cases where GOD will not allow anyone else to be able to bring a release to your situation. It will depend on how bad you want GOD to move for you. Although GOD is omniscient, all knowing,

He will not intrude on anyone. The Bible gives three good sound simple instructions: **A.S.K. {Matthew 7:7; Luke 11:9-13} Ask! Seek! Knock!** Prayer, a form of communication, is a dialogue not monolog. Just as you talk to the Lord, He is listening to your heart and longs to respond back to you according to His provision for you. ABBA provision is the divine justice tailored for your soul, situation and sphere. There are different types of prayers and levels to reach as you stretch in GOD. He knows by the spiritual radar how to locate you in the spirit. He desires to speak to you to give peace and guidance through the existing suffering. Many may not believe GOD still speaks. He may speak in a small audible or still voice by His Holy Spirit, through others whom He has given divine wisdom and divine insight to, through the written Living Word and through other avenues of His chosen, like billboards or commercials. He is not limited.

The distress of suffering may consist of suffering short or long term, suffering a need, a loss, shame, violence or other. As you have read in the previous chapter, one form of suffering is due to the adversities a person undergoes through distinctive experience; while another form of suffering is related for the sake of righteousness which is called persecution, still distinctive, but at a more intense level which results in being martyred while contending for faith in Christ. Pain and suffering aren't desires at the top of anyone shopping list. You should not desire or want what another person has because you don't know what they may have had to endure in order to reach their goal *good or bad* or victory successfully. When GOD created us, He put all we needed of Him in us; for we are created in the image of Yahweh Elohim. In the fall the shift robbed humanity of true riches of dominance. But because Jesus suffered the penalty for all those that would turn to him, he restored us through regeneration, the Cross and His Ruach *(Spirit)*. Therefore, what the believer needs in order to rule, conquer and possess is *Already* inside of our spirit by the Spirit. The Kingdom of God within by way of Holy Spirit's regeneration work! However, most of us have not realized the treasure of gold that is hidden inside of us. In our humanity we have to go through fires for that which is spiritual to come forth. Because GOD is holy and is bringing us into complete perfection in Christ, He allows suffering to come for the birthing of what is *Already* in you in seed form to come forward. This is His Will. It is in you to be great, to be holy, to be brilliant, to be above average, purposeful, anointed, creative, gifted, talented, an overcomer, royal kings and priests *(Kingdom conditions)*, to rise out and above troubles. It is in you, but the developmental stages come through the valley of suffering.

GOD will allow a spiritual peeling back of the soul that will bring tears of emotional distress to take place in order for the gold in us to be seen, received, appreciated, honored and respected. Faith and the Glory of the LORD is priceless and of great value like gold. Each believer has within their human spirit the seed of righteousness; all that is glorified by the Father is to be a duplicate reflection in the mirror. Suffering with endurance moves the spirit of fear out of the way in order for divine purpose, courage, integrity and divine boldness will rise to the surface by the working of the Holy

Spirit. Suffering on the outward side doesn't appear to be working in our favor when we are in the fog of it. But as we reach to GOD he will intervene as he did with Brother Job and myself in our dilemmas; developing the story for His Glory. What the Lord has invested and placed in us at the cost of His BLOOD is of great worth and is given in manifested measure over time. It is there, but time has its place in the new renovation of you in the image of GOD. The believer's gifts or graces that came by the Promise, Holy Spirit, are in you. The Power of Faith authorizes us to speak things that are not as though they were into your atmosphere. In the sphere where there is power to lay hands on the sick and see them recover, the power to release those that may have wounded you and the power to complete a task under pressure without being consumed by the pressure or the power to perform the skills of a job gracefully, power to humble self, the power to talk right, power to embrace the testing, power to heed the Holy Spirit, power to get a prayer through and the power over all the power of the enemy. All these spiritual blessings plus more are equipped in the Holy Seed of Righteousness within you; yet will rise with mature effectiveness in time as you yield. The **Anointing** *(the Oil, Supernatural ability, influencer)* will come through the pathway of suffering. Even to live holy will cause friction from the inside out, but as Apostle Paul informs us of the joy to live *(new nature)* is Christ and to die *(old nature)* is gain {**Philippians 1:21**}. Suffering with supernatural endurance will instruct, lead and show us how to **suffer well** and that is victory. The supernatural security... Peace of GOD is a reality to be received that cannot be bought.

Innocent suffering, even though it is undesired should also be viewed through supernatural spiritual lens as an instrument or tool for each of us to learn how to draw closer to the Lord, how to hear, how to war in the Spirit, how to stand still to see the salvation of the Lord, suffer long, agape, forgiveness, contentment, integrity, discipline, loyalty and not to compromise. Yes, I feel one's pain and thoughts; it's not easy and it is not to be done in your own strength. Remember, we will be devoured in our strength. Perhaps, we may say we possess those virtues; suffering will work for our good to promote the **pure persuasion** of our testimony in Christ to the next level. It is under pressure a sufferer will find out what virtues are truly possessed in their character. Suffering can bring the worst out of anyone if not humbled in the storm that rages. It is possible to become bitter in the midst of troubled times. The unfruitful fruit of bitterness can spring up like monkey grass to choke life out of you and bring in desolation, depression, coldness, sadness, misery and despondency because the personal distress one is experiencing is non-favorable to them. The unfruitful fruit of bitterness works undercover slowly spreading up inner sabotage, anger, animosity and deep hatred, etc. Beware people of GOD, satan will use your emotional feelings as a door to your soul to detour your grow, faith, hope and trust in the Lord, as your savior, deliverer, healer, as the Truth and to blind you. The accuser of the children of Yahweh, our adversary the devil, does not play fair. He will come in appearing like a flood to overpower you and drown out the voice of God, kill your relationship with GOD and others, to seize your faith; from faith to fear, to doubt, to unbelief and destroy any form of communication with GOD. But the Lord is able to raise a blood banner against him. The devil knows that when the Hand of Yahweh bring you fully out you will have a divine revelatory understanding of your real identity in Christ and will be a powerful force against the gates of hell. When suffering, pain, anxiety, frustrations, depression and crisis want to linger, it is crucial that the believer who suffers tarry diligently in worship, prayer and in the Word. The forces against you will appear great in strength, but know that evil force is only as powerful as you magnify it to be. You may not see it that way, but there is a force behind pain which will grab you for the worst.

When all the bad is continually talked up, all the negative, all the hurt, all the what if's or whatever it may be that doesn't align itself with TRUTH, this is described as the spiritual process of building a fortified fortress or force field, a sphere of negativity, that will build bars around your thought- mind sphere to uphold carnality as ruler. The Bible refers to it as a stronghold. Overthrow the evil of your lower mind, your feelings, emotions, your desires and your affections by the washing of the WORD. In other words, magnify, make large and enlarge the WORD like a tent over the dwelling of your mind and heart. "Overthrow all persuasion of the soul- heart that is wicked; out of holy alignment." The WORD of GOD will stand like a barrier and a flood in your spirit against the works of darkness, spiritual snares, weakness and stumbling blocks. Ask GOD to remove blinders and all callousness and hardness of heart so you can respond to His TRUTH, Repent and Settle in the code of Favor. As you begin to cry out to the

Lord, put time in with the LORD and He will manifest the healing process of deflating by destroying that atmospheric spiritual disturbance on your behalf; Glory to GOD, taking life from that which sucks life from you. Let the process begin. But you must whole-heartily turn and trust GOD while suffering. The GOD in us is greater than anything we face {**1 John 4:4**}. Let Him Rise!

The pressure produced during suffering is to crucify and purify the deeds of the flesh and its dependency on self. In suffering we realize how weak the flesh is and how we sink into sin so easily. Suffering will show us the lack of endurance, strength and ability to regain control over crisis or inability to erase the situation. In suffering the sufferer learns to withdrawn from self and draw to the fountain of refreshing waters which is the Lord. Suffering can cause the heart and will of man to bow its will; to rethink things over, to repent of arrogance, stubbornness and independence apart from GOD. Suffering dethrones self off of the throne to give Yeshua access to the throne of your heart as Redeemer, Lord, Healer and Counselor.

Coming into such powerful revelation will change your reflection to reflect the way of the Master in one's life. The Potter cannot reshape the clay if the clay does not surrender its will and desires in the fire. This is a heart/soul condition known by several names: rebellion, stiff-neck, stubbornness, hard hearted and strong willed. This condition can result in the withdrawal of the Hand of the Lord for the enemy to come in because of a rebellious heart that continues in pride and refuses to humble. This is a condemning action to place one's self in. Suffering acts like a chisel that strips and peel with no boundaries; regardless of the neighborhood you reside in, the model of your car, the school you attend, the job title or position you hold, your income bracket, the color of your skin, the side of town you live or who you may or may not be married to or how often to give to charities. Suffering does not discriminate against any person. It has no regards to respect of persons. Suffering is always personal and emotional.

Suffering persecution is the reason why Yeshua HaMashiach *(Messiah, Anointed One)* came into this dying naked perverse world to do the Will of the Father, as the suffering servant and to conquer the crime of sin in His flesh. As born again believers, we must prepare ourselves spiritually to suffer for righteousness sake or persecution for what we believe. Just as Yeshua suffered for righteousness sake, the believer will suffer as a son *(position, heir)* for righteousness also. We must stand for Christ at all cost knowing that our eternal hope is not in vain. Seeing that our afflictions, our troubles are declared to be light at this very instant compared to the blood covenant cost of Yeshua *(Jesus)* which has *already* purchased our redemption and given us victory, power and strength to overthrow the weights that lead into sin. For this cause it is through the blood, death, burial and resurrection of Jesus the Christ, that the Ecclesia has eternal victory which bypasses the distresses of this age. This is our hope. When you find yourself in the furnace of trials, you are not alone, because the Spirit of the Lord is in the furnace with you to sustain you, speak to you, comfort you, direct you, reveal, reaffirm His Eternal Word, Glory and give you mighty power to bring you into a *wealthy place* of experiencing real peace, safety, abounding faith and assurance in Him. Those are riches that man cannot give another person nor be purchased with money. **Peter said silver and gold *(material)* have I none, but what I do possess I give unto you {Acts 3:6}.** Peter sowed the seed of the Kingdom of God that was needed for a distressed soul in trouble. The spiritual authority and command demonstrated by Peter released from heaven in the midst manifested restoration which qualified that soul for greatness and unlocked hidden potential. The Kingdom's demonstrative power source transcends the limitations that you may have bound yourself to in mind and deed. This is the dimension of the dominion of GOD that is within you. This dimension summons believers to arise to the occasion that is set before us in faith persistence will-power. GOD has doors unlocked waiting for you access with your name on it. God has put a hidden treasure in you filled with gold and silver, to access His Kingdom in the Heaven, *"LET YOUR KINGDOM COME, LET IT BE DONE ON EARTH JUST AS IT IS IN HEAVEN."*

FAITH DECREE

I Decree That As You Holdfast To the Living Hope, Not Giving Into The Pain of Suffering or Disappointment From Temporal Things Which All Suffer, That You Be Found With Supernatural Confidence, Knowing Without

Wavering In Faith Your Answer Is Already Prepared ready to be pulled down by the power of praise and worship (seeking) from your soul, prayer, obedience, love and faith.

And It Is So In Jesus Name. Hallelujah.

This is faith present tense: to believe it is done in order to receive; your faith is the evidence of it, according to the written word {**Hebrew 11:1**}. Things which are seen are temporal, they don't last forever, yet things that are unseen are eternal. Let's keep our eyes on the mark, Christ Crucified! Christ Resurrected! Now at the Right Hand of Authority, Power and Majesty; making intercession for the Ecclesia that our faith fails us not. GLORY!

Your faith in Christ will be tested; whether on your job, in the mission field, ministry, marriage, divorce, single, church leadership, college, schools, family, personal and in the market place. When your faith is being proven for greatness, it will be the evidence through you that you're no longer sinking, but walking on water. No longer overcome by what was formed to destroy or count you out. The thing you thought you couldn't do, couldn't achieve, wasn't qualified for or spoken against… faith has declared it achievable. Divine-faith transfers you out of regress into progress. No one can truly stand strong *effectively* against opposition until their faith has been proven. Even then, we must remain prayerful that GOD empowers us spiritually, emotionally and mentally with His Ruach

HaKodesh *(Holy Spirit)* to become flint toward all that the devil will use in this world against us and our faith confession. Ruach HaKodesh is working it out for your good in the bad, the ugly, the impossible and the unthinkable. There is a shifting in the realm of the spirit of agreement through your act of confidence and obedience. We must become concrete proof in the spirit of our mind regarding what we believe, why we believe what we believe and that there is no shadow of turning in your walk of faith. In your storm when active faith is to be presently working, the storm should produce a righteous anger that erects Holy Spirit authority to stand up in you giving off the fragrance in your spirit that you are persuaded in mind, persuaded in heart, persuaded in behavior and persuaded in soul that nothing or nobody will separate you from the love of God {**Romans 8:38-39**}. Holy Spirit helps you to engage forward from the current condition in your **psuche** to gain closure. Holy Spirit is at work developing a spiritual building, refining character and building spiritual credentials. Therefore, be confident in the declared promise that every good work which Yeshua has begun in you He will perfect until it is finished {**Philippians 1:6**}. The question is, "Are you allowing the work of the Holy Spirit to work perfection in you or have you blocked the work of Holy Spirit? Yes, all things do work together for them that love the Lord and who are called according to His purpose, but He will not work against your will. **Surrendering, humility and submission** are key elements for the Lord to work in your soul. God doesn't force His will, His way or His love upon anyone. He gives every heart the freedom of choice called free-will. So allow Holy Spirit to perfect you in Christ. I repeat "In Christ."

Trials and tribulations in this world help to prepare the church for such persecution that is coming to this world. If we go through life not being able to bear anything, withstand pressures, endure troubles, not applying the WORD of GOD for yourself, not stepping out on faith or not seeing the WORD manifest itself in your personal life that can be a leading cause for spiritual chaos, defeat and shame. Spiritual chaos equals a spiritual decline in faith. Where there is a faith decline the enemy has sown seeds of fear, doubt, confusion and unbelief. Beware of the devil's hidden devices. As children of God, we must not be naïve to Satan's strategies. God has already given a way of escape, it must be worked out by faith, obedience and He will give those that worship Him strategies. Remember, the scripture says when we have been proven, exercised, trained while suffering under pressure, only then will the fruit of righteousness yield peace and holiness as our reward. If we endure discipline God deals with believers as with sons {**Hebrew 12:6-11; Revelation 3:19**}. **The Bible tells us {Hebrew 12:29} God is a consuming fire.** He sanctifies the heart of those that are His sons through the pressure of suffering. We win because our GOD and His Kingdom cannot be shaken or compromised or overthrown. Therefore, this is His love and as a result of your endurance through Him you will win. He defeated **ALL** that would attempt to terminate you! Jesus finished it all at the cross; go through, the plan is designed for you to win. You'll come out victorious not defeated by the circumstances. All of us who have children and love them will correct and discipline them. This is for the advancement of their life's future; near and far, maturity, understanding, growth, safety, well being and as our responsibility as caring parents. ABBA, who is greater, does the same spiritually for His spiritual children, steering us into complete perfection in Christ. If we do not stand firm in faith, we will not stand at all. Because you now know the end result, you will remain in the race, overcome by activating faith which is supernatural and walking in agape.

There are varieties of levels of intensity in suffering that a person may experience. There are different levels of suffering, different levels of pain, different levels of anxiety that any normal person can cope with before breaking and even different levels of tolerance. Because there are levels, no one knows what they can handle until they are underneath or weighed down by pressures of whatever type of wind, hurricane or fire it may be symbolically. Which means each person's personal experience (*the focus here is on the crisis not the person),* the weight of the crisis itself will detail the response from that soul, but not necessarily the outcome. I repeat not necessarily the outcome. No two persons are made up of the same fibers; although, we are all flesh and blood. What we do share in common are emotions that are revealed after coming into a burdened situation, whether they are suppressed or released emotions. Be encouraged by knowing whatever storm may rise that as you bow your will, seek God's face and humble yourself the Potter is designing you as a weapon beaten by the fire to become a fierce warrior in the Kingdom of GOD in this world. A spiritual warrior who will be on watch on behalf of others assigned by GOD. He is molding in you resistance that will perform through you for the greater good. He will cause your spiritual eyes to see in the oncoming trials. As God translate your spiritual sight to see keen, the winds of change will no longer have an extreme effect over you. Because of grace God favors you and enhanced your character; you are capable by the Spirit to minister to others through their adversities. His Glory in you will break forth by His handy work of exalting you in due season. When you learn how to embrace afflictions by the Power of GOD which brings you into perfection in Christ Jesus, you will bear virtues of a sound, sober mind, sincerity and whole heartedness on the inner parts toward the provision of Yahweh in Christ.

FAITH DECREE

I Declare This Day That You Will Not Stagger Any Longer As One Drunk With Much Wine Or Mixed Drinks Who Knows Not Their Next Step Or Direction, But That You Be Filled With The Supernatural Wine Of Joy And Healing.

Spiritual posture is birthed forth during the adversities or trials that we encounter. The exalting from your weight of difficulty will denote the anointing placed on your life to give you vision, to keep you free and for the advancement of the Kingdom of Yahweh through you to others in need. In this world in which we live and are so easily drawn attached to is not under the ruling government of GOD. In this world everyone at some point will come face to face with some type of trouble in their personal life that may feel as if a millstone was wrapped around the neck holding one beneath their potential from accomplishing the fullness that life has to offer, such as, peace, success and joy. **The Bible tells us {2 Corinthians 4:4} that satan is the god of this world, the prince of the air.** Satan's assignment is to kill, to steal and to destroy. Knowing what the enemy's job consists of and how too effectively warfare against him will bring you into victory every time. All powers, all laws, all ways that opposes the ruling government of the Kingdom of Yahweh in the world are under satan's ruling power of the kingdom of darkness. The evil one rules from the second heavens at this appointed time until his doom day is fulfilled. As we war spiritually, our posture of prayer will elevate us above the dominion of the kingdom of darkness **{Ephesians 2:6}**. Yeshua declares in Him believers have *Already* won while waiting for the manifestation of promise to manifest.

Pressures, the weights of pain and anxiety, we face are not what moves GOD to act. We would think it would; however, God is bound only to Himself…by His Logos. Therefore, He is moved by Himself, the **WORD** made flesh. The test begins as pressures grow heavily and appear. The testing of suffering is a testing of our faith and its advancement. Each believer's faith will and must be put on trial to be proven to be genuine faith. Our faith muscle is to be increased under pressure. The testing of your faith is part of the refining process of cultivating us spiritually, as well as, naturally; in addition, disciplinary actions are apart of the process also. During these moments it is the time stay before the LORD in much prayer so you won't be overtaken by temptation. This is when we learn how to pour deeply from within our souls. When there is a desperate cry for help from a place of deep emotional anguish, a place of desperation, you will empty yourself on the altar. You will become the sacrifice laid upon the fire ready for the Master's touch. How GOD chose to turn it around is His choice. This is when the revelations of GOD may begin to unfold gradually in your life as you come to an end of self.

You know what you've heard or have been taught in church. Suffering will break down the limitations that were set up by traditional teachings of men or false teachings in the Body of Christ. Now you're in a state where the Spirit of GOD can meet your spirit to reveal divine revelation of His multifaceted Spirit, a level you have never experienced before. What you have been taught in church and believe will be tested in the fire. Will it burn or will it remain? Everything concerning your spirituality will go through the fire for purging. Life under the scope of GOD during suffering is between you and Him. The devil's target is for your destruction; lose sight and slip back to worldliness. But the plan of Yahweh is for divine purpose to arise in the supernatural Power which is not revealed by men, but by the Ruach of Yahweh. In the Lord's eye it doesn't matter how great the winds blow or how bad the storm looks, the pressure allowed is designed to squeeze you, break you, uproot old habits, old thinking, old ways, corrupt patterns, death cycles and to crush you for the divine makeover. It sounds horrible and harsh; But God never fails those that put their trust in Him. His purpose must be birthed. We were not created by design to carry burdens. He created us by design to commune, bathe in His Presence, not in the problems. Let this revelation soak daily for absorption. I testify of the purging and the crushing.

Psalm 139:8
Oh taste and see that the Lord is good blessed is every many that put there trust in Him.

Isaiah 40:31
But they that wait on the LORD shall renew their strength; they shall mount up with wings as eagles; they shall run, and not be weary; and they shall walk, and not faint.

FAITH DECLARATION

Open Your Mouth And Speak Life…

I DECREE MY FAITH WHILE UNDER THE FIRE, IN THE FIRE BE INCREASED, DEVELOPED, MAXIMIZED IN ABUNDANCE AND THE ADVERSITY THAT WAS FORMED TO BRING THE FIRE, ANOINTING OF HOLY SPIRIT OUT OF YOU; YET MEANT TO BURN…DESTROY ME, BE PUT OUT BY THE ARSENAL OF THE SPOKEN ETERNAL WORD OF GOD IN THE MATCHLESS, POWERFUL NAME OF YESHUA (JESUS) HAMASHIACH (MESSIAH) THE CHRIST (CHRISTOS). THERE IS A PROMOTION THROUGH THE FIRE. I WILL RECEIVE MY ROYAL PROMOTION IN JESUS NAME. THE SPIRIT OF GOD IS WITH THE CALLED OUT ONES HE CALLED OUT OF DARKNESS INTO THE LIGHT. THE LORD PROMISED NEVER TO LEAVE ME NOR FORSAKE ME.

RECEIVE IT IN FAITH IN JESUS NAME.

AMEN.

Once your soul is empty, then He's ready to pour into your spirit and fill your soul with fresh oil. You will not know when the time is, but He does. It is crucial to be in Christ, so you can experience the mixture of His peace, His love He speaks about Himself toward you. The WORD is the supernatural energy that comes alive and breathes on you, but you must trust Him and take Him at His Word without any hesitation. Your life depends on what you say you believe and how you respond to what you believe. When He's done pouring a portion, fruit will come forth, new **wine** *(fresh oil)* will burst forward. Even though pressure is the method used, faith and prayer are the antidotes to get to the other side in victory. It's something about the condition of brokenness *(crushed)* and a contrite *(remorseful)* spirit that GOD the Father will not despise. YHVH is the LORD GOD; holy, loving, infinite, longsuffering and eternal who sent Yeshua Hamashiach to be broken for the wickedness of wretched humanity. He is the lover of souls.

Beloved, be encouraged I am not saying these things to be mean, but to inform you of truth which brings deliverance, hope, vision and soberness. I am speaking to you from my personal experiences which took me into what I call the major encounter with the Father. When we are informed, then we can better be prepared. When our experiences do not resolve themselves in a proper time frame, yet continually to grow like contagious windstorms resulting in extreme pressure in our weary souls, they will crush us into pieces. While we live in this fading world trials will continue to exist and repeat the crazy cycle over and over and over, until all things are made new. Jesus told us a truth with a promise attached. **The Bible tells us {John 16: 33} that in me** *(Jesus)* **you might have peace, in the world ye will have tribulations.** Now He warned us troubles will be; we are not exempt from them, but the key to receive His peace *(wholeness, healthiness)* is we must be in Him. But if you notice He did not stop there and give us a pity party. He said, "Be of courage *(boldness, made up mind)* for I have overcome the world." Yeshua *(Jesus)* has completely conquered and provided a way of escape for every problem in this world that we may come in contact with during the course of life. We are commanded to be courageous, even in the dry places, by the Ruach of GOD to advance in the supernatural as Yeshua demonstrated while on earth. He also tells us to take heart, be strong, bold in Him, trust Him, and depend on the provision-care that has been completed through Him for us. The LORD is saying, "Since I *(Jesus-blood-keys)* have already overcome the world then, you will overcome by the same power if you be in me, take courage and faint not. **"HE WILLS THAT YOU OVERCOME!"** What awesome news of assurance for today. Receive It!

FAITH DECREE

The LORD Declares For You To Place Your Confidence In Him, Take Courage, Keep On And Don't Faint! I, The Lord, I AM Is Making You To Mount Up As An Eagle To Soar With Eagles Wings And To Conquer. "I AM MAKING YOU!" The Pruning Must Come First, Then The Oil.

Receive It by Faith and tell the Lord Thank You. The Lord said you are special to Him. GOD loves you unconditionally. He knows our corrupt character during the storm, but He loves us so much that His Agape continues toward us in our metaphoric stages of ugliness through the transitions. Love Him back by coming out of that season before the season is up and pass you by to die in the pass, spiritually first…choose life and live.

Now some issues are created by our own selfish desires and over ambitious ways, which will cause unnecessary suffering. Sometimes decisions, choices or practices whether good or bad will cause distress, maybe from of lack of knowledge, experience, stubbornness or lack of self control. Ask the Lord to increase within your spirit the fruit of self-control in all areas the fruit needs to be sown and developed. "It is Oil of the Supernatural; Oil to deepen the inner-man's strength." It does not matter if the affliction is minor or major. What is huge to my eyes may be small in someone else's eyes and what is huge in your eyes may be nothing in someone else's eyes. GOD will use small things to get your attention as well. Then there are major afflictions that may come; due to the magnitude of the heaviness of the weight, the enemy will use the pressure of the pain to kill, steal and destroy you through whatever door he can get a foot hold. Those areas under attack start within the realm of our soul *(psuche)* will-power, intellect, thoughts, feelings, intuition, perception and lead toward our faith being attacked. Whatever the devil attempts to rob, if the door is open he will take all it.

GOD wants fresh Oil *(New Wine)* dripping in the lives of believers. And when oil is dripping something happens in the atmosphere around you and with others, especially those who are receivers, waiting to be fed. Yes, it is a deep revelation of GOD that will unfold in the next chapter. The Lord will fill you with His New Wine in measure as He determines; spiritually traveling, growing from little faith to great faith, to abounding faith and growing in the perfection of the sanctifying work of Ruach Hakodesh is the reward of another measure of fresh oil through **suffering well**. Holy Spirit proportionally perfects in us how to suffer-well. We need Fresh Oil to break cycles, yokes, to build up family structures, to accomplish daily tasks, walk in His love, walk in loyalty, to govern well in the earth, to witness effectively, to walk in kingdom dominion with royal power, to dispel bush fires in our lives and etc,. Believers need Fresh Oil to withstand the physical forces that will rise in life in this world, to fulfill the mandated divine purpose on our lives in the earth, to saturate us with the Fear of the Lord and to be effective in witnessing wherever you are called to be light. Your going through the fire was intentional for the motivation of revealing the purposes you were created for. We Are Overcomers In Christ Alone!

FAITH DECLARATION

Open Your Mouth, Speak Forth Life…

I Decree by the Power And the Authority Invested In Me In the Name of Jesus, devil, You Will Not Take Anything from Me (*name(s)* _____) That I Am Fully Aware of That Belongs to Me as the Redeemed of the Lord. I am Blessed And Walking Under The Fragrance of the Oil of Joy. I Am Favored Even In the Midst Of My Distress. I Am Faithful To the One Who Hears My Cry And Answers By Fire. ABBA's Word Does Not Return To Him Void, But Accomplishes Where Forth It Is Sent. The Living Word Is Working It Out For My Good. I Am Blessed Coming In And Going Out. I Am Blessed When I Rise And When I Lye Down To Rest. I Am Blessed To Be Above My Problems And Not Beneath Them. The LORD Has Appointed Me And Anointed Me (_____, _____) As The Head And Not The Tail. I Am Who GOD Says I Am; Nothing Less And Nothing More In Jesus Name. I Decree A Hedge of Protection Around All That Concerns Me (_____), Because The LORD GOD, my Master and King, Cares For Me…I Am. I Am His. Lord, I Thank You For Empowering Me With Your Anointing To Live And Not Die, To Rise And Not Sink In Jesus Name.

Amen.

Believers Build Yourself Up In Your Most Holy Faith

Hebrew 12:11

For the moment all discipline seems painful rather than pleasant, but later it yields the peaceful fruit of righteousness to those who have been trained by it.

Revelation 21:4

He will wipe away every tear from their eyes, and death shall be no more, neither shall there be morning, nor crying, nor pain anymore, for the former things, have passed away.

1 Peter 4:12-19

Beloved, do not be surprised at the fiery trial when it comes upon you to test you, as though something strange were happening to you. But rejoice insofar as you share Christ's sufferings that you may also rejoice and be glad when his glory is revealed. If you are insulted for the name of Christ, you are blessed, because the Spirit of glory and of God rests upon you. But let none of you sufferer as a murderer (hatred) or a thief or an evildoer or as a meddler. Yet if anyone suffer as a Christian, let him not be ashamed, but let him glorify God in that name.

Romans 8:18

For I consider that the sufferings of this present time are not worth comparing with the glory that is to be revealed to us.

1 Peter 5:10
And after you have suffered a little while, the God of all grace, who has called you to his eternal glory in Christ, will himself restore, confirm, strengthen, and establish you.

2 Timothy 3:12
Indeed, all those who desire to live a godly life in Christ Jesus will be persecuted.

Psalm 34:19
Many are the afflictions of the righteous, but the Lord delivers him out of them all.

Psalm 119:71
It is good for me that I was afflicted, that I might learn your statues.

Isaiah 43:2
When you pass through the waters, I will be with you; and through the rivers, they shall not overwhelm you; when you walk through the fire you shall not be burnt, and the flame shall not consume you.

Matthew 24:13
But the one who endures to the end will be saved.

Romans 8:35
Who shall separate us from the love of Christ? Shall tribulation, or distress, or persecution, or famine, or nakedness, or danger, or sword?

John 3:16

For God so loved the world, that he gave his only Son, that whoever believes in him should not perish but have eternal life.

James 1:12

Blessed is the man who remains steadfast under trial, for when he has stood the test he will receive the crown of life, which God has promised to those who love him.

Jeremiah 29:11

For I know the plans I have for you, declares the Lord, plans for welfare and for evil, to give you a future and a hope.

Luke 9:23-25

And he said to all, if anyone would come after me, let him deny himself and take up his cross daily and follow me. For whoever would save his life will lose it, but whoever loses his life for my sake will save it. For what does it profit a man if he gains the whole world and loses or forfeits himself?

Review: the Behavior, Heart, Mind and Soul

1. We must put into habitual practice Ephesians 4:26-27. Write it.

_____

_____

_____

2. What possibly could out of suffering over bearing crisis in anyone's life?

_____

_____

_____

3. Since adversity occurs at unknown times in the life cycle, how should you engage in any case of suffering *knowing* the Lord will not leave you nor forsake you? What should your deposition and tone reflect *knowing* GOD is your source?

_____

_____

_____

4. What would be the reason for an outward cause of emotional breakdown uproar in the soul of a person?

_____

_____

_____

5. What would be a purpose for God to allow such dramatizing distresses to occur, after all He is God?

_____

_____

_____

6. What does the word *sovereign* means and how does the definition reveals the nature of the Lord to you personally?

_____

_____

_____

7. What are the three key elements mentioned in this chapter that gives God access to work in your soul at all times?

   • _____

   • _____

   • _____

8. What is the Hebraic meaning and word of the English term church? _____.

9. What does endurance mean in your own words?

_____

_____

_____

NOTES:

CHAPTER FIVE

PENETRATING OIL AT THE ALTAR

The stress of burdens can be parallel to weights or a stone being carried across the shoulders and chest over an intense period of time. The weight of suffering can bring on shortness of breath, deranged thoughts and numbness to feelings and others, a mental disconnection, nightmares or blankness to reality. Such physical forces will weigh on one's ability to focus, make accurate decisions and responses. These weights are not easily shaken. They're not easily forgotten, forgiven, handled or easily overcome with your human ability. The weights can cause disarray to your mind that may lead to negative actions. We were not created anew to carry the pressures that come upon us as the world does; those who have no hope, no grace card or no concrete foundation. When the Lord stretches us to know Him in a greater way that stretch alone can cause deterioration. GOD created mankind in His image with purpose to worship, meet with Him, reign, regulate, subdue and conquer in the earth through His divine providence. Therefore, when we encounter sorrows at our front door we must not allow the pain of suffering to over take our thoughts or willpower. When we find ourselves in places of exertion due to long term suffering, we must press out of that arena by the Supernatural Power of Christ**.** I repeat the Supernatural Power of GOD made available through Christ. Those wilderness places will attempt to destroy the divine order of God's creative design if you bow in weakness to the pressures of limitations in the flesh. Yes, we all will confront something at sometime or another; however, you have been sanctioned and infused being a new creature in Christ to arise to the occasion in the **Strength of the Lord**, not your strength. That's a Kingdom benefit. What you are facing is bigger than you alone, but it's no match for GOD, Holy Spirit in you and Holy Spirit upon you or the Rock of your salvation. Yahweh unveiled in Christ *(Christos-Messiah)* the inaugurated course for you and me to obtain triumph and success through the blood of Jesus. It Is At Your Altar Where You Will Die To Self and Meet *(commune)* Him and Rise Under the Supernatural Power of Jehovah God, the place of sacrifice. I'm saying it again, *"IT IS AT THE ALTAR WHERE YOU'RE CONSUMED AND BECOME THE LIVING SACRIFICE CHOSEN FOR GREATNESS." HE IS THERE WAITING!* Yahweh wants your heart. He jealous over His child and wants all of you. This is not a worldly jealousy, but a holy and righteous jealousy. God's jealousy isn't tainted, corrupt or polluted.

The windstorms we're in and must face are permitted for the spiritual act of being the altar designed for us to become the sacrifice offered; the giving of ourself. This is what is meant to give or lay our lives prostrate before Him; the releasing of the old and familiar ways. The altar where Fresh Oil is poured is the place for release, exchange and vindication.

Hebrew word for the English term Sacrifice, Offering
Karbon: derived from the word karbonot,
"To draw near to God"
Zebach: the act of offering to God for the purpose of winning favor, security, involving a loss for a greater good

Hebrew word for the English word Altar
Mizbeah: giving up of something, to slaughter, a place of sacrifice

It is the penetrating Oil of the Glory of Yahweh, when released upon the person suffering that will break the yoke of strain and in return bring out the sacredness from within the disturbance. My altar, the place of sacrifice, from a dying of myself to God began in the storm duration of my pregnancy with my first born, Isaac DeShaun Tipton; his birth and his suffering from a birth abnormality from the beginning to the end. I endured for a season in sadness, confusion, pain, grief and agony; even in the hurt, there was strength not my own that was drawing me. I communicated all I new how to GOD, the bitter and the sweet. I was in a back and forth emotional sweeping with the Lord due to the intensity of the pressure turning me into ashes like unto a sacrifice. It's at the altar that we pour out, undress our heart and lay it all bare for Him to dress. Many of us do not understand or recognize ordained seasons that the LORD will use for plowing the soil of the heart to bring us to an end of ourselves or preparing to do a makeover in your soul for redirecting your life. GOD will use suffering to exhaust carnality in order to present another revelation of Himself to the sufferer. When disorder invades your comfort and all that you know seems to be in a far away land of the untouchable, your pain will erect thoughts and questions toward Yahweh in your mind as if to put Yahweh, who is All Powerful, on trial as if I was the judge. Is this not what many hearts have been or are guilty of? In this state of mind compared to that of Job would be considered normal for the preparation of being offered as a sacrifice for the slaughtering of the mind of the flesh that rise to persecute what it doesn't justify. The LORD foresees the agony, the pain, character content and the impurities of floating bitterness that is on the rise. The LORD foresees all the sleepless nights, the crying, the slobbering, the grief, the begging in prayer concerning the situation and the fear of receiving even more bad news at each doctor visit not knowing what was next. My God, My God.

The LORD in His sovereignty foresees all. Just as Jesus stated My God, my God why have you forsaken me, I personal believe ABBA looked away at some point for the natural force to accomplish its allowed ordained assignment…became the offering of substitute. Satan was allowed to move against Job for that season by getting permission first from Yahweh at the meeting {**Job 1:6-8**}. Is there a meeting about you in the heavenly courts? Just as ABBA turned His head away as Yeshua HaMashiach hung on that Cross at Calvary, taking the sins, the punishment and the curse of the world upon Himself to rectify the spiritual condition of humanity in order to be in a state worthy to be presented to ABBA {**Galatians 3:13-14**}. ABBA, Father willed Himself within Him to be the substitute for humanity in becoming the peace offering, burnt offering, sin offering, grain offering with oil and wine to be slaughtered. Yeshua, the sacrificial offering that released the Grace-Unmerited Favor Anointing with all its multifaceted forms and measurements unto mankind as the Will of the New Covenant. Yahweh's love is unlimited in all that He performs. We have to wait in anticipation, eagerness and look for the LORD who will answer. The Ecclesia is not to coward or drawback when it looks as if the LORD is far away that He can't be touched. I am declaring to you through word of knowledge, one on one, from GOD, Truth. **The Bible tells us {Psalm 145:18} The LORD is near to all who call on him, to all who call in truth.** The declaration stated is a promise with a condition to be met by the caller. GOD has a master plan and for that reason the believer in Christ will suffer well in JESUS Name.

Of course in our human condition we have emotions that will get out of control. We cry, shout at people, we get angry, give up, say ugly things, talk negatively, knock holes in the walls, kick doors, slam doors, cuss, fault-find, point fingers, have pity parties, stop praying, stop going to church, just attend the church, condemn the pastor or others that may get in the path and etc., things of the sort. All these things are related to the flesh, carnal mind, the sinful nature manifesting a spiritual tantrum; these are blemishes and the inner bleeding of the soul crying out *(spiritually)* for help. This is the state of peeling, stripping and pruning the undersurface of corruption that is to be laid on the altar for sacrifice. If you notice it starts within the human spirit traveling, affecting the mind and the soul; without us noticing due to the exertion of pain one begins to act the pain out negatively through the body of flesh. If the sufferer does not yield to the voice of GOD that will speak directly into their spirit or through someone or something else, that very innocent being may become tainted and deadly in the depth of their soul. The actions of the sufferer then may become justified in their eyes as being right because of the bitter taste of distress. The LORD knows these impurities will surface outwardly from one's spirit, attitude or behavior in undergoing seasons of distress. **The Bible tells us {Psalm 34:19} the righteous, upright person may have many troubles, but the Lord delivers him from them all. That's A Promised!** Because difficulties will arise in your life, the promise is He will, not might, not maybe, not if, but He will deliver the upright from them all. The soul must be in Him for remaining. All that contends against the one who puts his/her trust in the Lord, the Lord will contend against that very thing. This promise is the result of your faith stance in Christ as the redeemed of the LORD. Believers are the seed of righteousness {**Galatians 3:29**} engrafted in by *The Seed of Righteousness*; to be in Christ- signifies a bond, a merging, a uniting, a union and Lordship; and if Lordship, then ownership, if ownership, then you're His possession. The LORD is breaking off the old and replenishing with the new. There is a gold treasure in you, and that gold will catch ablaze in the heat of the storm and be activated in the spirit of your mind in Christ. Christ is not defeated, twisted, confused, sad, downcast, competitive, broke or disgusted. El-Elyon, God Most High, Possessor and Maker of heaven and earth is He who possesses what you need. **YOU ARE A NEW CREATION IN CHRIST JESUS OLD THINGS ARE PASSED AWAY AND BEHOLD ALL THINGS HAVE BEEN MADE NEW {2 Corinthians 5:17}.**

There is an anointing of fire in your spiritual womb awaiting to explode in the storm's bitter season that blows harsh winds in your life. The windstorm is position for the upgrade of your spiritual walk of faith in Christ for Kingdom advancement by the Power of the Ruach of Yahweh. The LORD is the GOD of elevation and promotion. Some sooner than others will walk with divine crowns in the realm of the spirit on this side of glory. In the realm of the spirit some have qualified through perseverance in faith by GOD, not self effort or man placing and are wearing a supernatural crown of victory. This is Holy Spirit's reward badge from the Royal Kingdom of Yahweh. Flesh and blood has not revealed this unto me, but Ruach Hakodesh. There is no demonic spiritual activity of competition or comparison in the

Kingdom of Yahweh. The KINGDOM is not divided, but is one unified Spirit. **The Name of the LORD is a fortified tower; the righteous RUN to it and are SAFE {Proverbs 18:10}.** The spiritual condition is that you must be righteous *(upright, right standing in the eyes of the LORD)*; the divine position to receive His promises, in order to take shelter. The refuge is a shift into His Presence by faith into another dimension. Divine-faith is not dead, not little, not blind, but faith that takes your spirit out of one location and to secure you in another in reality or existence. Faith does not leave us abandon or in the same location of thought. **"The Shift Is A Supernatural Shift!"** When JESUS bid Peter to step forward out of the boat *ONTO* the water, JESUS demonstrated His Kingdom principle over the laws of nature for transitioning Peter's faith to enter another dimension of faith which opens doors of miracles of the supernatural into actual time outside of Peter's familiar place of time…God-faith. You are a Peter. *HALLELUJAH! Glory To GOD of Miracles!* Holy Spirit Is Breathing On You. The devil does not want you to act on divine-faith. He's A Liar and Defeated. Receive It!

PROPHETIC DECLARATION

I Prophesy That You Will Run Swiftly To Him In Perseverance And Swiftly For Safety. He Is Your Shield And Your Fortress, Your DELIVERER In the TIME of Need. Where His Presence Is, Is Also His Glory. GLORY HALLELUJAH!

Your time is now to call upon HIM, who is Healer. GOD out of His goodness and holiness has declared away of escape for your victory. All which He promises **"SHALL COME TO PASS,"** because you place your trust in Him, you're His property and you act upon His Eternal Word that is forever settled in heaven. The LORD promised that with the same temptation that He has *ALREADY* made the way of escape tailored just for you during your season of testing. This season has not taken Him by surprised, as they do us; however, GOD has been expecting it for the purpose of a divine transfer of manifestations of His Glory toward you. ***Glory Hallelujah, I AM THAT I AM SAITH THE LORD***. The Lord also revealed that He will not put more on us than what we can bear. The way of escaped is your testimony that is going to verify that the demonstrating Oil of GOD is activated in and resting upon you. Wow! Hallelujah. I am humbled even the more as I am receiving revelation from Holy Spirit for you, as well as, for myself.

Now when the Lord declares a word of promise, that lets you know it isn't over until He has done His justice on your behalf for His Name Sake. Then it's just really getting started for the Glory to be revealed in you and upon you toward others for the purpose of walking the straight and narrow path of righteousness, breaking chains, destroying unclean yokes of bondage and transforming mindsets as you abide in His Presence of holiness. Ruach Hakodesh does not release the Fresh Oil of anointing for you, but for others in need of what you have received from on high as the Oil *(Wine)* permeate your spirit-being, because you are spirit. Just as He uses the oil spiritually, the fragrance of His Oil extends with you wherever you go; on your job, around friends, family, gatherings and isn't bound to areas of location.

PROPHETIC DECLARATION

GOD SAID AS YOU SEEK HIM THE REVELATION THAT HE IS DISCLOSING TO YOU IN THIS SEASON AND FOR THE SEASONS TO COME IS TO ESTABLISH, GROUND, STORE THE REVELATION OF WHO HE IS, WHO AND WHOSE YOU ARE HIDDEN IN HIM AND YOUR KINGDOM PURPOSE IN THE EARTH. THE LORD SAID WHAT HE REVEALS TO THOSE DILIGENTLY SEEKING HIM FROM A HEART OF HUMILITY WILL BE REVEALED NOT BY FLESH BUT BY HIS SPIRIT.

When you meet *(commune)* with GOD to lay your burdens down at the feet of the Jesus, there will be a paradigm shift in your mind which works by faith to remove the pressure, moods and bitterness. He wants you not to just talk about him, sing about, quote scripture verses, tell stories about him, attend church ritualistically, go to church, church hop or leave the same way you came in, but Messiah, the Lover of your soul, is expecting a personally **one on one** intimate encounter with you and Him…the meeting place. The benefits of salvation gave us Holy Spirit to Dwell In us and To Be Upon us no matter what surrounds us. That is the Super on top of our natural abilities and inabilities. Yes, that means He has given believers what is required to rise above what we face for the simple truth that His KINGDOM lives within believers. It is through the Anointing, the Wine of GOD which enables you to rise up soberly and focus and determined in the *Dunamis* of the LORD. However, first you must recognize in your own physical weakness that it is possible to be done through you and for you. **The Bible tells us {2 Corinthians 12:10} For when I am weak, then I am strong.** It has *already* been done and completed for you, but you got to see it the way GOD is seeing the outcome. He said it is *already* done; therefore, the next step is to give power to your faith *(what do you believe)*, put crazy faith to work in the face of the impossible. Apostle Paul said your boast should be in your weakness due to the Truth {**2 Corinthians 12:9a**}. It is the **Strength of the Lord** that carries you over to the other side of the mountain. GOD never fails and His WORD never returns to Him void, but you must believe, trust and step out of the boat that you think is secure. GOD knows that there are stages for the human mind to go through for processing truth; believe it or not, the storm plays a part of that process of evacuation for you; again shifting from the natural reality to the spiritual reality in Christ. Only the **Anointing of Yahweh**, Fresh Oil, will destroy the yokes that want to execute your potential, faith increase, destiny and bring shame about your GOD and alter your future hope.

HaMashiach Yeshua *(Messiah-Christ, Jesus)* prayed a powerful life altering prayer in his time of tremendous pressure of overwhelmed sorrow to the point of sweating drops of blood at the Olive Grove location of Gethsemane. Yeshua's prayer meeting held with ABBA **one on one** prior to the Cup of Suffering that he was about to partake of at the Cross of Calvary for the judgment, punishment and humanity redemption cost {**Matthew 26:36-56**}. Yeshua *(Jesus)* pressed his way through the tormenting and bitterness of soul. First, with humility, because the redemptive act was the Will of Yahweh, the Father, to purposely fulfill at all cost, his life. Second, by obedience, because Yeshua understood the fullness of eternal joy, faithfulness, victory and reward that was on the other side of this selfless sacrificial act of unfailing love to institute the only door to be established before the world for mankind to be reconciled back to the Holy Father. Although Jesus was God in the flesh and could have called a legion of angels to prevail against all that was about to transpire…He was ordained for this very **cup of suffering** for the release of the Cup of Blessings. The weight of sin, perverse wickedness and a self-gratifying world crushed him to the point of bearing humanity's sins in His flesh to render its power defeated. Jesus was sent for that very purpose of dying for sinful humanity.

The name of the garden holds extremely great significance. Gat Shmanim *(Hebraic)* details the spiritual deftness of what possibly takes place deeply within the human soul of them who suffers and surrenders during seasons of sorrow bitterness; and are torn spiritually from them self. We cannot see the Fire of the Holy Spirit burning to consume the bitterness which surface within our soul in grievous times with the physical eye; only through spiritual lens can these things be spiritually discerned. Ruach Hakodesh *(Holy Spirit)* is symbolically referred to in the Bible as **Oil, Wine, Wind, Breath, Fire** and **New Wine** among other titles. As Jesus travailed through the pressing of the emotional crushing, the anointing within him and upon him burst forth in **mighty** *(ischus)* **power** *(kratos)* to complete His redemption plan for all eternity. God desires new wine of Himself to penetrate our spirit from His Spirit with detail workmanship of His hand in His Church, the purifying refining fire of holiness. This is part of our preparation for the wedding; to ensure the right garment is worn at the wedding feast to become one eternally forever with the Bridegroom, King Jesus.

Fresh Oil [Hebraic word **Yit shar**]
means anointing produce light
Fresh [Hebraic word **Raanan**] means green, newness

Wine, grain and oil are gifts from Yahweh. These are natural materials of blessings with a single spiritual meaning that points to the Kingdom, covenant bond-ship with His saints, their prosperity and position in Christ while in this world and the demonstrative Power of Holy Spirit abiding in them and resting upon them. Although they are material the symbolism points to the Anointing Favor of Yahweh in Christ. The wine and the oil symbolized God's divine supernatural pleasure; His aroma of undeserved favor and covenant blessings upon His chosen people verses the judgment resulting from disobedience and from emptiness of Holy Spirit. Wine and oil where also agricultural products which represented increase, wealth and prosperity in the land of the people of Jehovah. As long as the chosen people were not in disobedience, idolatry or placed their alliance in any graven images, place or thing Jehovah was bound by Himself to provide for them wealth to sustain there welfare in the land. This was His promise. In their seasons of hardship, distress, disappointments or crisis if the saints turn to another to worship and turn from Yahweh *(Jehovah)*, then judgment would follow as a consequence of their action at heart. In their time of wilderness testing, Yahweh used the bitter wilderness seasons to reveal to them His **identity, character, nature** and in return they where to display faith, trust, obey and depend solely upon Yahweh for deliverance. **No one else!** God's people bare His Name. He would deliver, sustain and provide for his chosen people by the guidance of His Spirit upon the vessel He chose to bring deliverance. This principle applies to the Ekklesia today. **The Bible tells us {Psalm 104:14-15} wine gladdens the heart of man, oil makes the countenance shine and bread strengthens the soul.** This is parallel to the joy we are to experience even in the midst of trials and tribulations in this present world and the joy that is the eternal glory of our hope. As we abide in the Lord, He is bound by Himself to preserve the believers going and coming; the well-being of His elect. That's the expression of joy **{References: Joel 2:24; Hosea 2:8, 21-22}.**

We are not exempt from any pain, heart-arch, hardship, rough times or struggles or trials. And the people of GOD do not escape them. Suffering is a part of our human condition that came through the fall in the Garden of Eden. The trials and sufferings we may experience under the sun are common to man. GOD through them wills to birth forth spiritual maturity, spiritual direction and total dependence on him, soberness and integrity, holiness into our hearts, behavior and life style. God will use the heat from the furnace in which a soul may be in to release His fire; for purification and identification of the soul and to generate New Wine and Fresh Oil. The pain may be extreme, but the reward from GOD is greater than the storm. The storms in life are lessons for the natural, as well as, for the teaching of spiritual things. If we do not learn from them, bow under them and seek GOD in the midst another test will come around again and again and again for the discipline and the promoting of your faith to be Kingdom secure and fit. When the obstacles rise against you, you will find out actually where you stand in your faith in the Lord. We can say we have faith all day long, but **tests** will demand the testing of your words and evidence of faith to align and expose itself. That is good a thing. Tests will always come.

Many souls that say they believe yet turn their way back to the way of the world while still attending church. One reason being is the familiarity with the world atmospheric system, not familiar with believing what they cannot see and having no true revelation of who Yahweh is, other than Yeshua saved me by grace. It is a crutch for any soul to gravitate to the familiar ways of life in any season. This is the spirit of fear at work to shut down the supernatural advancement for the soul to overcome and develop in faith reality. Remember, in the distressful times there is another who resides in the believer's soul, the Spirit of Christ *(Holy Spirit)*. Don't hold Him hostage. Holy Spirit confirms to you greater is He which is in you than he that is in this world **{1 John 4:4}**. Yeshua commands you to speak to your condition from your position as a son of Yahweh, whether you are seasoned or a baby in the LORD. Ruach Hakodesh *(Holy Spirit)* is your helper and teacher. The Lord hears the call of humbled souls.

New Wine Experience: Joy is to be experienced even in distress moments. Joy Is Fruit that Is Evident of Supply of the True Vine Connection.

Put on the *garment* of Praise for the *spirit* of heaviness {**Isaiah 61:3**}
• Let the Weak Say I Am Strong! I Say I Am Strong! For it is not your strength, but the power of Holy Ghost who you allow to filter through in your matters to overthrow the work of defeat.
This is your Strength: • I Shall Not Be Moved!
• I Shall Stand On God's Unchanging Word.
This is your Strength as you prophesy life over yourself: • I Refused To Give Up, I Refuse To Give In • I Refused to Be Defeated • I Refused To Be Sad, Unhappy, Or Despondent! • I Refuse To Be Broke • I Refuse to Let the Devil Take What Belongs to Me! • I Refuse Because GOD Will Prevail In My Life
• This is your Joy: I Shall Live and Not Die.
• This is your Joy: I Am the Head and Not the Tail.
• This is your Joy: No Weapon Formed Against Me Shall Prosper!
• This is your Joy: Even Though It Might not Look like Nothing Is Happening, I Say It Is Well In My Soul. I Trust God To Manifest the Promise In the Presence of My Enemies!
• This is your Joy: As Wine Gladdens the Heart!

Let the Light be your declaration and watch GOD prepare a table before the enemies of your soul. Be Revived! Stay faithful! **The Bible tells us {Nehemiah 8:10} the joy of the Lord is my Strength and {Psalm 27:1} whom shall I fear.** You will become what you are in Christ, fully persuaded in the Light, a force to be reckoned with in Christ and unstoppable by the power of Yahweh. Hallelujah!

Although temptations will appear, Yeshua' command was to pray that you enter not into temptation. Just as Yeshua *(Jesus)* defeated temptations, He has given us the **Power** key to succeed. Looking back will be in the pass no longer ruling the future. When a soul truly comes out of the fire with the fire of revelation proof of the Anointing Oil, their life will never be the same. This process will not happen overnight because Holy Spirit does not give all the pieces to the puzzle at one time, but in measure as you commune with the Lord and walk in holiness. That is my personal testimony of how powerful the Presence of GOD is with those that wait on Him in the midst of the storms that rage in life. You may be wondering, "if I expected my end result to be a success before the storm or during my time of suffering?" No, Beloved, I did not expect victory. I couldn't even see how victory was possible. I humbly say if someone had prophesied that I would've been entering a furnace for a season of testing, but when it was over my life would have the Oil of GOD dripping from it and my faith will be transforming continually as gold is purified; I would not had believed it. In devastation emotional storms, the normal way of life dealings and church as we traditionally were taught will become abnormal, because at this point everything may become questioned by you. Therefore, a spiritual reality of the divine advancement of God's Breath is required to fill the void in the soul. Just talk and compromising will not get a soul to this point. You must become the sacrifice, dying to self, in order to live. Anytime a person has had a major encounter with The Lord and has been touched by the Finger of GOD, be assured your life no longer is your life and you feel the Presence of the Power of Christ that has humbled you. These types of experiences bring the fear of the Lord upon us. Your eyes become open to unveiled unexplainable revelation of what GOD has done. You recognize without Him you would not have made it through. And how He did it completely is amazingly a miracle.

Greek words for the English term Power
Dunamis, Ischus and Kratos
dunamis (power) means ability, strength, miracles
dunamis is the root word of our English
word dynamite, dynamic
ischus (mighty) means to hold on or
to possess something, strong
kratos (power) manifested power with
force, to seize, to arrest, to imprison

There is untapped potential of greatness, divine potential that ABBA has placed in your spiritual *DNA* before the world was created. You were only a spirit form existing without body. The potential of greatness is *already* done. Okay, I am shouting it. ***THE POTENTIAL AND THE GREATNESS IN YOU IS ALREADY DONE!*** However, it does not manifest without diligence, devotion, a lifestyle pleasing to ABBA and an ear to hear what the Spirit is saying to you. Be assured as you humble, **Humble, Seek and Commune** with the Lord, He will exalt you with the grace, the anointing, mantle, gifts, divine revelation and counsel beyond what your imagination-thoughts could ever have shown you. GOD makes this supernatural divine transfer possible. As ABBA exalts you by His Spirit you must shrink to grow and expand in true humility. Ask Brother Job, King David, the three Hebrew boys, Hannah and Apostle Paul there testimony account. They would confirm they knew not what the outcome was going to be like, but they admonish you by their testimony to work faith and trust in season and out of season in a spirit of humility. They would also tell you it wasn't picture perfect or microwave, fly by night or instant recovery. A touch from the Master's hand to man's heart, mind and soul will resuscitate you. The Master's touch will call you to respond to divine purpose through breathing another wind in you; to humble you, draw you to your knees to cry out, to lay your life prostrate before him and to yearn for Him with a life long thirst and hungry heart. Which all is a gradual elevation released from the faith dimension in a humble servant's walk in complete measure. For the believer in Christ Jesus is to be confident, **The Just Shall Live by Faith, Not by Sight {Habakkuk 2:4}**. This is the believer's confident, GOD said it and that is all that matters. It is a lifestyle of practice, learned mostly through the fire of suffering and waiting on the Lord. Therefore, when the next windstorm blows weighty pressures it will not take you by surprise or off course, because you have personally experienced deep revelation of the Hand of Jehovah *(Yahweh, LORD)* for yourself. It is also the detailing workmanship of Holy Spirit and not man.

• Faith revelation will carry you through any wilderness experience
• Faith revelation establishes your faith to become unmovable, unshakeable
• Faith revelation establishes the true identity and nature of GOD
• Faith revelation unlocks mysteries
• Faith revelation reveals to you new territories eyes have not seen ears have not heard, nor feet have trotted

A sorcerer by the name of Simon fixed his eyes on what the disciples possessed supernaturally; the priceless royal Gift of the Kingdom of GOD. The Gift demonstrative power unveiled which could not be bought for money or produced through unregenerate souls or meaningless talk. There are many today, want what GOD has; yet, covet the anointing that someone else operates under, failing to realize a blood price involving suffering and pain with humility is attached to such and given only by the Ruach of Yahweh.

Hebrew & Greek words for the English term Gethsemane
Gat [gimel, tav] means winepress.
Shemanim [Shemen] means oil
Gat Shemanim means a press of oils, it is an olive press

Hebrew word for the English term Messiah
Mashiach: Anointed One [Christos-
Christ] holds office of authority

THE OLIVE OIL PROCESS

Gat Shmanim hold revelations of truth for us, unfolding the natural work of an olive press or press beam to the inward working of the Spirit of God in the soul of man. The Garden of Gethsemane is a place where Olive Orchard are grown and in this location is a Gethsemane press where olives are pressed from the fruit of the olive tree, a unique place with a unique name designed with a unique purpose. The concrete function of the meaning is to press until oil is obtained. I repeat, **"To Press Under Extreme Pressure Until Pure Virgin Oil Is Evident On The Surface."** There is a separation of the natural material and the sacredness of the raw material. The skin and pit are strained for separating bitter content resulting in pure fresh oil. Oil is produced under pressure and it brings joy to those who produce it. At an olive press, olives were gathered into rough sacks and stacked one on top of each other. A beam was lowered onto the stack with increasing weight being added to the end of the beam to press oil from the olives. Olives are crushed into a paste form and smeared on mats *{Bible History Online}*. Olive oil symbolism in the Bible is the presence of the Holy Spirit. Oil was used in the Old Testament to anoint priest, prophets, the tabernacle furnishings and kings and to bring light from the menorah which was located in the Holy Place inside the Tabernacle. Olive oil symbolically is also used today to smear, anoint in consecration and as a point of contact. The fresh oil or new wine was not to be used unholy, but had to be handled appropriately as the things of Yahweh. The same instructions also apply for the Church today. The anointing oil was used for the consecration of those in the kingdom and not for the degenerated person. This is Holy unto the LORD. Those such as the Kohathites were not to come in direct contact with what was sacred as GOD had commanded, they where doorkeepers or caretakers of the tabernacle not priest. Due to their open rebellion they where destroyed by the same Hand that bless those who heeded and obeyed the instructions. The Church is not to mishandle or take lightly the things of Yahweh in Christ Jesus. It is better not to touch than to touch or partake or walk unworthy before GOD due to pride and the lack of knowledge. The Bible calls it ignorance.

The pressure of any trial, no matter how devastating, GOD can use it in His sovereignty to exhibit divine manifestations and to bring Him glory and to elevate that soul from glory to glory. Unfortunately, without the fire to initiate the press there will be no fresh oil, no anointing, no transformation, no smearing, no fruit and no genuine character or substance developed by the Spirit of GOD. On the other side, the heavier the pressure, the more oil the more anointing is released from GOD upon a person life for the mantle already established before he or she were formed in the womb. Everybody has a purpose; however, a divine purpose can be missed or neglected due to the spirit of fear and the lack of faith. Pressure can become overwhelming during the process of a life crisis. But in my spirit, I know without a doubt, there is a purposeful calling for you that you are obligated to respond to by faith, untapped greatness to be accessed. It has nothing to do with your age, sex, race, title, degrees, deformity or finances. The potential is vivid in the midst under the scope of the eye of GOD. He sees the gold in you. Our faith is never at no point or time, to stop increasing. ABBA GOD *already* had it planned before the foundation of the worlds was spoken, for you a tailor made detailed purpose and destiny entwined together. No one else has the exact fit. I repeat, **"No One Else Has Your Fit. It is tailored, designed and detailed only for you."**

After praying three times, Jesus prayer ended in this manner: ***FATHER, NEVERTHELESS, NOT AS I WILL, BUT THOU WILL BE DONE.*** *Our prayer petitions must arise to this love, faith and obedience level. Heavenly Father, If this cup may not pass unless I partake of it, Nevertheless, LORD; not my will, but* *let thy will be done. The answer has never been in our human strength or knowledge outside of God's wisdom.*

Hebrews 12:2b

That Jesus, who for the joy that was set before him endured the cross, despising the shame, and is set down at the right hand of the throne of God.

Hebrew 1:9b

Therefore God, even thy God, hath anointed you with the oil of joy [that brings Gladness] above thy companions.

The Lord allowed a storm with fire to come into the life of David and me. I can't speak on behalf of husband, but this storm shook my world and almost the foundation of my faith. The Lord knows the outcome when we are tried by fire. We had no idea or clue this was coming. Satan was allowed to move against us. The advancement of the Kingdom of GOD in the earth realm starts with us first through suffering. Did I know and understand that then? No, I had very little spiritual insight. I would not have been able to tell you anything, other than, this isn't right. How could this have happened to me? Why? Why Me? It has been eighteen years later at the time of the writing and publishing of this book. Yahweh predestined His righteous government through His election before time existed out of eternal time. Predestination! It is foreordained, predetermined for the children of GOD in Christ Jesus to live in faith and obedience no matter what comes our way. Who we are in Christ is not determined by the pressure of the storm, but by the Blood of Christ, the Word and Holy Spirit who lives on the inside of us. The Spirit is like an umbilical cord attaching us vertically to the Father and the transmitter so we can communicate with Yahweh. Remember, the storm is an instrument used to recover the deep hidden sacred treasure value from within the clay, just as gold, diamonds and pearls are surface deep. Anytime GOD predestinates, it refers to His KINGDOM RULE of GOVERNMENT. He's speaking of His sovereign perfect will outside of unrighteousness, His ruling Government of Righteousness. On the flip side, all who chose to live in disobedience and rebellion are predestined to eat the fruit of being in a barren state separated from GOD eternally forever. **The Bible tells us {Romans 8:1} that there is no condemnation to those who are in Christ.** Selah! No deception only love and truth.

I never considered thinking of what I had been taught or believed about GOD would be challenged, tested or weighed. As I did others still do; I read the Bible, but didn't absorb the Spirit reality of the Bible verses revelation. It is part of the makeover of the clay by the Potter through His Spirit making a deposit into man's spiritual account. However, my thought was: "What kind of GOD who is supposed to be loving would allow such devastation to happen to his child that He suppose to protect and keep from circumstances of this magnitude." That is how many of many hurt confused souls feel in the world today, just as I did with intensified grief. Grief can grow, if not handled properly. And my frame of thought and emotional feeling was my immature conscious view of GOD. I did not picture GOD like this. I had painted a one-sided picture of Him. There was an unrevealed side of Yahweh, the Father, *not the Son* that I would not ever have fathom. Because He is all knowing *(omniscience)* knew it was part of the human condition under pain. Just as our Christ suffered as the suffering servant, then we also will suffer for the cause of awakening the spirit. We don't perceive this in moments of suffering; as Job did not know what each day from the next would result in through his season of testing.

This windstorm crushed me into pieces. I literally melted. ABBA wants brokenness in your inward parts. ADONAI *(Hebraic title Master)* has to begin the process to detoxify and sanctify you before He does a new thing completely within you. He always by nature sets aside what is of Him and separates or cut away what is not of Him. Glory to Yahweh! He will not pour something new *(fresh wine)* into something old *(old wineskin)* that does not have the structure, capacity or wherewithal to hold the wealth of true spiritual riches. Your spirit must cry out unto the deep…the meeting, His Presence. A believer's walk of faith is just that, a walk of faith. It is spirit form not carnal or fleshly. Therefore, the measure of faith in you speaks to the volume of Him who is faith far above all the heavens; to bring you by His Spirit to the place rightfully yours by spiritual birthright, your testimony and the blood of Jesus, to accomplish the Will of the Father in your life. You are here to occupy until Jesus return for His

Bride and to be victoriously, successful in this walk of life according to His perfect will. I am not speaking of material success, but that which is spirit. A soul can gain the whole world of materialistic things such as cars, houses, clothes, jewelry and the best of so call friends, popularity, money and vanity; yet, be unhappy and not fit to meet the LORD of eternity. GOD Forbid! {**Luke 9:25**} Why gain the whole world and lose your soul? GOD will allow such conflict of soul for the purpose of detaching us from the attachments, self gratifications and cravings of this world. Satan, the god of this world, sets up unseen tentacles for people to become slowly hypnotize, a desensitizing through trickery leading away from God's Truth. Whatever soul is available the devil will seek to devour it. **Fresh Oil** will keep us prepared, set apart, watchful, sober, diligent, in loving fellowship with GOD, loving people, occupying the land with purpose, forgiving and not lovers of the sway of the world.

INVITATION TO CHRIST

Heavenly Father, in the Name of Jesus Christ, I acknowledge my failures, my weakness, my transgression, my iniquities and my inability to keep or save myself in this world and the eternal world to come. I have done it my way for so long with nothing good coming from it. I repent for my sinful, rebellious ways and I humbly ask you to forgive me of all sins of holding grudges, lying, stealing, sexual sins, lust, greed, pride and all other sins that I am not aware of. Come into my heart and dwell and fill me your Holy Spirit. Wash my heart, sanctify, cleanse me and make me holy LORD. I release all those who I have held guilty that I felt wronged me in my times of self centeredness, retaliation, distress and hardship. I acknowledge my alliance to you LORD and I denounce and sever all alliances to other idols and falsehood. Thank you Lord for not letting me die in my shame and guilty condition. Thank you for removing the blinders off my spiritual eyes so that I can grow in spiritual understanding. Father GOD I believe Jesus is your son raised from the dead and seated at your right hand. I receive your grace Father GOD through faith in Jesus name.

Amen.

Beloved, if you have sincerely prayed this prayer the Lord Jesus has extended to you his unmerited favor and power to overcome in this world. Welcome to the household of faith. Now you need to be baptized with water and the fire of the Holy Ghost, power in you and power upon you. Jesus said go and sin no more; therefore, the power must be within. The fruit of repentance is to come forth out of your heart in your daily living. I pray that Holy Spirit will guide and plant you in a Faith-base Spirit-filled Word Church where you will be spiritually nourished and equipped for the fulfillment of your divine purpose.

Shalom.

PRAYER FOR DIVINE HEALING: JEHOVAH RAPHA

GRACIOUS ETERNAL FATHER, IN THE NAME OF YESHUA, I REPENT AND ASK YOU TO FORGIVE ME OF ALL MY SINS. YOUR WORD DECLARES THAT YOU ARE FAITHFUL AND JUST TO FORGIVE ME OF ALL UNRIGHTEOUSNESS. YOUR WORD DECLARES THAT YOU WILL KEEP ME IN PERFECT PEACE AS MY MIND IS STAYED ON YOU! YOUR WORD DECLARES THAT YOU ARE THE HEALER OF MY SOUL, OF MY MIND AND OF MY BODY! I PUT MY HOPE AND TRUST IN YOU! I ASK FOR HEALING IN MY BODY AND HEALING IN MY SOUL...TOUCH ME LORD! I ASK THAT YOU OVERSHADOW ME AND TOUCH MY CAUSE! I ASK THAT YOU TOUCH EVERY AREA OF BODY, MY LIMBS, MY MUSCLES, MY VISION, MY HEARING, MY EMOTIONS, MY NERVES, MY BLOOD PRESSURE AND MY BREATHING; I CAST ALL OTHER PERSONAL ISSUES UPON YOU IN YESHUA'S NAME! I TURN FROM UNBELIEF, STUBBORNESS, GAMBLING, DRINKING AND SMOKING, _____ AND SURRENDER COMPLETELY TO YOU IN THE NAME OF YESHUA! I DECREE THE LAW OF YOUR PROMISE DAILY BY FAITH FOR COMPLETE HEALING MANIFESTATIONS! THANK YOU FATHER FOR MY HEALING MADE AVAILABLE THROUGH THE BLOOD AND THE BODY AND THE RESURRECTION OF YOUR SON, YESHUA! I RECEIVE MY TOTAL HEALING BY FAITH NOW IN YESHUA'S NAME!

AMEN.

**Write the <u>verses</u> on the tablet of your heart for daily use...
study**

Hebrew 11:6

_____

_____

_____

James 2:8

_____

_____

_____

Psalm 34:19

_____

_____

_____

Psalm 45:7

_____

_____

_____

Review: New Wine

1. a) How is New Wine/ Fresh Oil received in your own words?

   _____

   _____

   _____

   b) Is there a method? _____.

   c) Scripture verse? _____.

2. Why should this be of great concern, after all I am already saved? Align long lines under questions not numbers

   _____

   _____

   _____

3. How would this come about since we are flesh and blood?

   _____

   _____

   _____

4. What is "Fresh Oil" purpose in your own words?

   _____

   _____

   _____

5. What is the difference between new wine skin, old and oil?

_____

_____

_____

NOTES:

CHAPTER SIX

IN THE MIDST OF

Appointed seasons will come that will push you and shake the very foundation you stand on for the reconstruction and paradigm shift in the mind, pattern of things and spiritual things. As you have read most of the chapters in this book you understand that in the midst of a crisis, especially if you have never been through anything severe, they are experiences that come to usher you into another chapter in your life pertaining to reality, truth, purpose and to expose the fact that there is more to life than that which is seen. Yes, this is the real reality of real life. It's not what we see circumspective on the surface. What you see is what you get, Nope. What you see may be driven by something behind the law of cause and effect. Cause and effect is spiritual as much as natural also. Your existence has a cause. You do not exist on earth by accident or coincident. We have been desensitized through television, radio, technology, the good life, the sway of the world and media to think everything is grand before our very eyes, that things just happen just because or it's the normal way of life or to think nothing devastating could possibly happen. But how many of you know that is so far from the truth? Anything at any given moment can happen to anyone.

The time came that seemed to be the right time that my hubby and I decided to begin our family by getting pregnant. I was very happy to be pregnant and excited about this first baby addition coming into the family. The pregnancy for a few weeks was going great, prenatal visits good, but down toward the latter part of the first trimester going into the second, I began to have complications so the doctor put me on a close schedule to watch the pregnancy. At some point in that second trimester all panic broke through and I thought my baby was gone. I had an extremely bloody flow and ladies know when that happens that is not a good sign for any normal pregnancy. As I stood in the kitchen in one place, I yell to the top of my voice NO, because what was happening was off course and out of timing. I was taken to Methodist South Hospital immediately due to the bleeding; there weren't any abdominal cramps or pain. Along the way, I am praying JESUS Please…out of fear of losing my baby. The doctor I saw was very direct, to the point, without any tact or bedside manners; just cold in spirit. As I lay on the examining table afraid, the doctor's immediate response to me was, "I recommend that you have an abortion; look for the fetus to abort itself." I was all choked up, speechless with tears in my eyes as I prepared myself to leave the hospital. At that point, I began to petition GOD, fearing that the very words the doctor spoke would happen any day at any moment. What I did know was I wasn't about to have an abortion. Weeks later my OB/GYN eventually referred me to a group specialist: Genetic for Prenatal Screening and Diagnostic Testing due to more developing factors. They probed me for weeks and later determined after the screening test I needed to have an amniocentesis done. At this point, I held it together until I was alone. The weeping and the crying were consistent, sometimes harder than other moments. We just believed GOD that all will be made right. I believed and hoped that GOD, who is Healer, was going to heal all that they said was wrong. Amniocentesis is a test that determines the sex of the baby and examines the fetus's chromosome pieces for abnormality genetic conditions by surgically inserting a 12 inch hollow needle through the navel into the uterus to obtain amniotic fluid. The doctor informed us that the puncture could possibly work against me by causing fluid to leak at some point. The usual puncture is only one time, but for some reason they had to insert me twice through the navel to remove fluid for testing that same hour. After the numbing of the area, I watched the insertion of this needle enter and exit my stomach twice with no fear, only faith. My pregnancy was placed in the high risk category. After several weeks, the results came back for my husband and I to view with the genetic counselor. The news was not good, but in spite of what they called it and what photos they showed us I held on to the Lord. He was all we had for hope. The genetic doctors, prenatal tests nor fear was going to overtake me; although I was being crushed inwardly. They told us the baby was a boy during the second trimester and the genetic abnormality he was diagnosed with was called Wolf-Hirschorn Syndrome II. This is a genetic syndrome that static say happens one out of every hundred million. We were told it was due to the short arm of a chromosome deletion; meaning the loss of multiple genes on the missing chromosome. The syndrome effect many parts of the body such as the development of the organs, nervous system, growth and body functions. *BUT, I BELIEVED GOD!* Wolf-Hirschorn syndrome II is not inherited as we thought it was. The devil tried to sow a seed of discord between my husband and I by causing us to point fingers and blame each other. I desperately wanted to know where it came from. How it happened? What will it take to fix his issue? I wanted answers that no one could give me, including the doctors. And how did something so rare happen to us out of millions of people? I had many questions? Some things we come face to face with in life will cause one to question everything in search for a relief that will counteract the situation. My pastor and family were praying for this situation that we did not have a clue which way it was going to turn. We just hoped for complete healing. That was my only prayer because again I wanted my baby to survive. Fear tried to grip my husband with thoughts, but the only way this baby was leaving was that GOD who gave Isaac life would be the one who takes that life.

I dealt with the discomfort pressure of pain and difficulty during the term of my pregnancy, while still working in the salon for a half of year in segments; securing my stomach weight with pregnancy lift straps to help with the pulling, tighten and the pressure of the baby's position. The doctor constantly took me off my feet due the high risk and fluid leakage that began to take place. I suffered major loss in business clientele, as well as, loss in income. Everything was headed downhill for us. Meanwhile, my husband's job was in the process of relocating to another city two hours away one way. Everything began to happen right behind each other, like a domino effect. When the windstorms come you cannot see your way clearly, just the step in front of the next and just the day with its hours, minutes, tears, pains and thoughts of what will happen next. Fear of the unknown will paralyze one's will not to act in faith and encourage one to shutdown due to the uncertainties that life deals out without asking for it. *"BUT I BELIEVED GOD AND HOPE WAS ALIVE!"*

The Lord was gracious in many ways throughout our pregnancy, mainly by counteracting what could have been a miscarriage or an abortion due to all the facts from the tests. The Lord allowed baby Isaac not only to be formed in the wound as a baby, but to be born into this world without being destroyed out of unwantedness, fear and shame. I've always have said, after the fact, that I was carrying an angel in the form of a baby for a purposeful call ordained by Yahweh. And now I do realize he was a miracle that took place. Into the beginning of the eight month or last trimester I begin to lose amniotic fluid quickly without any labor contractions, the baby had not dropped and my water had not broken; immediately rushed to the hospital in tears, scared, put in a room, hooked up to I.V. pumps with fluids *(Intra Venous:*

into the vein), asked questions about the pregnancy history, the genetic condition, which delivery method and a few hours later was informed they would have to speed up my labor for a vaginal delivery for the safety of the baby and for me due to the uncertainties of health disorders. This process is known as Inducing Labor. And throughout my whole pregnancy I was fearful of the unknown, not knowing what to expect each step of the way. This is similar to how GOD works with His children. We have no idea how things are going to turn out before us, but faith is the substance that secures, breaks the fall that leads to disaster and removes the factors of fear.

The Ecclesia is commanded to walk and follow the leading of Ruach Hakodesh and not the spirit of fear. Some things are induced to bring about the mysteries of the unknown territory for a move forward and download in the course of your faith walk with the Lord Jesus Christ. The children of Israel made unnecessary laps around a mountain that could have been done in eleven years. WHY? Because they feared the unknown, **refused** to step out of their known comfort zone and **reverted** by to the old way, which took them out of the provision of Yahweh. The Lord doesn't want any soul to fall victimize to a drawback spirit; an unclean spirit that comes cleverly through the gate of fear with no signals. The LORD will use the suffering and the timing as an incubator process to reprogram the mind and heart of His children *(chapter 3)*. In the season of the children of Israel wilderness experience they were to seek GOD instead of turning from him going back to the past. The situations were induced. The downfall is that they, like most of us, run from the answer which was extended from fully manifesting, instead of running into the Ark of Safety, JESUS. The wilderness is designed to induce spiritual labor pains to birth forth supernatural **purpose**, **newness**, **humility**, **obedience** and **reliance** for the promotion of GOD in us, upon and toward us and then back to Him from us to others. The wilderness also teaches us how to yield. It teaches us as we yield **to be still**, **to recognize**, **to know**, **to develop an ear to hear spiritually** and **to respond** to the LORD in faith. GOD IS SPIRIT. When we come face to face with high risk or low risk distress, we must learn and be willing to take the leap from **weak faith** to **consistent** to **growing faith.** Having roots planted securely for the journey of unknown territories with a readiness to challenge what is challenging you out of a *zealous (God-fearing, fervent, fierce, energetic)* heart, from **common faith** to **great faith**; not being insincere or wavering in faith any longer. By faith this is equivalent to making each of your steps fixed onto uncertain grounds into a walk of certainty without having the manifested evidence before your eyes, **unwavering faith {Mark 11:22-24}**. That walk on water *regulates (control, supervise)* how you conduct yourself to make progress and one's way in the midst of troubles that will come your way. **The Bible tells us {Job 14:1} man that is born of a woman is full of trouble.** When humanity *(male/ female)* was born out of the fallen human condition of weakness and corruption into this world, trouble was induced and assigned to all with no exemptions. All are **exposed** to joy, happiness, labor, hardship, disaster, disappointments, turmoil, pain, grief, sorrow, distress, defilement and disorders in this life and land at some point. We must become like a sideward, upright mountain climber who stays fixed to the course up the mountain as he pulled and plant each upward step upon the ridges of the surface, going upward in bold, secure, **strong faith**, not allowing the rough or shadow places to dictate how he will finish the course.

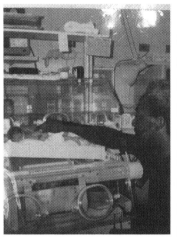

Several things happened after arriving at the hospital and being assigned to a room: the process of inducing labor, the response after the induction, the birth of our baby, tests on baby Isaac, NICU, the incubator, surgery, feeding and back to the incubator environment and then home. Remember, the photos that were shown to my husband and I earlier in the second trimester by the specialist concerning the outward appearance were somewhat negative. Isaac did not have eyes that sat spaced apart from one another, he did not have the cleft lip or nose deformity, he did not have the syndrome look that was expected, he did not have the short fingers, but he had internal issues. Although, I was in my eighth month, we were told that baby Isaac had stopped developing and was the size of a seven-month old baby. Actually, everything I encountered I can whole heartily now say was a miracle in my eyes from the intervening act of the LORD responding to the prayers of the righteous on our behalf. Isaac DeShaun Tipton was born June 17, 1997 at 11:13pm. The very thought of carrying Isaac and vaginal delivery that was not supposed to have existed by man's diagnosis came to pass and was sustained by the command of the LORD. The Hand of GOD and the prayers that merged together as a kiss touched heaven for the purpose of holding Isaac in my wound that extended time. Mercy and Grace like a kiss preserved the pregnancy.

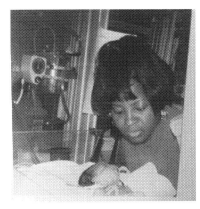

Baby Isaac came through the delivery looking around. When they put him in my arms in tears I was amazed, in tears and speechless to behold a miracle, such a fine looking newborn baby with direct attention response to sound and light. It was as if he was looking around to see all the people that cared to see the success of his arrival come forth. The syndrome baby Isaac was diagnosed with baffled the doctors in the hospital, due to the fact they only detected by sight a premature birth with premature disorders. GOD allowed me to care, comfort, love and provide for him as a mother even in his stay at the hospital. Nevertheless, GOD, the Author and the Finisher of my faith had the last word in this unfinished matter that was at hand. I called Isaac "Little Fighter", he underwent a dual surgery at one time. The doctors wanted the heart condition to function at a proper level because of his low

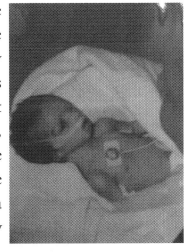

weight…2lbs 11 1/2oz. at birth. He was sent to the best care facility, St Jude Children's Hospital, where they placed a stomach tube for feeding and a valve for the two holes in his lower and upper heart chamber for heart volume medication. He thrived successfully over the months that he stayed at Methodist Central Hospital. I went faithfully to the hospital daily three times for the complete remainder of his stay; morning, afternoon and evening/ night. I breasted pumped and stored up breast milk for all Isaac feedings to store at the hospital for his consumption for the nurses to use in between my visits. After the doctor and nurses had done all that was assigned to their hands to be done, baby Isaac was released to go home after two months. He came home with the feeding tube and a heart monitor. The valve stem to his heart was removed and sealed before leaving the hospital for home.

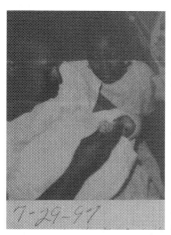

We had all the hope that a mom and dad could expect to have for life to be completely extended for a wholesome living. After a few days the home care nurse made her first visit and the photographer came to take baby Isaac pictures, he was thriving well, but by the second home care nurse visit he had passed. The morning Isaac passed-on; I was awakened before day break after my husband had gone to work. Isaac was not looking well, he was not receptive to his feeding and the motion of his arm movement was slow, then the heart monitor began to sound off, but it stopped. When the monitor alarmed it put me on alert. After the early morning hours in the kitchen after everything calmed down as he lay in the bassinet, I remembered looking at my baby boy with compassion; yet, helpless to fix the problem and not wanting him to suffer. I laid my hand upon his little chest and begin to pray the Will of Yahweh. I remembered praying, "LORD Heal Him," and then, "LORD, Don't Let Him Suffer," and then, finally I uttered the words "LORD, Let Your Will

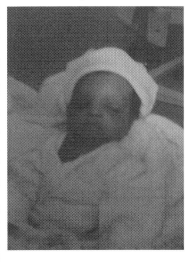

Be Done." Sometimes we don't even realize we are praying the Will of GOD, and when that happens it is Holy Spirit praying through a sincere, contrite heart. Within the hour the monitor's alarmed sounded off again and would not stop. I called 911. Before my very own eyes, I begin to see the breath of life escape my baby's body with outward visual signs. These were signs that no one wants to see, imagine or experience. I know GOD was there holding me together so I could function as I wept frantically. We were taught, trained and certified for infant CPR at the hospital, but I never thought that I would've had to use it on my baby boy. I performed infant CPR until the ambulance arrived. He was responding off and on when the ambulance arrived. When they

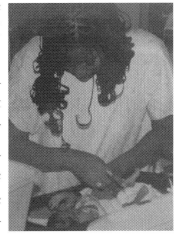

brought the family into the hospital holding room where he was wrapped secure, it was as if he was sleeping in the bosom of GOD in peace and victory. As family looked and some held Isaac aka Lil' Fighter, as I sat in the chair being comforted by love ones. I was limp and numb; yet, responsive. Now, something supernaturally happened to me in that small room during that time when everyone was around that no one heard or witness, but me. The SPIRIT of GOD opened my spiritual ear to hear in a higher dimension. I've never experienced this until that moment. A spiritual portal *(window)* was opened. I thought I was going into shock. As I looked at Isaac, eyes filled with tears, I was spiritually enabled to hear the cry of his voice by the Power of GOD. The cry elevated from the upward perimeter of the room in a motion, like he was being carried away. The area we were in was secluded from the main parts of the hospital. Isaac had a whimper of a cry; never as a regular full strength baby cry

and for most of the time he slept. I attempt to ask others there, "Do you hear what I hear?" "Do you hear him crying?" And the sound of the cry was a comfort cry tone, a tone as to say mommy, I am whole. And the cry suddenly went away. It wasn't a cry of distress, chronic in or out or painful. Mothers have the intuition of the meaning of their baby cries. But 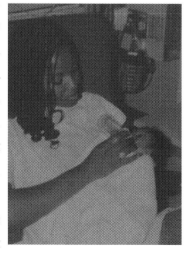 The LORD was not allowing my mouth to open. I remember that cry oh so well to this today. GOD didn't just allow me to hear baby Isaac in the realm of the spirit, but GOD confirmed to me that Isaac was healed, restored, in a safe place, made whole and that His Will was being done when I released Isaac back unto him in prayer that morning. I received revelation as time went by. Over the last eighteen years the Spirit of the LORD has unveiled revelation from that season on different levels for me to minister to others that are wounded, shackled and in need of liberty by His Spirit or to show me something. Isaac's body stayed warm and his complexion blush pinkish for a long period of time, not like the average death. Isaac passed on Sunday, September 7, 1997, at Baptist Desoto Hospital and was buried on Wednesday, September 10, 1997. The death certificate stated cause of death was congestive heart failure.

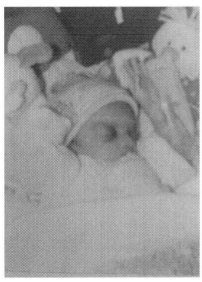

The ancient question that comes out of our mouth when under severe pressure, stress and anxiety rest upon us: *WHY? WHY THIS…. HAPPEN? WHY Me?….STOP IT?* After All You Are God? It is human nature that poses to ask questions, even to question GOD about himself and his dealings. We all have different reactions, but pain and deep hurt will speak out. When we don't know GOD or understand his ways or thoughts, the fallen nature or sinful nature will rise. Although I did it, I also had to repent of my sarcastic remarks that came out of emotional hurt and ignorance. When we read the Book of Job, we find in Job's windstorm, although a righteous, upright, devote man of Yahweh even questioned the Creator. What audacity or legal right do we think we have? When the flesh goes into shock mode it sends out shocking, disturbing responses. This is part of the surfacing of impurities of the soul, for the change that must take place after self is removed out of the way and for us to see our nakedness and vulnerability. The old man/nature will bow to understand naked I entered and naked I will leave. In other words, we brought nothing in this world and we certainly have no power within ourselves to make something remain. It is nothing wrong with asking that famous ancient old question. Why? However, we will never get the satisfaction of what we want to here, and if we did it still will not replace what or who we have lost or gratify our selfishness to hold on and never let go. Therefore, the healing is not in the answer you are expecting to receive from GOD on your policy term. The Lord asked me several breathtaking questions that provoked me to think, be quiet and review my crisis. And the answers were not what I was expecting or wanting to hear. All the answers we will ever get from the Lord by His Spirit will line up with His holiness, His character and His nature. The WORD of GOD tells us that every knee shall bow and tongue will acknowledge the LORD God {**Romans 14:11**}, even in the dry places. Our wilderness experiences is the place purposefully designed to teach us that even you must bow in this situation and lay your life prostate before the LORD God that He may bring closure. When GOD speaks to us, first He opens our spiritual ear to hear Him in the realm of the spirit in order to hear what he wants you to hear and secondly, to see as He will's by getting our attention to receive. Whether you believe or not ***GOD IS STILL SPEAKING EXPRESSIVELY IN THESE LAST DAYS*** to His elect by His Ruach HaKodesh. GOD responded by asking me questions, to answer your questions… daughter…your answers will come through answering these questions:

1. WHY NOT YOU?
2. ARE YOU NOT SAVED?
3. DID YOU NOT GIVE HIM A CHANCE AT LIFE AND TRUST ME?
4. I DID NOT ONLY ALLOW HIM TO EXIST, BUT YOU MOTHERED HIM!

Now the LORD placed these questions before me that I could not refute in my time of devastation, because they were true. The devil also will appear throwing fiery darts with his ancient old vices to hurting hearts. And those darts, if they pierce, will cause open wound bleeding and leakage of the soul. When a person doesn't know the scripture the enemy will pull covers over the ears and eyes; assign deafness to such ears and plant seeds of stubbornness in the heart. The devil plows the twisting of words and emotions when we are in a fragile stage. However, many courageous believers have *already* faith-walked our course in suffering. We can learn the revelatory insight and instructions from their testimonies to apply to our cases on trial. The devil like a persecuting attorney only knows slander and accusations and destruction. At the time, I didn't know what the Book of Job consisted of in counsel until I begin to study, research, meditate and prepare to preach my first message in 2006, which happens to be the title of this teaching manual. The devil said to me, "What kind of GOD do you serve?" He let your baby die. Why would you serve him? Walk Away! There were many, many counterattacks by Holy Spirit against the assaults when the adversary was targeting my mind like a dart board. When you approach seasons of testing in your life that are not favorable to your feelings, sight, hearing, health, finances, family, job, relationship, marriage or being, turn off all voices that send assault threats against you. Turn your mind off to them. The assaults are sent to assassinate your next level in GOD. GOD promotes the release of your spiritual and natural blessings in life. Promotion releases come through your personal time in prayer with GOD, searching the scriptures and meditating on the Word day in and day out for your way to be made successful {**Joshua 1:8**}. You don't have to know the whole Bible, but you need to have some *faith-Word* in you which is your defense and constitution. Your success or victory is sure to manifest.

Due to what I faced, the questions stopped, but then I begin to put demands on GOD, on His KINGDOM. At the time, I did not know about decreeing and declaring the laws of the Kingdom of Yahweh in Christ that are already established for each blood redeemed believer. Your miracle is in your mouth. Your situation can change when your heart and talk transition to align with the Kingdom's demand for counteraction against defeat. Many of us in the Church must experience a meeting with the KING personally. No one can enter into that secret chamber for you when GOD has ordained a meeting for you to meet with Him, *one on one* in your season. All that you saw in church growing up, the praises of his goodness and mighty acts, the blood songs, how He would keep you, the preaching of the cross, God will bring you out, God will rock you and not suffer your foot to be moved: all the church living for me was becoming empty, not real. I was searching. I tested GOD to be GOD. I told Him he would have to do something before I go back to the world, before I walk away from all that he had blessed me with. In all my pain, anger and bitterness I told GOD if you are who you say you are do something. I even questioned if He was even sitting where He said He was on the throne in heaven. My pain, bitterness and agony were becoming intense. I was on the verge of accepting the lie from the accuser of the brethren, this is real talk. The enemy had almost convinced me that GOD had forsaken me and that He didn't love me. Then, during my ride to work, taking the long way and driving slow, slobbering with tears swelled up in my eyes. I could barely see how to drive. The Spirit of the Living GOD began to speak to me in silence, not an audible voice or still voice. Because I was talking so much out of hurt, desperation and not listening; His Presence came into my car and His Presence got my attention. I stopped talking altogether! I was listening for something while groaning, moaning and crying, but that something I did not know. I did not know what was taking place. It was if His Presence arrested my attention and my emotions; calmed me down and said, **I Am That I Am** is going to show you visually.

ADONAI *(Master, Lord)* has a way of silencing us in the hope for the promise of assurance.

My salon business had lost major income and my clientele had dropped tremendously; business overhead was overbearing and out of six stylists only three remained. My husband was graced quickly to be hired at another company. **I AM THAT I AM** was showing me. GOD gave me double for all my troubles which included spiritual blessings also. Are you hearing me! He supplied me double-fold all around. When the LORD delivers us He also desires for His children to be equipped with His KINGDOM appetite. All that I demanded through decreeing from the Kingdom was supplied in three weeks. I opened my mouth to a barber that GOD had placed before me about working in my barber/beauty salon. Even though the barber said he wasn't currently looking to relocate; suddenly, that same week I received a call from him saying he needed somewhere to work because the owner was mistreating him and told him to pack his things. I asked no questions. Are you seeing the setup in the spirit? *"WHAT IS FOR YOU IS FOR YOU (your breakthrough) AND THE GATES OF HELL SHALL NOT PREVAIL IN YOUR APPOINTED SEASON TO COME OUT OF THE PIT INTO THE PLACE OF VICTORY WHEN HOPE IS ALIVE."* The following week after he started he referred three others, whom I interviewed and they began working at Studio of Styles Beauty & Barber Salon. And then another stylist which I was told about, started the same month. The overdraft took me into the Supernatural overflow of abundantly being blessed in my faith walk and arising in my spirit. GOD reversed all the lies the devil had ever told me; even those lies told since I've been in ministry to this day. The enemy doesn't stop at his assignment. Therefore, the Ecclesia-Church *(Body of Christ, Spiritual Organism in the earth)* is to continue to progress, pursue, push, press, produce and prosper in the Might of the LORD and counteract with the WORD of GOD. GOD Is Great And Greatly To Be Praised! Hallelujah to my KING!

However, my deliverance which was the major portion of the overflow release came first. Jehovah Jireh *(God's Provision provides)* supplied the spiritual need first; shattered the chains, all related bondage, clothe me with that which surpass all understanding and excelled my spirit- mind *(psuche)* to another dimension bringing His set time into the space of time. He supplied the material need, displaying His concern for me. My deliverance was all at once. It's like the moment an addict get delivered from an addiction and never turns to walk in that pathway again. It was phenomenally powerful and still impacts my life today; especially, in the sphere of the supernatural. Even though I was bitter, mad and disappointed toward GOD and the Pastor at church at the time, I was yet drawn to continue to attend worship service. My spirit was in a tug of war, but Holy Spirit overshadowed me with unction. After returning back to work, I often found myself witnessing out of my weakness and love to clients about the LORD when the opportunity presented itself, not realizing GOD was working to build my inner spiritual esteem of value of Himself in me. I was at church one Sunday and I had shifted from the front rows to the back where no one could see me closely; crying hard to the point I could feel the veins in my forehead with my hands as I covered my face. That Sunday in worship, I heard Holy Spirit say, "Go Testify." I didn't know I had a testimony, but out of obedience to His unction, **Go Testify**; I rose with a puffed up face from crying and went to the pulpit during testimonial time. I remembered as I opened my mouth I could hardly speak to get my words out clearly. There was a supernatural invasion that took place; a release came into the atmosphere, only the people and GOD knew what all was said. It was as if the chains and strongholds and grips of agony were being loosened through the breath that breathed into the breath of my spirit…Revival…Fire. When I got off the floor from the saturation of the Fire, Anointing and Favor of Yahweh, the church was on Fire. Ruach Hakodesh was moving; arresting every demonic hostile presence, rendering them powerless, breaking chains, setting minds free, healing and restoring by His Anointing. **OH, YES, HE DID IT**…from that day forward, I walk liberated and delivered…it was **SUDDENLY. GOD DID IT BY THE AUTHORITY OF HIS WORD!** Even to this day I can't explain what took place other than the *SUPERNATURAL POWER* of Yahweh Presences' invaded the camp; spoiled the plans and plots of the enemy against all that were under the Glory Cloud *(YHWH Presence)*, establishing assurance of an expected end. It was cloudy in the temple. The GLORY of the LORD was resting in full manifestation on my day. GLORY HALLELUJAH! He will remove the grave clothes with its residue of death, defeat, sickness, torment, isolation and clothe you with divine garments of peace, dreams, favor, vision and purpose.

The LORD desires to reveal and manifest Himself to you in his multifaceted nature. He did just as He had said to show the children of Israel who He was and reveal who they were over and over. He is willing to do same in a greater measure *(New Covenant Blood)* for those that obey and seek His face. When you arrive or approach those challenging or distress seasons that bring different windstorms toward you, He said, **fear not take courage** this is the tool being used to reveal to you another part of Himself and to increase His Power in you as you decrease. He doesn't want you tossed to and fro in dry places, because He is there with you; yet, desiring for you to thirst to know Him through the bond of Covenant. GOD desires for you to depend dependently on Him as your source of supply for all your needs spiritually, as well as, physically. The wilderness is not designed to kill believers, but to equip us for an encounter and an invasion of the Supernatural Wisdom of Yahweh through Yeshua for the unlocking of God-ordained greatness to unveil within you. He put Himself in us, which is the **Treasure of Greatness** sealed in the soul. Selah! Reflect on that thought for a moment. **"Be All You Are To Be In CHRIST JESUS."** Jesus asked Peter a question which only he could answer through revelation and a personal walk experience with the Christ. **The Bible tells us {Mark 8:29} But what about you? Yeshua asked. Who do you say I am? Peter answered, you are the Messiah.** This is what GOD is asking you personally. **WHO DO YOU SAY THAT I AM?** Divine revelation only comes through experiential revelation which brings about transformation in the soul, spirit and mind and pathway. Whatever your case may be, place it before the LORD. There is a place called *THERE* where meetings are to continue **one on one** and mysteries will be revealed unto them that belong to Yahweh in Christ by His Ruach.

The ancient enemy of our souls known as the accuser of the brethren, the adversary, the destroyer and deceiver will play tricks with your mind, your thinking, your imagination, your will, your reasoning and your thoughts. Our minds are dimensional; the seat- soil of the seed or generation or beginning of thoughts which creates. Satan will appear with smooth sensible words to attempt to entice or draw a soul when they are at their weakest state like the coward he is. Satan comes to manipulate, maneuver and to convince your heart *(mind-soul-spirit)* to curse God to his face and die. That is the lie he spoke to Job's wife and in return she attempted to plant the lie in Jobs heart and mind. "Die," literally means to turn from the One True Living GOD to your own way, a spiritual separation or division; and physical death. That is alienation from Yahweh who is Holy, which is led by the spirit of deception; the enemy's strategy to rear a soul in their own path to consider that there is no GOD. Before I knew with understanding and revelation what the scriptures said to me, especially the Old Testament; Ruach Hakodesh in this experience, along with others, started me on the journey called the School of the Holy Ghost. What Yahweh by His Ruach *(Spirit)* teaches, exposes, reveals, educates, influences, empowers and clothe doesn't come from the seminary school. It comes from being in His Presence. I had a supernatural spiritual awakening encounter for several months, in intervals. Each time I broke down, yet calling unto the LORD God for help, He met me where I was to bring me into a place of prosperity. Now the meetings weren't the same: some encounters were not exposed in a small still voice or a wind, but in the form of a Canopy or a Shield as a hedge of divine protection.

These are two encounters that I recall while alone, depressed and in agony: I had thoughts of suicide…killing myself; the pressure was overwhelming. The enemy gave me step by step visual instructions, I could see it. But the evil presence that was trying to sway and overtake me was overthrown by JESUS…His Presence. I heard and saw in the realm of the spirit the devil or demonic presence over my shoulder on one side and JESUS or an Angelic presence in one form over the other shoulder in a battle concerning me. I heard the commotion in the spirit and I sat at a halt listening. I don't remember the exact words, which I don't believe were meant for me to remember. This blew me away and caused me to become alert and sober in thought; snatching me out of the delusion of despair. My worst battle to conquer was being alone. Through all my questions, pain, sleepless nights, visiting and sitting in the cemetery and crying spells GOD was with me in the darkest hours of what I thought to be despair. No Hope, I imagined could have come out of this at this point. **BUT GOD!** Another encounter happened when I would look in the mirror at myself in confusion, bitterness the enemy would sow discouraging thoughts/words which I would repeat at myself, which is call death confessions, but GOD reversed the curse the enemy was attempting to plant. Remember words are spirit, seed; good or bad, and many voices may be heard in dark moments. Yet they fall into to categories: evil or good. When we are ignorant to the weapons and ways of Yahweh or the devil's vices, yet are seeking the LORD all we know how, even in the darkness, hopeless moment He will show up as your defender against the persecutor that is trying to take you out. **HOLD ON!** To those who visit the cemetery like going on a lunch date, like I was faithfully, GOD wants you to Stop! **Stop Going!** It is a hold on you mentally, as well as, spiritually and is a blocking vice that will retard and revert your healing, deliverance and restoration process. The pain will ensnare you to the grave where only dust is located, not the soul or spirit of the person. The grave presence can drain vitality, fights inner healing, attach a chain to your destiny, stir up idolatry, familiar spirits and/ or hold any soul hostage. The grave know no answers, holds no healing and no promises; although loves remains are there. The LORD wants to heal every pain, every deep hurt, every imbalanced unstable emotion, wrong thoughts, weak hearts, attachments and bring prosperity into your spirit and your soul. The devil knows the shift is the Supernatural Presence of the LORD. You must not only know it's the Supernatural Presence of the Lord, but you must shift, relocate and move into the Supernatural Presence in your spirit- mind. Don't allow the devil to use your present status to cheat you out of your divine supernatural benefits as a believer in Christ. The benefits materialize for believers. You have a legal right by birthright to silence the voice of darkness according to scripture. Don't think about, entertain or believe or accept the devil lies.

Satan's Characteristic Worth
• Imposter
• Without Principle
• Counterfeiter
• Sow Discord
• Sow Confusion
• Sow Unbelief
• Thief/ Robber
• Father of Lies/ Liar/ Deceiver
• Tempter
• Destroyer
• Murderer
• Crafty/ Cunning/ Scheming
• Manipulative
• Defeated

Jesus knows what you are in need of and how to deliver the grace to be effectively working for you against all the odds that **appear** with a look to be greater. **Believers Are Winners!** Just as Lazarus died and laid in that tomb, wrapped, bound, secure in separation and with odor arising from the corpse as a result from being dead for four days. The cemetery holds life with vitality back from you and will hold you captive with pass regrets, hurts or resentment, although you may think it to be an innocent act or harmless to the natural eye, could in fact be deadly to your character and spiritual development. These doors must be shut down in the spirit and in the physical realm or they will spiritual shut you down; moment by moment. Allow Jehovah Rophi *(Hebraic title: the Lord that heals)* to heal you, then you will be able to see the difference and the outlook from a higher mind perspective, the **mind of Christ**. At this moment, if this is you it may not make sense. What is spiritual is nonsense to the carnal mind and unrestored emotions. Remember, satan will steal, destroy and kill by any method, window or door that remains open that should be closed. **There is a season, a time for everything under the heavens {Ecclesiastes 3:1-8}**. We do not want to be caught in a place out of season! That is not the perfect Will of Yahweh for you. When and if GOD release you to go to the cemetery it will be totally opposite of your motive beforehand. My healing deliverance elevated to another level when I stopped going to the cemetery. JESUS wants you to know the situation may look bad, clothe you with the stench from darkness, be uncomfortable, make you feel as if you are empty on the inside with nothing to live for or offer, no reason to carry on afterwards and the hurt you are feeling may be overbearing; yet Yahweh God declares it's not never to late in His eyes or on His divine clock *(appointed time)* to resurrect you from the ashes or resuscitate you to exist with purpose beyond just existing without purpose. He removes the face mask; phony smiles, wrong disposition, and visage out of the heart that we can display so well and give us inner beauty, integrity and healing. Mary, the sister of Lazarus, told Yeshua if you would have only been present *(on the seen)* this could have been prevented. Lazarus would still be alive, *only if.* JESUS was then, and even now still full of compassion wants us to trust and believe that what may seem to be a dead situation, there is still something great that can be revived from it *only if* you believe. I was revived fully. It is by His Power and Divine Revelation that when you receive what He has *already* spoken that supernatural freshness will clothe you with Kingdom garments. It's like the wind blowing, His Presence that you can feel upon you, but can't explain the change or the touch you just know that you know you know in your knower something is happening that you can't put your hands on and that you are falling in love all over again with your first true love, Yeshua HaMashiach. JESUS has a special way of wrapping us in swallowing clothes like a new born baby; symbolizing His unconditional unfailing love, His arms, His touch, His mercy, His compassion, His security, His care, His presence, His covering and His closeness during and after a crisis.

INTERCESSION FOR SOULS

Heavenly Father, I Give You Honor Praise And Thanks For Your Many Spiritual Blessings. Lord I Worship You In Spirit And Truth. I Ask For Your Forgiveness On Behalf Of The Souls Who Are Partaking Of This Mandate In Prayer To Come Clean And Pure In Conscience Before You. Forgive Us Of Our Sins As We Forgive Our Debtors. I Thank You For The Privilege And Honor To Come Before Your Throne Of Grace And Mercy To Lift Up The Many Hearts And Souls That Are Bleeding From Unhealed Wounds. LORD You Said In Your Word That You Are No Respect Of Persons And That There Is No Partiality To Be Found In You. Because You Are Holy, Righteous And Just. The Heart That Is Bleeding Lay Their Wounds Down At The Feet Of The Cross, LORD We Ask You To Lift This Soul Out Of The Miry Clay. They Release There Hurt, Angry, Pain, Frustrations, Low Esteem, Depressions, Panic Attacks, Deep Hurt, Quick Temper, Bad Habits, Bitterness, Sharp Tone, Callous Heart And All Other Vices That Have Formed And Manifested To You In Exchange For Your Healing Balm. I Command Every Intruding Evil Vice To Leave Now In the Name Of JESUS CHRIST. And By the Authority And the Power of Holy Spirit I Command The Enemy Taunting Of Their Souls And Minds To Seize In JESUS NAME. I Plea The Blood Of JESUS Over Their Sleep, Thoughts, Dream Life And I Plead the Blood of JESUS Against Idleness, Pride, Recognition, Prayerlessness And Murmuring In JESUS Name. I Loose The Spirit of Holy Conviction to Arrest Every Wayward Plan And Evil Plot In JESUS Name By The Authority And Power Of Holy Spirit. I Bind And Break the Power of Every Deviating, Counterfeit, Masquerading Demonic Spirit In the Name of JESUS CHRIST. I Command Truth And Holy Conviction To Be Bind to Their Reasoning In JESUS Name. I Command Your Sinews To Be Strengthened And Fresh Oil To Supernaturally Empower Your Mind And Will To Be In JESUS Name. I Decree Healing To Be So.

Receive divine healing and walk in divine deliverance daily.

Amen.

The Lord forethought to reveal who He is as *ADONAI (Lord, Master, Owner)* in these experiences and whose you are through Covenant Birth-Right. As I went through my storm a part of me died with my baby, but it was designed that way in order for me and you in the midst of crisis to search out who this JESUS is that we say love us, saved us and died for us by drawing closer in our daily walk. All which has been touched by the storm: the reasoning, the relationship, the finances, the job, business, security and stability are no comparison to the overshadowing of His Presence and Promises. Now is the place and time where GOD says it is His turn to prove Himself to you if you will take Him at His Word and trust His provision advancement in advance. Everything that was lost can be recovered greater by faith; this portion is beyond material gain, yet part of the wealth increase. When we have been stripped of self, we will desire more than material gain. As we rest in Him, Holy Spirit will supernaturally fill us with that which expands into a broader knowledge, width, depth, breadth and wisdom of JESUS CHRIST. **The Bible tells us {Proverbs 4:7} Wisdom is the principal or first thing: Get wisdom, in all thy getting, get understanding. The World English Bible says: Yes, though it cost you all your possessions.** Wow! That is deep revelation. Ask Holy Spirit for divine understanding. The LORD God wants us to have a clear and better revelatory understanding of His holiness, character and nature and as this take place the true image rise forward from within.

When we hurt and the hurt goes unhealed, it grows deeper and darker in the soul even though it is an emotion. That emotion can awake disturbances and open doors that you would never had second thought to walk through when the mind is sound, whole, sober and at peace. Unhealed pain or anger outward response is like a swinging door on loose hinges with no self-control. When we walk around deeply wounded we may just accept the next quick fix that seems like it will heal the problem. These are a few manifested behaviors resulting from a spiritual portal or window that may be opened and wants to remain open without being detected. Some doors walked into are the tattooing of the body, body piercing, social or occasional drinking, partying spirit, malice, drugs, excess spending or borrowing, don't care attitude *(that manifested through a door)*, turning to the same gender for relations, illicit sex, laughing at everything, walking out on your spouse, isolation, outburst of anger and/ or lashing out and many other unlisted factors. This is meant to bash anyone, but to alert your heart. These are evil tunics or garments out the realm of darkness that have or will manifest with the attempt to clothe and entwine themselves with a person's being to become one, but we can cut the cord when aware. These are persuasions of another voice and another source; swaying the heart to another path or compromise. Beloved of GOD stuffed just don't happen without a cause to bring the effect into open view. Portals are like gateway entrances that connect the spirit realm to the physical realm releasing good or evil forces into the natural realm through the Law of Attraction. **In the Name of JESUS rebuke All demonic energies in your home, in you, from you, over your children, relatives and in your atmosphere by the Authority and Power of Holy Spirit.** Many times they are called vibes, but those vibes may well be unclean spirits. **Remember the Bible tells the Church that Spirit discerns things of the spirit and a natural mind can not discern spiritual things {1Corinthians 2:14; John 3:6}.** Yahweh only releases His Gift(s) through His Holy Spirit. My husband was the one that stepped up to my rescue to help me to rethink soberly about some choice doors I was about to open that would've cost the both of us additional chaos. JESUS is the Answer to your needs the world does not have the answers to your spiritual need or insight. Every case may differ, but pain has no limitations on how far it will take you off course and out of sync with Truth and GOD reality. Glory Be to Yahweh God who hears and sees the tears on top of tears that seem to be never ending; who sees the bruise, broken, and crushed soul that pours out to Him. He will perform, promote and fill His Promises. ADONAI will not forsake us. He will not allow the pearl *(you)* of a great price to go unrewarded in this life…His Bride.

As Yahweh revealed himself to Abraham, Isaac, Jacob, Moses and to the children of Israel, He still acts to work in revealing Himself to the sons and daughters of the household of faith in Christ Jesus during dry places. Revelation and wisdom is given by Him attached to great responsibility, loyalty and devotion. When we face those hardships where is He? Who has He unveiled Himself as? Do you know Him in that grace code or do you only speak well of Him of the grace? Each destination we arrive to that seems to be a test is there with a purpose for you to humble and for Yahweh in Christ to unveiled another measure of Himself to you which elevates you from Glory to Glory, Faith to Faith. The LORD displays His work in you and through you. When He heals, revive, restore and deliver us that is a work of Ruach Hakodesh *(Holy Spirit)* to testify of His Glory in the earth. It is the Lord's doing and it is marvelous in His children's eyes. GOD wants you to know Him so you will be able to stand in your faith in this evil day in which we live that is closing JESUS slowly out of its dealings. You are the temple of GOD. You must be built on the Solid Rock Foundation and filled with His Holy Spirit and found in Faith when Jesus returns.

The prayer on the next page is a prayer for all those that have lost their babies to premature death in any form and are still suffering with emotional hurt from death of love ones that can stain the soul. This prayer is also for those that have lost love ones to premature death in any form or fashion. Premature death is also related to early death of any soul and age. And this prayer is also for those who are struggling with the sickness, other ailments themselves, pressure, the grief or even those which have buried the pain *(covered it up with busyness, unwholesomeness, negativity, idleness or drinking, etc)* which causes that emotion to lay dormant leading and secretly inviting other familiar spirits. Holy Spirit revealed to me that this is known as the inner spiritual bleeding of the soul crying out for help. JESUS is Still in the business of Healing and Delivering. It's only to late when you are in denial, rejection or do not recognize and respond to the call for resuscitation from JESUS. New beginnings and freshness is available to start at any given moment. Just because it *(the distress)* is happening to you is not the end of your life, but the start of another chapter for you to expand and succeed in areas that could not be revealed to you in your prior state. Now is your season to arise.

PRAYER OF ACKNOWLEDGMENT AND HUMILITY

Heavenly Father, In The Name Of Jesus Christ The Name That Is Above Every Name, I Am Empty And I Come Naked Before You Acknowledging My Weakness, My Anger, My Pity And My Little Faith, Even For Questioning Your Supreme Existence And Your Position, I Ask You To Forgive Me While You Where Stretching Me To Know You. You Have Kept Me Thus Far And Because I Was Blinded By Bitterness, I Didn't Realize You Were There In the Fire With Me And That I Was Not Alone. Your Love Has Not Failed Me Yet. Lord You Know My Uprising. You Know My Down sitting; My Going And My Coming, Even My Thoughts And Actions Before I Take Them. I Invoke Your Presence To Cover My Mental And Emotional Being, For You Are The Lifter Of My Head, And The Restorer Of My Soul, Without You I Have Nothing And I Am Nothing. Therefore I Stretch My Hand To Thee And Surrender For You To Intervene On My Behalf In Jesus Name. I Have No Fight Left So I Plea My Case For Your Help As I Humble Myself. Let thou Will be Done In Jesus Name.

Amen.

Write & Memorize this Promise which comes with a reward and what it means in your own words:

Psalm 56:8

Hebrews 3:8

Do not harden your heart as when they provoked me, as in the day of the trial in the wilderness.

1. a) How does Hebrew 3:8 relates to you today? What is God saying to you?

Deuteronomy 1:31

And in the wilderness, there you saw the LORD your God carried you, as a father carries his son, all the way you went until you reached this place.

Deuteronomy 8:2

Remember how the LORD your God led you all the way in the wilderness to humble you in order to know what was in your heart, whether or not you would keep his commands (instructions).

Psalm 139:23-24

Search me, O God, and know my heart. Try me and know my thoughts. And see if there be any grievous way in me, and lead me in the way everlasting.

Ezekiel 36:26

And I will give you a new heart and a new spirit I will put within you. And I will remove the heart of stone from your flesh and give you a heart of flesh.

Romans 12:2

Do not be conformed to this world, but be transformed by the renewal of the mind, that by testing you may discern what is the will of God, what is good and acceptable and perfect.

2. a) How does <u>Romans 12:2</u> relate to you in times of lack, distress, hardship or identity?

_____

_____

_____

b) Write and heart memorize <u>Jeremiah 29:11</u>

_____

_____

_____

Healing and Restoration: "You Are A Miracle"

1. What is the revelation of your wilderness experience? Ask Holy Spirit?

   _____

   _____

   _____

2. What is the transition in your wilderness experience?

   _____

   _____

   _____

3. What was the transformation in your wilderness experience?

   _____

   _____

   _____

4. What did you learn from your wilderness experience?

   _____

   _____

   _____

5. How have you used your testimonies to impact the lives around you and to build up the wounded and to advance the Kingdom of God in the earth?

   _____

   _____

   _____

CHAPTER SEVEN

AVAILING PURPOSE

There is purpose to be unveiled in anything that comes by our way if we wait it out through the power of prayer at the altar. Purpose will manifest through **transition**, **revelation** and **transformation**. The altar has that affect on thirsty souls, like a deer that pants for flowing water {**Psalm 42:1**}. We'll begin to thirst for Him and only the LORD can fill this void because it is spiritual. And the Father knows how to nurture the need of weary souls. The spirit of worldliness, sex, drugs, hanging out, idleness, the bottle, quick fixes or such like will not fill this thirst or void. Have you experienced any tornados or tsunamis in your life in which divine purpose was revealed to you at set times by Ruach HaKodesh or vessels of honor sent that crossed your path with a true Word from The Lord? I literally mean heavy winds in life which could be parallel to harsh weather with form to takeout anything in its pathway and be life threatening.

In the midst of any windstorm are located pressures or weights which can escalate in strength. When there are high windstorms, heavy rains, hailstorms, tornado or tsunami, if the pressure of the storms were removed, the effect would be different altogether. As beautiful as snow is when it comes down heavy, moderate or light, the snow within itself differ from the snow with an ice mixture. The pressure of the storm is then maximized with the possibility of a chain reaction. In my view, this is the same formula hidden under the surface of devastations that will build upon other influences during seasons of suffering in a person's life. However, each personal experience and reaction differs. Where pressures or weights seize to exist, we have a tendency not to depend on GOD as much, but until there is a right now desperate dying need the tendency changes. We as a people with carnal instinct gravitate to fixing problems or situations independently void of GOD, because the flesh or carnal inclinations are hostile toward God. The mind of the flesh inclinations do not see or recognize the need that self is in need of a spiritual awakening of transitioning and examination through the spiritual lens of *The Eternal Word*. The weight has appeared to show you (us) your fleshly ways, fleshly thoughts, fleshly response, fleshly appetite, fleshly insignificance, fleshly path which is separate from Truth and Holiness and the spiritual need for divine guidance and deliverance. GOD wants the Church, believers, to mature, to be sound and whole beyond using Him for convenience or selfish reasons. That course of action will run out. Among many, the LORD delivered me by the ***Power of Holy Spirit*** from a character flaw called impure motives of the heart…using him like a vacuum cleaner among a lot of other selfish flaws….wanting His blessings, but not His corrections or way. Self must see it is self that needs to die, the flesh; so the work and Spirit of Christ can live through you continually. He doesn't want to be pimped by the one He has redeemed from the curse of sin, death and eternal separation. And neither does the LORD wants His redeem to prostitute His Word, gifts, talents and anointing for the purpose of worldly recognition or greed. The Ecclesia which is soon to be the Eternal Bride of Christ is betrothal to Christ by blood covenant. We are in the preparation stages for the wedding of our glorified lives hidden in the resurrection life of Christ.

Some of us in the Body of Christ comfortably make the affirmation I ***know*** GOD and GOD is good all the time, without having experiential revelation of ***knowing*** who the LORD really is personally; quick to repeat catchy phrases that may not be in agreement with the heart condition of that soul. When things are done repetitiously we can pick them up, seemingly innocent or not, without understanding how to discern our heart through Holy Spirit. Knowing Yahweh through Christ intimately and that He is most certainly good all the time isn't to be just a sound good phrase that's catchy, but a revelatory knowledge of truth confession through your life changing experiences with Him. Your testimony should be a proof of you growing in the revelations of knowing The LORD personally. I am persuaded by the Bible's supernatural testimonies that the storms' pressures are allowed for more purposes such as; to usher in divine transition, uprooting, revelation and transformation in the child of Yahweh through the *Messiah (Anointed One, Christos)* about whom we declare as The GOD of Our Salvation in the midst of dry places. The pressures in life will put this belief with many others affirmations to the test for the testing of developing genuine moral fiber approval that extends beyond the five natural senses. Even our emotional senses have to be sanctified and immersed in the Spirit of Christ. Christ wants all of you not just the portion that you picked out for Him, but all to be completely baptized into His body by the Ruach.

When immerged into the bitter cup of suffering often times the soul can get stuck in this transitioning stage, but you must not remain there because you will suffocate. This stage is a process of your soul dying for the purpose of emerging or submerging into the Perfect Will of GOD that pertains to your destiny. Remember, this is as much spiritual as it is natural. Under the spiritual lens you must not stop during the delivery stage, yes a spiritual birthing is to come forth. Our testimonies aren't only tests passed, but a divine promotion toward the greater things to come as we continue the course. What is invested in the believer through the **Seed of Righteousness** will be revealed in portion during the transition stage of coming out. This stage can be straining, but yet profitable as you push and press yourself out of yourself into the Presence of the Lord. If you are seeking and waiting on the LORD, then you are spiritually pregnant in your spiritual womb with a spiritual baby by the Supernatural Power of YHWH in Christ. This has nothing to do with your gender. There will be purpose birthed if you do not let go or terminate before the delivery. The **Seed** contains purpose, substance, destiny, greatness, anointing, gifts, graces, plans, strategy, promotions, power, revelation, wisdom, counsel and promise for those whose paths are tailored to reveal or expose the pathway of GOD through faith; without seeing the full manifestations of their deliverance. Yet, believing that it is *already* done in the Spirit which gives supernatural peace and supernatural stamina.

When the angels were sent to Sodom and Gomorrah to rescue Lot along with his family and to destroy the city completely, Lot's household was given instructions during the transition *"Not To Look Back."* Often times when a believer looks back when transitioning out of distress and suffering this very act will put a strain and block on your future, dreams, corrupt or poison others close to you or cause a decline from GOD. Looking back can paralyze your future. What one tends to believe, negative or positive; truth or a lie, will become a visible part of their being evident in behavior and conversation. Yahweh's instructions to believer's is *"Don't Look Back"* with remorse, regret, attachment, sorrow or demands, but let go and look forward in the Power of Grace that is carrying you to your destiny with promises and benefits attached. Anytime we suffer lost, looking back will appear innocent, but beguile us to indulge although a soul may not see its trap. This negative energy will absorb your strength and focus and future. This looking back differs from remembering where the LORD "BROUGHT" you from in order to give praise and thanks. In time that promotion of strength moves us forward in delight with no questions asked or second thoughts which builds up fortitude.

I remember telling Jesus how much I love him…how I want to be more like you…LORD make me into what you would have me to be…LORD nothing will separate me from you; and all these things are what we should ask for. Little did I understand that my faith in Jesus who is GOD would be allowed to be put through fire. My spoken soul confession was going to be tested for genuine faith to come forth and for pure wine to spew out from my inner man. This is the stage where the Body of Christ will be proven to be genuine in their faith walk with active inner evidence and not active lip service. **The Bible tells us {Isaiah 29:13} and the Lord said, Because this people draw near with their mouth and honor me not with their lips, and their hearts are far from me, and their fear of me is a commandments taught by men; {Matthew 15:8}.** Yahweh wants *His Redeemed* to have a personal spiritual encounter of who He is as *I AM THAT I AM (I will be)* and who you are as a son *(lead by the Spirit, no gender)* in Christ Jesus as you go through the pressure allowed for His disciplinary purpose to show forth increase. The five natural senses cannot wrap themselves around how the DNA spiritual anatomy senses will become awaken by the Spirit of GOD. ABBA wants each believer roots to be planted deep so that whatever comes against the redeemed of the Lord in this world, that you will be willing and able to stand like flint on the Rock *(Yeshua)* and not faint under the roar of the adversary who has no authority over believers hidden in Christ. As we are taught by Holy Spirit through other trials that will appear, we will learn to embrace it because of the divine impartation of the last triumph GOD delivered you through has taken your faith root deeper in Christ; making your foundation sure and steady. As the Lord finishes with us in each process, we become less dependent on flesh and the warrior within is rising in readiness to take the fight in the spirit realm by the leading of Holy Spirit. It is the working of the divine Counsel of Yahweh, as He increases the persuasion of the faith gift in your heart. Our embracing will come from the infusion, boldness of faith and confidence in The LORD by *knowing* through covenant experience that He is with you and will not suffer the faithful foot to be moved off the Rock of Salvation nor your pain to destroy you.

When the Body of Christ confesses that we *know* Yahweh in Christ, there should be proof of fruit and power as the reward within the confession of faith in *knowing* the Lord. Now, the word *to know* means to recognize, perceive, to have a revelatory understanding of what is known. This *to know* is beyond head knowledge, it's beyond all formalism of church attendance and it's beyond what you may think to know. It is an exposed divine revelation downloaded from Holy Spirit to the redeemed of the Lord, the faithful. How many say, **"I know the LORD?"** Sometimes it is simply what one may think to understand or have heard about the LORD that can lead to misconception of the real *knowing* that is needed in deep waters or troubled times. But even in this, if one is willing to seek the Lord, meditate day in and day out, He will remove what makes the soul unstable by replacing error with Truth which comes from the Spirit of

Truth. It is in deep waters that we *(you)* must call unto the deep, for the Lord to intervene with divine interference in your condition. When our souls thirst for an encounter, thirst for a divine breakthrough, thirst to get into the Presence of Yahweh for answers of assurance, answers of peace, thirst to hear the LORD speak a declaration to your atmosphere, a thirst just to be in His Presence to feel His approval of your life, decisions or a thirst to know the revelation of who GOD really is…that thirsty soul will cry out unto the deep. There is a spiritual well in you that must be filled continually with Living Water to satisfy the thirst and hungry of the soul which draws to the fountain that supply forever and ever. The LORD, who is *Living Water*, is ready to fill your spiritual well.

The Bible tells us {Romans 10:17} faith cometh by hearing and hearing by the WORD of GOD. This is an active impartation of faith from GOD to any yielded soul. The impartation of faith is to take the believer through the suffering processes that will rise. For us to become increasingly acquainted with His nature, intimately in personal experiences as He reveals Himself and download in measure the Supernatural DNA into your spirit from His Spirit. Remember, we have not the power source to impart faith into our spirit by self efforts. Therefore, when Holy Spirit breathes to quicken, make you alive for the cause that has approached you, receive the impartation at that divine appointment when He comes. It is in what you may know or what you have been told or taught about GOD that must become a truth reality to you for the sake of victory, your soul remaining faithful to GOD and remaining in the kingdom of Yahweh. And if what you have heard as Truth does not line up with what you are seeing, then this isn't the time to run out from Jesus, but it is the season to embrace with purpose, to soul search for yourself what Jesus meant concerning His promises, His will and the unveiling of heaven's mysteries to you from the Father. Jesus confirms His purpose to us in scripture that he came not to make a reputation for Himself; for whatever the Son sees the Father doing that I *(Yeshua)* do also {**John 5:19**}.

Holy Spirit wants to teach you all thing pertaining to your citizenship in the Kingdom of Yahweh. GOD said you are healed, but the doctors may have said differently. The doctors are used by Yahweh, but the doctors do not have the last word about your healing condition. But the **test** of fires is to direct you to run into Christ to see what the Lord has to say about any given situation. And to see Him reveal Himself to you as *I AM THAT I AM,* the LORD will be whatever you need Him to be to you. GOD is Spirit and healing is spiritual, supernaturally manifested in the physical realm. God created our bodies to heal themselves and the medicine only treats the symptoms that appear. We seek the one whose image we are created in, who is the Great Physician. All that GOD has for us is spiritual when he releases His blessings of promise, light which is uncalculated in eternity approaches time which is calculated in the earth atmospheric zone. There is war in the heavens. Yahweh's joy is to show you His love at all times and in all that pertain to your welfare. Therefore, as you hear Him…follow and obey Him.

Many forfeit their birthright when windstorms or distresses come by turning from the Lord to another god or false religion which has no eternal salvation with benefits to offer; while some are led astray into deception by things with a temporarily shade of countenance appearing as a covering for a wounded heart. And some souls drift away because the spirit of doubt began to grow and festered in the inward parts. Remember, the devil will lie anyway he can to gain a foothold in your imagination to paint a hopeless image or word in your spirit in difficult seasons. Just as the LORD has a purpose in the midst of any type of crisis, the devil which is subtle and crafty in schemes has a wicked device of purpose also. The devil, the Father of Lies, was a liar from the beginning and a defeated foe of Yahweh. Therefore, the same way ABBA sees the devil is the same way the Church is to see him. The devil along with his demonic kingdom of darkness is coming to an end at that last day. Judgment Day Is Coming!

The devil will make false accusations
• About you to the Lord
• Through others to assassinate your character
• Yahweh doesn't hear you when you call
• God is not even real or there is no God
• God is disappointed in you
• Your God sent me to destroy you
• Yahweh has forsaken you

Yeshua HaMashiach is the Head of the Body of Christ, so the body is to respond and follow the head. Holy Spirit has revealed that many in the church are walking in emotional hurt, wearing masks, coming in and leaving out the same way they entered, hiding from Him due to the shame, pride, lack of understanding and the lack of ***knowing*** him beyond church services; in church yet really disconnected with a cliché of GOD which will cause open resentment toward GOD grace covenant. When Yahweh called Abram out of his homeland and gave him instructions with promise, Abraham after awhile developed a growing bond-ship of ***knowing*** who Yahweh was through trial and error. Yet, Sarah only knew what her husband had related to her about the Promise of the promised seed. Sarah's response was a laugh of contempt not at Abraham, but at the divine interruption of Yahweh **{Genesis 18:12-14}** that sounded ridicules in her old age. The contempt served as a purpose for testing, cutting away unbelief, circumcising the mind, teaching and developing Yahweh's character in their inner being. She had not yet developed an intimate relationship with Yahweh until the set time of purpose was exposed in her body which brought the reality of divine manifestations. However, reality was established at the moment GOD opened His mouth and declared the *Spoken Word* in the form of the Promise unto Abraham. Sarah represents souls that have a need to see before believing, which is not of faith, the divine persuasion from the LORD. GOD declares souls to trust Him because He has spoken and broken covenant with Himself before time exist in time and He is bound to Himself to fulfill all that He speaks through personal covenant with believers.

Anytime the LORD tells us or promises us something that WORD may not match the current condition in the season/time that you are presently experiencing. GOD does not seek to match in time, but seek to establish what is *already* established before time into time. Praise The Lord! Receive the prophetic release…just receive it and don't try to figure it out. Faith is now, not what we are to figure out to make it happen. Hallelujah to the Lamb of Yahweh! What the LORD says is manifested upon faith, obedience, following the Will of GOD and asking the LORD to release His provision in the areas you have need in. If that area is patience, then your petition is Heavenly Father, in the Name of Jesus, I pray that you release your provision in my life for divine patience; strengthen and condition my heart when the test comes to teach and prove me that I might *know* you.

Hebrew and Greek words for the term Know
Yada (Ginosko): confess, perceive by experience, recognize, acknowledge, skilled in, acquainted with, intimacy

A person can live next door or in your neighborhood or work right by you for years, but that doesn't mean you *know* them. Some people know people on the account of what others have said about them which isn't truly *knowing* a person either. This is how GOD is too many in the church, at a distance. It is in the dry places in life, I repeat again, the dry places that Yahweh will allow to come upon his children for his disciplinary purpose to expose, reveal, train, revive and create in us His newness. This is the opportunity for the Church, the believer, to seek GOD personally to enter an intimate personal one on one experience in the Presence of Yahweh. The reward that *ADONAI (Master)* desires upon His body is to be able to arise under any pressure that life will bring toward you for the destruction of your destiny in Him that we as believers may not be condemned in the judgment that is coming upon the unbelieving, rebellious world. Other purposes for the wilderness is to judge, rebuke, correct, build, settle and to present us holy *(set apart)*, unblameable and unrebukeable in His sight as we continue in the faith.

Do you understand that what we face and experience in this world may perhaps be a fact, but it is not necessarily the reality or mirror of **TRUTH**. I know that sounds ridiculous and it is to the natural mindset. But the believer is a spirit-being with a new nature which is born from above not from this world, born of GOD, Spirit **{1 John 3:9}**. I can see that a condition is real, but the condition is not from **TRUTH**. It was allowed through the permissive Will of Yahweh not His perfect Will. Yes, our condition came as a result of the fall; stealing our identity, but our reinstated position *(sons)* came at the moment of salvation; restoring our true identity. Remember, you are a spirit with a soul that possesses a body. The Spirit of Christ in you is greater than any storm against you. That reveals that if GOD is for you, He is more than anything or anybody the devil uses to rise up against you

{**Romans 8:31**}. But you must comprehend that actuality personally for yourself. The LORD will allow these things to promote and develop us in Him. You got to catch this revelation from Holy Spirit. The *TRUTH* of what GOD has **declared** and **promised** to you as an heir and joint heir about any circumstance or any crisis is not only fact but *TRUTH*. And *TRUTH* Is The Only Reality in the Kingdom of GOD. All which is outside of faith is sin. If we revert in fear our conditions will hold us hostage leading into sin and that is the trick and trap of the devil, but JESUS has *already* provided the way of escape. Yes, there are after shocks to crisis, but the *TRUTH* and the *Power of the SPIRIT* is able to over power any after shock or panic attack you may face. So why are many held prison, locked up in their minds about *TRUTH*? Is the Spirit of TRUTH revealing or are the spirit of doubt and the spirit of unbelief blocking? Identify the unclean spirit and command that demon to go in Jesus name. Hold On and Grab the towel, you will not throw it in or give up the fight because Yahweh has revealed and promised that He is with those that trust in Him. He declares even in the desert I Am there. I Am there with you in the dessert, in the storm and in the blizzards. He's there to supply your need of hope, strength and deliverance. He is healing and gathering the tears. He sees the sleepless nights. He sees the pacing of the floor. He sees the hair falling out and He sees the pain and all the needs. Yet, He declares that He is the Restorer of the soul, His testimony is sure. Let the healing begin.

Hear the Word of the Lord…Rhema

THE LORD SAYS COME TO HIM, COME! THE BURDEN WAS NOT MEANT FOR YOU TO CARRY, THE WEIGHT WAS NOT MEANT FOR YOU TO CARRY, BRING IT TO ME, BRING IT TO ME, BRING IT TO ME MY CHILD. LEAVE IT! I'M PROCESSING YOUR MIND, I'M PROCESSING YOUR HEART, I'M PROCESSING YOU FOR YOUR RIGHTEOUS HOLY GARMENT, YOUR HEAVENLY CROWN…STAND… RESIST TEMPTATION, I'M PROCESSING. I'M HERE…YOU WILL KNOW ME FOR YOURSELF! SEEK ME! WORSHIP ME! PRAISE ME! I WILL REVEAL MYSELF TO YOU! YOU WILL OVERCOME! YOU WILL IN ME, IN ME, ABIDE IN THE SECRET PLACE, SECRET PLACE…ABIDE IN ME…ABIDE… AND I WILL ABIDE IN YOU SAITH THE LORD.

Receive By Faith.

How big is GOD in your life? Take the limitations off of Him! He is all of that and much more. You must reach beyond what you may presently feel or think, what it is looking like or how long you've been in the predicament. Your direction of thought will change because you are coming into agreement with the LORD JESUS *(Yeshua),* making a supernatural conscious decision by faith to reach for ABBA's unchanging hand to help you understand according to His provision. The acknowledgment is a sweet aroma toward GOD and you bowing your will for His wisdom to be birth forward continually in your development. Just as Daniel sought GOD not for things, but for the divine wisdom of Yahweh for understanding the seasons in which he was experiencing.

He understood his position in Yahweh, but his request was for wisdom to rise above and not faint in the midst of the crisis. Daniel learned to embrace his seasons in the ***Power of the LORD***. This is powerful when we recognize the seasons we're in and how to demonstrate in delegated Power the Kingdom of GOD in those difficult seasons. When you cast your faith like an anchor to GOD in the seasons of heaviness it activates the anointing of GOD upon you to resuscitate you during the process. The casting of our faith acts the same as sowing to initiate. The provision purpose of the LORD will plant, cultivate, expand, spread, grow, water, breathe and bring forth that sacred treasure which he has invested within each saint during our life span on earth. He is calling forth Himself out of your being to be displayed, demonstrated to the backslider and to the heathen, as well as, to the masses for deliverance of souls and a testimony that He is still on the Throne of Glory. **The Bible tells us {Philippians 1:6} be confident of this very thing, that he who began a good work within you will carry it on to completion until the day of Christ Jesus.** People of GOD we do not need victory, deliverance, restoration, the mind of Christ, holiness, sanctification, warfare, righteousness, faith, hope, self control, mercy, love, compassion, desires of our heart or needs met in Glory; we need the manifestations of the Kingdom of GOD to be demonstrated here on earth from heaven…this is the Apostolic Mission in the earth. When it's all over with at the Shofar Blast of Yahweh the glorified state of the saint will be completely whole and perfect in the full perfection of Yeshua HaMashiach.

The Fire of the LORD wills to transform our perception to reflect His perception; our outlook on life transformed to reflect His outlook on life. Our view of others transformed to reflect His spiritual view of the spiritual condition of the heart; our conversation, our behavior, our deposition, our attitude and our character is to be transformed to reflect His desires, thoughts, holiness, perfection, righteousness, compassion, grace and love within our new nature. **The purpose in the midst of the storm is for transformation of your in mind, thought, deed, spirit renewal and disposition and the identity renovation.** Remember, as believers live and grow, Christ is to forever expand in us.

⌣⟶

Jeremiah 29:11
I know the plans I have for you declares the LORD, plans to prosper you and not to harm you, plans to give you hope and a future.

Isaiah 55:8-9
For my thoughts are not your thoughts neither are your ways my ways, declares the LORD. As the heavens are higher than the earth, so are my ways higher than your ways and my thoughts higher than your thoughts.

⌣⟶

The Church has limited salvation to one step, receiving grace and receiving and receiving. The Favor of Yahweh wants to enlarge our boundaries. It is good for continual receiving; however, something will be required of us at some appointed time, which happens to be in the moment of distress when we need to give up carnal thoughts and ways. These are ways and thoughts that lead hearts gradually away from Him or to render our bodies as instruments of sin {**Romans 6:13; Colossians 3:1-10**}. There Is An Exchange! Now the Grace of GOD is needed to be received by all in all areas, His undeserved favor released, but with **TRUTH**, Grace is completed in the duration of the Body of Christ existence on earth. The Church is to desire Yahweh fully, **Grace and Truth** for balance and completion {**John 1:17**}. **TRUTH** is revealed by the Favor of GOD under pressure removing the scales from eyes, spiritual handicaps, rejection and clearing the pathway. The devil doesn't want this revelation to get out. The unveiling of the divine revelation of the wisdom of Yahweh through the finished work of Christ on the Cross concerning our ordeals undergoing discipline by His fire while under pressure points. This is what we do not want, the fire, the pressure; yet, we want the promotions. That's normal, but there is a cost. Oh, what a wonderful price to be paid by surrendering our all to Him, dying to our flesh, carnal ways and rising in the Power of Yahweh given in Christ by His Holy Spirit. As GOD reveals revelation through your intimacy of quality time, He will help you to embrace suffering as the apostles and other saints have done. Your outcome is greater in Christ. ***Repeat: My Outcome Is GREATER in CHRIST!*** Our promotions come through God's vision.

Since the church is the spiritual organism in the earth in which the Spirit of God dwells, the believers are to be living sanctuaries. It is not by the Lord's design that when we experience windstorms in our personal lives that we remain without supernatural fruit that come from the **Seed of Righteousness…SEED.** Believers are to mature spiritually in the spiritual things of GOD which in return governs the natural. We cannot afford to stay on milk. Trials and tribulations will destroy a person that has no growing… steadfast substance…divine faith in motion. Circumstances do not wait on anyone to be weaned off of milk. Certain seasons when extreme situations occur at different times bringing different winds will provoke a baby believer to be weaned off the breast and the milk soon; spiritual baby food. For example, some children or teens that have had to step out into adult roles quicker by getting a job to help make ends meet or maybe caring for sick parents or younger siblings before time. These children mature faster and sometimes learn how to overcome difficulties due to responsibilities that called them forward to take a giant step without physical preparation. In the natural sphere a toddler the age of three is not expected to think or behave as a child the age of seven; nor a teenager the age of eighteen is expected to think or behave like a twenty six year old. Now with those examples in mind that which has happened in the natural is a similar copy of what the spiritual side resembles. If a child that is sixteen still behaves with the same thought and behavior at thirty, some of us would say their elevator stopped along the way. Transfer that concept to the spiritual essences of believers. Some that has been in church seven or seventy years, but lack spiritual maturity, behave or look as the world looks, instead of reflecting the life of the one who they belong to, ABBA, through the grace code. There are many that attend church services ritualistically, yet there may be little or no genuine substance of fruit in there life giving off the aroma that I been dipped in the blood. Therefore, Truth is needed to make equal Grace for the transfer of spiritual meat to the spirit; graduating from milk to substance.

Before marriage I straddled the horse for a while, not really thinking nothing was wrong with my lifestyle, as long as, I attended church regularly, sang in the choir as my duty, made it to choir rehearsals, maybe bible studies and attended some of the programs. But after church it was my time to do what made me tick. Well, not only me decades ago, there are many of all ages in the Body of Christ with these ungodly, lukewarm desires, behavior traits, sending up strange fire to a Holy GOD, not aware that judgment is coming on this side for the sake of Christ to straighten out crooked paths of those that say they belong to the LORD. When a peach tree, plum tree or banana tree seed is planted it sprouts forth the fruit of that seed only, none other. Believers are to birth forth Christ-likeness. Some windstorms are allowed in order to cut away the stoniness out of the believer's heart, thoughts, to purify the motives, bring forth sanctification, honesty and overthrow generational patterns. Many think once they accepted Christ Jesus as savior then all is well done. And all is well, but there is a spiritual well in you that must be filled frequently with living water. The LORD wants not only to be Savior, but also

LORD; our personal Master of influential power in our new life hidden through the Blood of Christ.

When we measure ourselves by the supernatural spiritual attributes of GOD who is infinite, righteous and holy, we in our flesh are doomed and purposeless. When we reflect back over our lives after windstorms pass there should be a reflection of vivid light that was dim or dimming before the dry place exposed the areas for reproof. When we look through the spiritual lens as we are in Christ, we see a glimpse of what we are to reflect. As a believer in Christ grows from glory to glory there is a shift in the desires, the motives, the vision, the heart and the will. We all have a small amount of virtue in our soul, but increase will be produced by the Ruach Hakodesh. Since believers are purchased by the cost of the Blood of Yeshua HaMashiach *(Jesus)* the soul must undergo purification. Our human love, peace, joy, goodness, perfection, mercy or compassion is limited and dispensed abroad at our will when not lead by the Spirit of GOD. The *Fruit of the Spirit* which are grace virtues come from the Spirit. Remember, God Is Spirit, not flesh. The graces are Spirit substances not flesh substances. These graces will bring the abundance of spiritual wealth into our natural lives that money cannot buy. We can have all types of material gain, positions, titles, cars, luxury, furs, diamonds, even a little money or maybe none of those; yet, still may lack the attributes of the Father. Wealth or poverty will not qualify anyone for supernatural greatness. Many love on the bases, as long as, it is convenient for them with no discrepancies to be dealt with that will prolonged the process of things going their way. Many have compassion as long as it is within a reasonable time frame of being compassionate in their view toward another. Many even show mercy until there strength shows up and the mercy they thought they had, has run its full course in their allowed time. Many may even show patience until there nerves rise and begin to show the natural weaknesses of the flesh. We all can validate what we thought we had until the wind or heat appeared and showed us that we need more of Jesus and less of ourselves. Abraham and Sarah knew not that it would take twenty years before they would experience the promise made by covenant. Yet through their course of revelation, Yahweh revealed Himself to them and as a result they developed through faith supernatural grace virtues such as longsuffering, patience, joy and temperance. I'm graced with His love to be transparent when the LORD leads me because someone else may be struggling in a similar area, not exactly the same, but need to know that someone else has been there and emerged out of that pit. However, the pit was established for the sake of stripping the mind of carnality, strong-will and desires that causes a decline in their covenant with the LORD and wicked works. I remember on several occasions when Holy Spirit spoke to me about me. He will deal with you while you are pointing your fingers at others. I remember on several occasions when Holy Spirit brought back to my remembrance just as I was merciful with you, in return you're to show the same grace virtue regardless if they deserve it or not. I shut my mouth tight as to pout. This requires His strength and our conformity. When I got this supernatural download I just couldn't dismiss it as if I did not understand or hear. I could have, but I feared the Lord too greatly from having revelation in part of His sovereignty and power. **Holy Spirit is forever training, equipping and teaching believers to bring us into true perfection in Christ Jesus, spotless, as the virgin bride.** However, what I done next is what is required of the Church for deliverance. I entered my closet, the secret place, consistently, regularly until my flesh began to die and not respond overly emotional, too quickly, sharply or sarcastically. You must know what your flesh smells and look like under the spiritual lens of the *Eternal Word*; the flesh is corrupted in the eyes of GOD. Fall out of love with the sinful or lower nature and its ways! He cautions believers that no good thing dwells in the flesh and the flesh profits nothing {**Romans 7:18; John 6:63**}. As you worship, seek and lay your life prostate before the LORD, He will enable you to spiritually discern when your flesh needs to die to, how it smells and its depravity. It will turn you OFF to the point that you desire not to please the flesh because it doesn't please ABBA…that's the love of GOD Grace abounding. The flesh will turn you OFF to the point you will learn to rebuke yourself. That confirms that the matter at hand has always been a spiritual matter from day one.

When we extend godly love, show mercy, compassion or patience…God's attributes it is completely different from our quality given. As we grow in grace *(taught in the fires and learn and implement)* Holy Spirit will oversupply our spirit with more of His eternal virtues. He cares what we look like, smell like, how we carry ourselves and how we think and react. Our character reveals our spiritual condition. We may miss it sometimes, but in those times of missing that gap will grow smaller if you continue to enter that secret place and put your flesh on the altar sincerely. This is the pattern of purpose for walking and living in Christ and being holy vessels unto the LORD and offering up pure spiritual sacrifices. In the Garden of Eden the LORD searched for *ADAM (both of them Yahweh called Adam, Adam named her Eve)* while their flesh was uncover; spiritually, as well as, naturally to make atonement for there sins and to restore broken fellowship. GOD was then and even now showing unconditional love, compassion and mercy in spite of there willful immoral acts. Yet, they didn't receive the benefit until they surrendered their will, desires and abandoned all forms of debate. And because of favor they did not get the judgment they deserved.

Yahweh's love is demonstrated far above all forms of mankind love. Yahweh's Love is an action that has been limited to just an emotion by mankind. **The Bible tells us {John 3:16} for GOD so Loved the world that he gave his only begotten Son.** The focus is on the Kingdom Government endorsement for a corrupted world's liberty...the life of His Son. **The Bible tells us {Isaiah 9:6-7} for unto us a Child is born, unto us a Son is given; and the government shall be upon His shoulder. And His name will be called Wonderful, Counselor, Mighty GOD, Everlasting Father, prince of Prince. Of the increase of his government and peace there will be no end.**

Greek terms for the English word Love
Eros: physical, sexual love that God purpose
between a married man and woman
Phileo: brotherly love, a tender affection, impulsive
(act without thinking)
Agapeo: unconditional love God has for mankind, to have
high esteem, high regards; Agapeo demonstrated in mercy,
favor, promise, grace, guidance, instructions, compassion

Hebrew term for the English word Love
Ahava: expressions of action to provide,
protect, oversee what is given as a privilege,
fellowship, intimacy between two parties

Therefore, a great portion of ***knowing*** GOD deals also with the manifestations of His nature and identity exposed in the nature of the believer; summed up in one word ***LOVE***. What is inwardly branded in the heart will come out. Remember, as the potter breaks, remolds and reshape the clay gradually to shape its purpose, potential, character and destiny in the restructuring, the grace's virtues are imparted by the working of the Spirit in the soul of the **yielded** believer. There are many cells of the Fruit of the Spirit, composed as one unit; **{Ephesians 4:5-6}** one Spirit, one GOD, one faith, one baptism…one Fruit that we as believers are to possess and show in our daily dealings toward others. **The Bible tells us in {Galatians 5:22-24} but the fruit of the Spirit if love, joy, peace, longsuffering, kindness, goodness, faithfulness, gentleness, self control. Against such there is no law. And those who are Christ's have crucified with its passions and desires. If we live in the Spirit, let us walk in the Spirit.** The verse started with the word "*but*" which implies there are some clause factors to walking such a course. The principle that opposes the **Law of the Spirit** is the **Law of Sin and Death** which is the works of the flesh followed by consequences regardless who a person may think they are in the church. No one is above the **Law** of the Spirit of Christ. It governs. **Grace** provided unmerited, undeserved favor and **Truth** came with correction and guidance.

Grace Virtues for the Perfecting of the Saints in Christ
•   Mercy
•   Compassion
•   The love of God
•   Humility
•   Slow to speak
•   Quick to listen
•   Singleness of heart
•   Christ-minded
•   Integrity
•   Diligence
•   Purifying the heart
•   Daily self examination

Each soul has a God-given purpose that will only be obtained through reaching for and seeking the LORD. Our purpose goes beyond our job skill or expertise or knowledge. However, it can work and may tie into your job. When we seize our purpose and know who GOD truly is to us personally that *knowing* will distinguish all forms of compromise and fluctuation in your faith walk; then and only then will we be as trees planted for the planting of the Lord, trees of righteousness displaying the Lord's Glory, firmly rooted in the source. Therefore, when the winds blow and the storms chatter we won't be so quick to give in, sink, walk in worry or fear and throw in the towel or fall short all the time. But we will exercise Kingdom Authority and Power. **The Bible tells us {Jeremiah 17:8} he will be like a tree planted by the water that sends out its root by streams. It does not fear when heat comes; its leaves are always green. It has no worries in a year of drought and never fails to bear fruit.**

FAITH DECLARATION

Heavenly Father, I Thank You For Your Grace, Mercy And Truth. I Praise You Alone And Magnify Your Holy Name, For You Are Worthy of All the Praise, All the Glory And All the Honor. I Bless You With The Fruit Of My Lips Out Of A Heart Of Gratitude. For You Are Faithful, You Are Just, You Are Compassionate, You Are Longsuffering, You Are Splendid, You Are Holy. You Are Good. You Are Patient With Me And I Say Thank You. Teach Me LORD By Your Holy Spirit To Persevere In Faith When I Am In Wilderness Experiences. Teach Me Your Statue, Your Will, Your Word When I Am In Distressful Places. Teach Me How To War In The Spirit And Fill Me With Your Holy Spirit With Evidence. ABBA Place A Hedge Of Protection Around Me As I Go In And Come Out Of My Wilderness. Help Me To Stand; Resist The Devil, Resist Temptation And Every Appearance Of Evil. Strengthen My Faith As I Go Through The Fire In Jesus Name. Here I Am LORD Purify, Sanctify And Make My Faith Pure As Gold And My Stance To Be Established In You. Encamp Your Angels That Are Assigned Around Me. ABBA Reveal To Me Your Character And Your Nature That I Will Know You And Trust You All The Days Of The Rest Of My Life And That I Not Be Moved By Every Wind Or Doctrine Nor That I Develop Itchy Ears. Open My Eyes And My Ears And Give Me Wings To Soar In The Spirit Above My Distresses With Arrows To Conquer That Which Rises

Against Me In Jesus Powerful, Majestic Name, Cause Me to Rise Out of The Grave. I Thank You For Not Leaving Me Nor Forsaken Me And For Keeping Your Promises Concerning Me As I Yield My Will And Obey You.

Amen.

Scripture Study & Mediation:

Proverbs 19:21
Many are the plans of man in the mind of a man, but it is the purpose of the Lord that will stand.

Proverbs 16: 9
The heart of man plans his way, but the Lord establishes his steps.

Job 42:2
I know that you (LORD) can do all things, and that no purpose of yours can be thwarted.

Psalm 138:8
The Lord will fulfill his purpose for me; your steadfast love, O Lord, endures forever.

Proverbs 22:4
Humility and the fear of the LORD are riches, honor and life.

Deuteronomy 4:29
But if from there you seek the Lord thy God, you shall find him, if you seek him with all your heart and with all your soul.

Colossians 3:23
And whatsoever you do, do it whole heartily as to the Lord and not unto men. Knowing that of the LORD, you shall receive the reward of inheritance, for you serve the Lord Christ.

Daniel 11:32
The people who know their God will be strong, stand firm, take action and will firmly resist opposition or do exploits.

Ephesians 1:5
He predestined us to be adopted as sons through Jesus Christ, in accordance with his pleasure and will

2 Thessalonians 1:8
In flaming fire, bringing judgment on those who don't know God and on those who refuse to obey the gospel of our lord Jesus.

2 Peter 1:2
May grace and peace be lavished on you as you grow in the rich knowledge of God and of Jesus our Lord

Philippians 4:6-7
Do not be anxious for nothing, but in everything by prayer and supplication with thanksgiving let your requests be made known to God. And the peace of God, which surpasses all understanding, will guard your hearts and your minds in Christ.

Jeremiah 29:11
For I know the plans I have for you, declares the Lord, plans for welfare and not for evil, to give you a future and a hope.

Proverbs 20:24
Man's steps are ordained by the Lord. How then can man (Ish: male or female) understand his (own) way?

CHAPTER EIGHT

SPIRITUAL AMMO

Whether we like it or not, the Body of Christ, the spiritual mechanism of Yahweh in the earth realm, is involved in an unseen spiritual conflict called warfare. When we translated camps *(new birth)* the enemy of our souls will still set up ambush in order to reclaim what was legally his through unrepentance, patterns of old and to bring chaos, confusion and attempt to sow lukewarm seed into the regenerated life of the believer. Deliverance and warfare involves the use of offensive and defensive spiritual weapons that will be necessary to use in each believer's walk of faith. As we go through or take others through deliverance believers must be equipped with knowledge and ammo. And as believers resist the works of darkness, resist darts sent toward us and pull down strongholds we must be equipped with the supernatural God-given ammo. Believers cannot approach the battlefield any kind of way you think is fitting or live in the world unprotected; through the outstretched arm of salvation we received victory benefits. The benefits flow **conditionally** to the believer through obedience, while yet are **unconditional** through the Blood of Yeshua. The spiritual weaponry used in the realm of the spirit are given to every believer through the finished work at the Cross, but in order for the weapons to work your heart must be turned toward the heart of GOD through faith, commitment and obedience.

The spiritual weaponry dipped in the blood came with the peace of Yahweh and reconciliation between GOD and the repentant…worshiper. Ruach Hakodesh teaches us the following graces: 1.) how to dress properly when engaging in spiritual warfare: 2.) how to hear His leading 3.) when to engage 4.) when not to engage and 5.) the law of following Holy Spirit rules of governing in the Kingdom of GOD. You can't engage based on what you think you may know or the experience you think you my have. When you dress properly with a genuine heart turned towards the LORD your aim will be to crucify the deeds of the flesh, walk in the Spirit, confront weaknesses through the weaponry of spiritual warfare and to please GOD. The spiritual weaponry cloak protects the spiritual anatomy that we can't physically see; your spiritual vitals from demonic darts during war assaults seen and unseen. The vitals include your mind, your soul, your vision, your hearing, your tongue, heart, feelings and choices.

When believers are walking in right standing before God, it will attract backlashes; backlashes will come with vengeance and manifest in the open through anything or anybody. Retaliations are consequences released openly on believers warring when certain arenas that the believer may have been authorized or may not have been authorized to come against in prayer. Backlashes are also a result of hitting targets in spiritual warfare that resist the dismantling of their assignments. The enemy of our souls does not give up territory willingly. Some backlashes may be avoided by knowing what is off limits in warring when engaging in spiritual warfare. Every battle is not yours to engage, whether in prayer or conversational, depending on your assignment from Holy Spirit and what the Word of God says; that is why we must be led by the Spirit of GOD and not by the flesh. This also comes through teaching and divine wisdom. There are ranks in the spirit world; just has there are mantles that are spiritual in the physical church. You don't beat against the air attracting high ranking demonic principalities *to you* as a result of praying wrong. Don't try to be or go deep when you haven't been taught by the deep or taking infant steps or in shadow water. A believer's lifestyle is accounted for when it comes to spiritual warfare.

Believers in Christ cannot live a mediocre lifestyle, one foot in the church and the other in the world or a life of prayerlessness or warring because somebody told you to or doing what you see somebody else doing that is anointed for the task. It will bring on repercussions. Beware of the many copycat spirits or false anointing in the church. GOD exposes all that is false; such as the spirit of error. He wills that believers be not deceived nor walk in a lie. The Spirit of Christ is Light and Truth, no lies and no darkness. The Spirit of the LORD is subject to teaching those who are hungry for revelation and have a teachable spirit. Even if you are not called to that level of spiritual warfare you will still need to use your spiritual weaponry in your prayer life and daily living.

The **Kingdom of Yahweh-GOD** and the **Kingdom of Darkness-*satan*** are two ancient kingdoms. They have existed before life existed on earth and spiritual things can escalade against you if improperly encountered. Our spiritual weaponry will impact three realms *(spheres or territories)*; the two that are mentioned above along with the physical sphere which we inhabit. Our spiritual ammo works effectively in all three realms when engagement is accordance to the leading of the Ruach Hakodesh who supplies by **Provision of Excellences.** That guidance is not to be ignored or taken lightly. When people are demon possessed, harassed, tormented by demons or influenced by them that picture in not tasteful. This is a reality. We can honestly see in our families, on our jobs, on the news and in the marketplaces-you name it; we can see visibly demonic influence, demonic presence and possession. Most describe what they see as the person's personality or up bringing; that isn't what that is. Those are open manifestations of unclean spirits that have taken up residence in the vitals of individuals…seed. This is why the Church needs the guidance, wisdom and the Power of Ruach Hakodesh working effectively within our sanctified vessels. It takes the Word of GOD sown to be received and activated. It takes the Anointing of GOD to set captives free and the Anointing works through the believer who is set apart in mind, thought, heart, behavior and spirit and filled with the infilling of the Ruach- the Holy Spirit of GOD. Therefore, at this stage, we understand our sins are covered and washed by the blood, we are covered in the blood and we are not practicing habitual sin or rendering our bodies as instruments of unrighteousness, but rather instruments of righteousness.

Now that you have read the previous chapters, you should have a great understanding and insight about what your posture should be during a challenging season. There are activations of the Spirit that must be put into action in your mind, heart and spirit. As revelation and the Supernatural Power of GOD fills you, your downtime seasons should be recognized as seasons of opportunity, seasons to witness, seasons of being reestablished, assignments or prayer flowing from your union with Christ in intercession and spiritual warfare to usher in change in the atmospheric winds that the LORD reveals for combat by His Ruach. The LORD gives the anointing in the forms of a spiritual eye to see, a spiritual ear to hear and the gift of discerning for the purpose of engaging with His mind and His heart on one accord in His time of pursuing. It is wise to ask the LORD, Shall I pursue this or not? Remember, those that **suffer-well** with evidence of a pure heart are rewarded the Kingdom of GOD {**Matthew 5:8**}. This reward allows us to behold visibly the access of the Kingdom's demonstrative power in the earth realm. Instead of running, talking about all that isn't right, people or situations that aren't changing, murmuring and complaining or fighting verbally among each other and other nonsense distractions; invoke the Kingdom of Yahweh in Christ Jesus which lives within you through Holy Spirit.

Holy Spirit will reveal strategies to those who answer and are faithful to the call of spiritual warfare intercession. Remember, conditions are temporary and will change due to the impartation of Holy Spirit's **Revelation, Wisdom, Knowledge and Counsel** for believers to war in the right spiritual posture in approaching seasons. Some blessings will be released through a spiritual posture such as the **Shofar** of your mouth and the Sword of the Spirit. Your mouth, speech and talk are weapons of influence and power in the spirit realm; then, the physical realm. If you speak death or life out of your mouth you will reap the fruit of what is sown. The fruit is an open manifestation of what type of seed was sown, conceived and birth. What you speak is evidence of what is in the soil, the condition of the heart. Your words have the power to create, change, establish your atmosphere, destroy others, tear down, shape, break and form or build up. Be mindful and watchful of what you speak out of your mouth gate. You reap what you sow and that is a law of the Kingdom of GOD: the Law of Sowing and Reaping. This law covers a lot of territory other than money and material possessions.

Psalm 141:3
Set a guard O LORD, over my mouth; keep watch over the door of my lips.

After you have come through the wilderness and have overcome, there will be other attacks sent your way. I am not speaking anything upon you, but revealing Truth to you for your preparation. Trials and temptations come in this life time. It is better to know in order to be prepared than not to know and not be unprepared and you desire to be prepared. Spiritual things call for Spirit things. What you see with your natural eyes is evidence of what has taken place in the spirit realm. The evidence of what was seen is not the root. It is a result of the root from a seed. When the root is revealed through spiritual revelation only then can the problem be dealt with from the root, not the surface along with the residue to be cast away by divine ammo. The Church's spiritual weapons are not of this world. **The Bible tells us {2 Corinthians 4:10} for the weapons of our warfare are not carnal but mighty through Yahweh to the pulling down of strongholds.** Just as the GOD of our salvation is not of this world all the benefits that come with our salvation likewise are not of this world. See it as this, JESUS the Son of GOD enthrones believers with the *Kingdom (Basileia:*

kingship rule of Christ in the hearts of believers) at the moment of salvation which is not of this world…Position and Power and Authorization and Dominion that's not of this world… ponder.

FAITH DECLARATION

In the Name Of YESHUA, Every Attack Sent To Cause Harm To Anything or Anybody I Am Connected To, By The Authority And the Power of the Holy Spirit I Command It To Be Sent Back To the Sender (Kingdom of darkness, satan). Satan, the LORD Rebukes You!

The decree is positioned in Christ against wicked assaults with your response as proof. Spiritual attacks can manifest through trials, tribulations, temptations, frustrations, worry, confusion, misunderstandings, anxiousness and human weakness directly or indirectly. But I admonish you to cling to the declaration of Apostle Paul, **If I must boast, I will boast in the things that show my weakness because I am made perfect in my weakness {2 Corinthians 11:30}.** Mercy constantly unveils the power and grace of Christ even more when we have been through the fire, through the desert and through the storm; yet, come out on the Lord's side…stronger, wiser and better. Our testimony should be because of the Power of Christ that showed up in our time of suffering to show us His power through our weaknesses. Now, I am fighting the cause of faith in the Spirit on behalf of the afflicted in mind, the bound up and the weak in faith. My advocate *(YESHUA- JESUS)* defends me in the heavenly courts in my down and up seasons and I overcome. Jesus is the lawyer with divine strategy in creation from the very beginning overthrowing all the vices, plots and charges the prosecuting attorney would bring forward against the repentant at heart. The Lord's weapons of war never fail. The LORD is a man of war; Yahweh *(LORD)* is His name {**Exodus 15:3**}. The same grace that Yeshua HaMashiach extended during times of trouble is the same grace that is sufficient in all of our weaknesses which calls us ***perfect*** in Christ *(Hebrew **Tah-meem:** blameless, complete, mature, healthy, whole, sound)* {**2 Corinthians 12:9**}. You are called in Christ in this hour to be holy, strong, courageous, valiant, exceptional, bold and humbled. The LORD of our salvation who has not only given you indwelling Power, but also His Anointing to rest upon you and to teach you how to take hold of the horns of the altar, to plead your case and invoke the heavens in the matchless and powerful name on the earth, in the earth and in heaven, JESUS the CHRIST; defender of faithful souls and the only name by which man shall be ***redeemed*** *(Hebrew **Ga'al**: bought back, rescued, delivered from the authority/ power of Satan)*. Remember, the children of GOD live by faith, and are begotten from above and belong to Yahweh GOD. **The Bible tells us {1 Peter 2:9} you are a Chosen People, a Royal Priesthood, a Holy Nation, a people for Yahweh's Own Possession, so that you can proclaim the Excellencies of the One who has Called You Out of darkness into the His marvelous light; once you were not a people, but now you are the people of Yahweh**

through the way of the bloody cross; once you had not received mercy, but Now you have received mercy.

Now, we are ready to take up the banner weaponry of intercessory prayer, a spiritual weapon, along with our Advocate to war against that which opposes the Light and decree what Yeshua *(Jesus)* has *Already* declared by continual faith on the believer's part. As new creatures in Christ Jesus, our Righteousness, Dominion, Power, Kingly Authority and Position imputed by faith restored by the death, burial and resurrection of JESUS CHRIST, the Son of the Living GOD, the first fruit from the dead. Our weapons are not carnal *(flesh and blood)*, not grievous or not earthly or of the occult activity *(demonic, witchcraft)* of those that bow to false gods or falsehood, but mighty in the LORD.

Hebrew word for the English term Stand
Yatsab: offer, station or place one self, take one's stand

Greek word for English term Standing
Histemi: establish, stand ready, firm, settle, set in balance

Greek word for English term Repent
Metanoia: change of mind- purpose; reflect in behavior and character of the inner man

Greek word for English term Holiness

Hagiasmos: sanctification, the process
of becoming, set apart

The believer's spiritual posture in the spirit is standing in the Strength of the LORD in the Beauty of His Holiness. Our Supernatural weaponry consists of the cloak of *Holiness, the Spoken Word, the Name of Jesus, Intercession, the Blood* and *Praise-Worship*. We must be clothed with these in the mind of our spirit just as clothes are worn on the body. If you go naked, exposed naturally or spiritually, you will be locked up in jail for physical exposure or bound spiritually from the lack of knowledge. These are important weapons of ammunition to be reinforced at anytime for protection, weakness, evil, sin and against the bands of wickedness; nevertheless along with putting on the *Whole Armor of God* spoken to the Ecclesia in Ephesians.

Holiness the cloak of the believer's spirit, is a spiritual standard against darkness; it shines bright like a reflector in the spirit realm signaling that the believer's life has been purchased with the Blood of Jesus, set apart from authorities of the power of this world, the god of this age and set apart to Yahweh's Dominion in faithfulness and loyalty. This does not mean the believer will not ever sin again, but it definitely means you recognize your allegiance is to the One True Living GOD and when you fall short that you will

not wallow in habitual sin, but **acknowledge** it and **repent.**
Repent of your sins so the persecuting attorney, the devil, will
not have a legal right to bring charges against you. **Practicing**
sin takes you *(us)* out of the Will of GOD, away from under
His covering of protection, bring separation and eternal
condemnation; rendering the weapons of power non-effective
in your life. **Confession and Holiness** are two strong internal
weapons against moral decline, sin, carnality and against
the accusations of the devil. The Holiness of GOD calls for
His children's purity to be the foundation of their covenant
relation with Him. Although, this will not stop the enemy
in his tracks; your faith however is another weapon of ammo
empowered to shield your uprightness *(righteousness)* in Christ
against fiery darts as you live in faith. In the face of conflict
Holiness confronts the devil on your behalf declaring private
property; they are my prized possession, my estate as Covenant
Keeper. Therefore, choose to fellowship with the Lord with
all your heart, mind and soul during conflicts because He
fights all your battles and intercedes on your behalf. ABBA,
by His Spirit will train you to use supernatural weapons of
victory in the valley places and has already declared and
command peace and comfort in the storms to manifest, be
transferred into the natural. ABBA through His Spirit will
teach your knees to bend in submission, your arms how to
archer the arrow of His Word and your mouth to sound as
a **Shofar** in the atmosphere of the spirit realm. The spiritual
cloak of holiness keeps us near the LORD, who secures with
guaranteed security and brings us into His Presence. This
attribute weapon is the radiances of our Heavenly Father
when it reflects off a saint spiritually *(believers)* it sends tidal

waves, vibrations in the spirit realm. These radiant light waves of electricity dispel the power of darkness assignments; because it is God's power not our source of power. Hallelujah! **The Bible tells us {Zechariah 4:6} this is the word of the LORD, Not by might nor by power, but by the Spirit of the LORD.**

When you draw near the Lord, He will draw nigh unto you and open up your heart to hear. The drawing near can be called spiritual union worship. As Holy Spirit trains your spiritual ear and your tongue believers will began to hear clearer to act and speak what Holy Spirit is revealing, such as, instructions to overcome, intercede, prophesy, stand firm on the Word, war the Promises of GOD, be the light in your home, among peers or on your job, shun evil or reveal warnings of danger. When we hear the voice of the LORD it is imperative to listen, to hearken, heed the instructions and obey. Yahweh commands all His children not certain nationalities **To Be Holy for I Am Is Holy {1 Peter 1:16}.** This command of action through the Spirit of Christ entails that those in union with Him through the Cross are to be governed by Him. This releases Him freely to act graciously when judgment should be expected. In addition, He is free to rebuke and to bring correction when discipline is needed. He will not share us with any idols, nor will He be shared by you among graven images. He is ADONAI, Master alone. Holiness tells the accuser of the brethren that you belong to the King and not to yourself or him, which results in Yahweh obligations by favor to believers as the GOD of Covenant, Lover, Healer, Deliverer, Shield, Sustainer, Protector, Provider,

Covering and All In All. Holiness is upright in the eye of Yahweh and should still be right in our eyes as His children. **The Bible clearly tells us {Hebrew 12:14} without holiness no** *(man, woman, boy or girl)* **will see the Lord.** This spiritual cloak is the saint's means of offense, as well as, line of defense. Holiness is a powerful supernatural stance with Kingdom benefits.

Spiritual *offense* ammo is used when the believer is engaged in tearing down the fortress of the enemy that has formed in the mind by using the WORD of GOD. Spiritual *defense* is the armor that we clothe ourselves to protect us against the enemy counterattacks and schemes. The devil wars against the spiritual cloak of holiness strongly to try to persuade believers who are weak in faith, babes, immature or don't know the Word that this attribute is not necessary and that no one is living holy lives because it is impossible. Remember, God's work is the realm of the impossible. The Bible Declares *"LET GOD BE TRUE AND EVERY MAN A LIAR."* The flesh will always seek to justify the flesh, but the Spirit will only justify what is of the Spirit of Yahweh. Just as the rib was taken from Adam's side is under his leadership, covering, provision care and protection, this is symbolic of the Ecclesia under the leadership, protection and provision care of Christ covering and dominion. Man cannot pervert what Yahweh has *ALREADY* justified through the Blood of the Lamb of GOD. The heart of man is twisted, but the BLOOD of YESHUA Is Still Washing and Cleansing souls, making crooked paths straight and turning hearts to GOD away from rebellion. You and I will chose to believe and fear the one who has the power to give everlasting life, as well as, to destroy the soul and the body to eternal condemnation. I also agree with other God-fearing leaders who believe and heed the report of the Master, *"HOLINESS IS STILL RIGHT!"* The reflection of Yahweh, who is holy, is the continual lifestyle to be demonstrated in the lives of every believer. Holiness is not something that you can pick or delete as you chose. It is a Law of the Kingdom of Yahweh. Just because someone may chose to believe otherwise does not delete or make this law less effective.

Spiritual weapons of ammo are used in the realm of the spirit and the physical realm against all appearances of evil that will expose itself through people or rise up in your flesh to shut you down so the Glory Grace within you will not avail. The believer's body is the temple or tabernacle, the dwelling place of the Spirit of the LORD. The Living Eternal Logos drives out unrighteousness and entered into creation creating His divine order in the earth. For these reasons spiritual weapons should be exercise in the life of each believer against diabolic outlaws that rise directly or indirectly to spiritually revert and rape believers of there state of purity in Christ.

Unclean Spirits Are Intruders To The Children of Yahweh
• Incubus / Succubus (sex demons)
• strong-willed demon
• spirit of disputing
• spirit of slander
• spirit of doubt mind
• spirit of control, manipulation
• spirit of division
• spirit of lack
• spirit of racism
• spirit of divination (fortunetelling, hypnosis, palm reading)
• spirit of idleness
• spirit of religion (a godly form denying the Power of God)
• spirit of confusion
• spirit of perversion
• spirit of deception
• spirit of importance
• spirit of fear
• spirit of haughtiness
• spirit of character assassination
• spirit of prayerlessness
• spirit of peer pressure
• spirit of competition
• spirit of loneliness
• spirit of lust
• spirit of unforgiving
• spirit of rage
• spirit of bitterness
• spirit of self centeredness
• spirit of whoremonger
• spirit of procrastination
• spirit of compromise

•	spirit of unbelief
•	spirit of greed
•	spirit of anger
•	spirit of rejection
•	spirit of worldliness
•	spirit of addiction
•	spirit of offense

You are not in the battle on your own accord; we have no power within our natural ability to fight in this dimension. The name Yeshua *(Jesus)* means Yahweh Is Salvation. Yahweh in Christ saves, rescues, delivers, reconciles, defends, wars and shields the believers. The Power Source *(Christ)* you're connected to is the Source of Triumph: **The Name and Sword of the Spirit.**

The **Name of Yeshua HaMashiach** implies Rank, Identity, Dominion, Majesty, Royalty, Redemption, Influence, Privilege, Honor, Character, Righteousness, Vision of the Father, Excellences, Favor, Authority and Kingship. Every battle fought in the **Name of the LORD** was then and is now victorious and every promise is binding {**Joshua 9:15-20; Numbers 30**}. **The Bible tells us {2 Chronicles 20:15} that the battle is not ours it is the LORD**. Which confirms that we have been quicken *(made alive)* in Christ Jesus and is *already* seated *(position)* with Him in heavenly places *(spiritually)*. We are hidden in Him, as you intercede using the Sword of the Spirit and the Name of JESUS, Supernaturally things will shift by faith in the realm of the spirit from kairos *(supreme)* into chronos zone. Yahweh acts to uphold His Word. Open your mouth let the Active Word sound out from a heart of divine-faith consistently and persistently and see before your very eyes the form shaping around the words you decree as images begin to form manifesting the material blessing. **Intercession** bathes and births prayer petitions into the earth; however, we must stay in the position of prayer and not give in. Intercession is like a birthing chamber. Our patience can be extremely short when waiting on GOD to answer prayers or to straighten out what we have messed up; therefore, we need the supernatural fruit of patience working inwardly to wait on the promise. It took twenty five years for the promise seed of the Promise to be birth through Abraham and Sarah. **The Bible tells us {1 John 4:17} as Christ is, so are we in this world.**

We are baptized, immersed into His perfection, position, identity, authority, dominion, soberness, power, victory, declarations, decrees, promises and essence through son-ship to confront, to overcome attacks of evil, temptation and sin and to obtain success. It is built in our regenerated spiritual DNA anatomy to conquer. Yahweh Sabaoth, a title distinguishing Yahweh's character and function, is LORD of the Hosts who will command the armies of heaven to accompany faithful believers in warfare, give us strategy to ambush the enemies of our souls and on behalf of others as we firmly rest strong in the mighty Power of the LORD. Warfare is conflicting war in the realm of the spirit. The Ruach Hakodesh residing in you warring against retaliation, accusation and temptation: holy versus unholy, evil versus good, and justice versus injustice. Many in the church that are fearful of spiritual warfare or do not teach the sheep will remain weak in their faith walk and live beneath the privilege of their GOD-given birthright. Awake! Awake you that sleep and realize the **mysteries** of Yahweh are revealed through Christ for the advancement of the Kingdom of Yahweh through the Church, the first Church Apostles and are not to be feared or afraid of. There will be many times a warrior must go and retrieve his goods through the aggression of spiritual warfare prayer; taking what is rightfully yours by the Supernatural Power given to you through the **Name of Jesus** and **the Blood of Yeshua HaMashiach** *(Jesus, Messiah)*. We lay claim to our Blood Covenant legal right of Dominion, Rule, Regal Authority and Command.

When believers have successfully overcome in the fire in which they have been in, with fruit and power as evidence, it is time to release the fire that has refined you for such a time as time. Now if you have not made it to this stage in your faith walk do not be discouraged, but continue because Holy Spirit is still working within the yielded thirsty heart of us all. The Refiner's Fire of Yahweh is a continual process of sharpening believers as iron sharpens iron. There is aggression in the realm of the spirit, the enemy does not release all so easily. He will attempt to block all that he can for you to give up the fight of faith and wear you out. Just as believers are commanded to resist him, he also will use resistance/ confrontation toward you. In the conflict of spiritual warfare believers are delegating and declaring what Yahweh Elohim has *Already* declared to be so in the Name of Jesus from the beginning, but if you don't act you will not get any results. Remove far from your mind the thought that whatever is meant to happen will happen; that is not in the Will of ABBA and it's a lazy, cop out speech for the believer that does not know the Will of ABBA. The people of GOD perish from the lack of knowledge that is not activated through faith, diligent seeking, studying and application with obedience. We see the spiritual aggression of **intercession** in the testimony of Daniel in the Lions Den, how he prayed and prayed and prayed for twenty one days, but for weeks there was not a manifested response from heaven. Why? As Daniel continually sought and waited on the LORD in spite of all that was taking place resulted in a divine interference. This is the revelation: the angel responding to the request was resisted *(confrontation)* by the prince of Persia who held up the answer to Daniel's prayers; Michael, one of the chief archangels was released to help **break** *(sever, shatter, demolish, warfare)* through the barrier of offense in the spirit realm of darkness where the answer was held up. Even in intercession we can see the outcome of a supernatural interference of forceful persistence. Well, the enemy back then is the same enemy now; satan's motto is still the same to kill, steal and to destroy by deception through confrontation. Yahweh tells us that he has given his angels charge over you **{Psalm 91:11}** and because He is LORD of SABAOTH *(of Armies)*, the angels wait on your mouth to release the **Spoken Word** so they can react. They do not need faith principles or maturity as we do, only to hear the WORD of the LORD. The angels hearken at the Spoken WORD from a faithful sincere heart.

As we engage in the spiritual conflict of warring, counter-attacking with the WORD of GOD and carrying the blood-stained banner of the Name of Jesus *(the Lion of Judah)* the blessings that may have been resisted, held up in the second heaven by evil forces will be released into the physical realm. Daniel's testimony was that he humbled himself first; then, sought GOD for understanding. Wow, that's supernatural and deep. He didn't allow the desert of dryness throw him into panic mode, because he knew the GOD of his salvation, the GOD of Abraham, Isaac and Jacob, would defend him in this case. Many of us need to humble ourselves and set our minds and hearts to seek ABBA for **understanding** and for His **wisdom** in all things pertaining to life and godliness. Instead of seeking the LORD for material things, there comes a time that maturity plays a part in taking a believer beyond material things into asking for spiritual attributes to support you in the midst of waiting for your blessings and manifested breakthroughs. **The Bible tells us {Matthew 6:33} seek ye first the KINGDOM of God and His righteousness and all these things shall be added unto you.** Understanding and Wisdom from GOD are silent weapons with a loud blast {**Proverbs 4:7**}. These are two combined, inseparable elements that work to promote your soul in Yeshua *(Jesus)* that Ruach Hakodesh *(Holy Spirit)* desires to produce in weighty matters in life. They should be worn as a garland to grace the head (***nous, mind***) and as a chain around the neck {**Proverbs 1:9**} to yoke us with Truth. This grace guides and instructs us into safety, directions and covers. Kingdom divine attributes will produce a lot of gold- substance that will sustain believer's health and mind through life conflicts and show us how to see it as GOD sees it while developing the Fruit of Spirit.

Spiritual warfare is real just as the power that uproots aged old trees. The Kingdom of God is set far above and against the work of the kingdom of darkness which breaks through the sphere of time to manifests its wicked deeds through the government of this worldly system. Therefore, as being children of light we recognize our identity and position in the Messiah is begotten of the Kingdom Government of Yahweh, existing in the earth in His Power to war spiritually against that which opposes divine order, light, worth, significance and justice. The Ecclesia *(called out ones)* is His body, His mouth, His hands, feet and habitation. The Ruach Hakodesh fills the body with His breath and His Oil to prevail against the gates of hell that they shall not prevail and to do greater works through the Ecclesia. We all enlisted as solders taking orders and learning; yet, it's through suffering, pain and the fire of God's discipline; the Fire of GOD births forth spiritual blessings to promote a warrior from within your being. We fight, but not as the world fights. We see, but not as the world sees. We hear, but not as the world hear. We exist, but not has the world exists. And we live, move and have our being in the Lord by faith, not as the world lives. Our source is supernatural, our strength is supernatural and our gain is supernaturally manifested in the natural. Ecclesia *(church, called out ones)* you are in this world, but not of this world. Our dependence is not in our own ability, but Yahweh's Might, Power and Spirit. Our **perfection** *(Greek **Teleios:** completeness, having reached its end)* is in Christ; the perfecting work at hand.

Furthermore, we enter warfare by putting on the **full spiritual armor of GOD**. It is His battle and the battle is to be engaged according to His plan, rule and authority for victory. When a soul goes into battle dressed in their own strength and manmade knowledge and pride they will be defeated, helpless and destroyed; the consequences are rewarded to the flesh. We are commanded to move when the Holy Spirit instructs us to move. Moving ahead of God will bring defeat, misery and delay which results from anxiousness, lack of trust, lack of patience and disobedience. I encourage your heart to take hold of your spiritual weapons and use them faithfully, honestly in the atmosphere of your home; pleading your case to GOD and warring in faith. **The Bible tells us in {Ephesians 6:10-18} to be strong, stand firmly in the Power of the LORD** and to dress daily in the full armor of

GOD to stand our ground against fiery assaults in these evil days that the accuser will charge against your mind, thoughts, imagination, against your faith foundation, your hope, your character, your life, family, health, job, ministry, marriage and your children destiny because of who you represent. We have to be ready at all times people of GOD. When your guard is down the adversary will come in appearing like a flood, but he will not win if you rise to the occasion to counteract his attacks through spiritual warfare using the Supernatural weaponry of the Government of Yahweh. The believer's **line of attack** is to 1.) Pray 2.) Decree and Declare 3.) Legislate 4.) Veto the mind and Will of GOD, **"Your Kingdom Come Yahweh Your Will Be Done Yahweh in Earth as It Is in Heaven In Jesus Name,** which nullifies the schemes of the devil. Don't you want the **Glory of the LORD** to show up on your behalf to shutdown oppositions against all that concerns you and to release the promises? Do not settle for defeat when there is no failure in Christ, whom you believe is Judge, Savior, Master, King and Ruler. It's nonsense to doubt Him. The Body of Christ wages war by the Power of Holy Spirit, the Ruach *(Spirit)* delegates the **Source of Power** to every believer, but the believer must partake. This is not to frighten you, but to alarm you to soberness in your faith walk. **The LORD has not given us the spirit of fear, but of love, peace and a sound mind {2 Timothy 1:7}.** Truth revealed is to induce authorize power toward and in us to act and not to demote us. The spiritual ammunitions are accessed to demolish the diabolic attacks and indictments thrown toward believers, to release blessings and to empower the believer's walk of victory. ABBA is concerned about all that concerns you and that which you see. His plan of purpose for each believer is to live life and life more abundantly in the Supernatural Increase of Holy Spirit. GOD is calling His Church to Holiness.

Remember, **Holiness** is an attribute of ABBA that should fit like a second skin; the condition comes with ease when you embrace and understand its' thought of action. Holiness stands unseen putting into effect the order for the full armor to be effective in your posture as you abide in faith. Holiness domination will push back the work of wickedness, due to its origin. **God's full armor** symbolically demands the protection for the physical vitals from the hostile response of darts thrown that may penetrate the physical, such as: 1.) mind-will 2.) reasoning-thoughts 3.) heart-emotions 4.) spirit-human spirit 5.) confidence-trust 6.) path-direction and 7.) your response-actions. Even though our fight is not against flesh and blood the devil can influence or possess individuals with unclean spirits *(open, unhealed minds)* and send them across your path. Sometimes people assignments *(uncovered)* that are not in favor of you will sow opposition, resentment or discord, but your fight is not against them. And when your flesh *(sinful nature: your intellect, will and emotions)* wants to rise and retaliate *(strike back)* that is a flashing red-light to let you know you need to die to the old man and cleave to the Spirit in that area. This calls for deliverance through the WORD of GOD, breaking legal grounds, severing cords and chains of demonic bondage. Those areas are calling for your carnal mind-will to be put on the altar to be purged by the Fire of GOD. Give the Holy Spirit access to the doors to the rooms you have closed Him out from *(surrender)*. He's waiting on you to grant Him freedom to sanctify those compartments in your heart and mind. You cannot war with a bad heart-spirit condition. This call for the need for self examination, repentance and to be prepared daily to combat the assaults of evil or challenges against you, suit up with the artillery armor **{Ephesians 6}.** It is for your greater good. The devil and his demons are disembodied spirits that are seeking whoever they can devour. When this manifests and you recognize what you see, your response is not to attack the person, but attack the root of the source through the keys of prayer, fasting, commanding, binding and loosing and be sure you are dressed in the proper spiritual protective covering.

Another weapon of power is **Discernment of Spirits**, a gift from Yahweh. You must purposefully seek and ask GOD for his anointing gifts. This supernatural gift as it increases helps you to determine the origin of the spirit that is operating in your view, whether the spirit is divine or wicked or if it is the human spirit. This gift equips the believer so they will not be tossed to and fro by deception, lying tongues that come through the church appearing to be light, but are full of darkness, masquerading as sheep; yet are goats. The Lord forbids His chosen sheep to walk in ignorance. This gift also functions to discern whether the spirit behind a preacher or prophetic message, apostolic anointing, teacher, prayer or whether the atmosphere or events are of Yahweh divinely or from another spirit *(wrong source)*. The other spirit is the devil working through that soul operating in their flesh which will open a portal-entry for demonic activity to manifest that looks right to the physical eye. This seducing spirit can seduce minds and redirect steps in the wrong direction. The devil will call you out if your spirit and lifestyle is not aligned with Truth. The Anointing of GOD attracts. **The Bible tells us {Acts 19:15} the evil spirit answered them, JESUS I know and Paul I know about, but who are you.** A lifestyle of holiness dipped in the blood *(being set apart-out from the worldliness unto the Lord in spirit-soul, mind-heart and deed)* is required which **identifies** you in the realm of the spirit as a son *(no gender)* of Yahweh through the door, JESUS. The enemy must see the blood banner applied to your spirit account because the flesh profits nothing. Believers this is not a game or show it is serious business, you must be prepared when confronting spiritual wickedness and when operating in spiritual reality. The Ecclesia Is A System, A Spiritual Institution of Divine Government that is Authorize in the earth by Yahweh to function under the KINGDOM Rule-Mandate set by CHRIST through Holy Spirit. That is what is meant "to be" the Head and Not the Tail, Above and Not Beneath and the First and Not the Last. It's Governmental Estate Policy, His Presence Unveils! The Church was never instituted to be traditional, comfortable or to sit idle, powerless and proclaiming Christ as the Head.

Psalm 119:89
Your word, LORD, is eternal it stands (firm, secure, fixed settle, established) in the heavens.

Jeremiah 23:29

Is not my word like fire, declares the LORD (Jehovah), and like a hammer that breaks a rock in pieces?

Praying the **WORD of GOD** is vital part of your spiritual DNA structure and is ammunition. Jesus is the Logos; the very thought and logic and expression of Yahweh Elohim manifested. Believers cannot go wrong when we open the Bible, stand on and pray Yahweh's promises back to him out of the abundance of the heart. **The Bible tells us {Hebrew 4:12} for the word of GOD is quick (alive) and powerful (active). Sharpen than any double-edge sword, it penetrates even to the dividing of soul and spirit, both joints and marrow, and able to judge the thoughts and intentions of the heart.** Now all the other weapons defend us from the attacks of the devil, but the **Sword of the Spirit** along with **Holiness** targets the enemy with no repercussions. The devil, sin, temptation, wickedness, deception, defeat, falsehood, low self esteem, alcoholism, sex addictions, pornography, lewdness, lust, greed and such like have no power against the **Sword of the Spirit** which is the **WORD of GOD**. Saints use your Sword. The angels hearken and bow at the Sword of the Spirit, demons Flee at the Sword, curses are broken by the Sword of the Spirit, bodies can be made whole by the Sword, holy conviction is released by the Sword of the Spirit, devils can be cast out by the Sword, chains can be broken by the Sword, sinful habits can be killed by the Sword, ungodly covenants can be severed by the Sword, blessings can be released by the Sword, minds can be transformed and conformed by the Sword, direction can be given by the Sword, reconciliation and healing can be established by the Sword and destiny can be spoken into your life by the Sword…the infallible **WORD of GOD**. Glory to God! Do you receive it? This undefeated mighty spiritual weaponry sown in faith will produce after its kind.

The **WORD of GOD** speaks and impart into our spirit by His Holy Spirit. The **WORD of GOD** reveals the Lord's mysteries unto believers, our destiny, our inheritance, warns of danger and falsehood, comforts, infuses us with the abundance of favor from ABBA, opens doors, gives insight, vision, patience, temperance, self control, mercy, counsel and wisdom. Oh, What A Mighty GOD We Serve! The Will of Yahweh will prevail in every single battle you may encounter by His Power in your lifetime as your will die…. conforming to His Will. **The Bible tells us {Isaiah 55:11} so is my word that goes out of my mouth: It will not return to me empty *(void)*, but will accomplish what I desire and achieve the purpose for which I the Lord sent it.** Believers are to seek or depend not on ideology, philosophy of man, sayings passed down from generation to generations, new era, hereditary, superstitions, self strength or self dependence, but should act on what the **WORD of GOD** is saying above all else; even testing all things by the **Sword of the Spirit**.

Ephesians 6:12-13

For our struggle is not against flesh and blood, but against rulers, against the authorities, against powers of this dark world and against the spiritual forces of evil in the heavenly realms. Therefore put on the whole armor of GOD, so that when the day of evil comes, you may be able to stand your ground and after you have done everything, to stand.

Colossians 2:15

And Jesus having stripped, disarmed the rulers and authorities (of there power) and made a public display over them openly, having triumph over them by the cross.

The **Blood of Yeshua HaMashiach** along with the SWORD are the major offensive ammo that completes and suffices all the other spiritual weaponry named and validates the perfection of all born again, blood washed, spirit-filled believers. The virgin, pure, untainted blood sets the only justice standard for righteousness, love, holiness, mercy, restitution and victory that Yahweh extended for the reunion of the broken fellowship and peace between a sinner and GOD that could be established through true repentance. **The Bible tells us {Hebrew 9:22} otherwise Christ would have had to suffer many times since the creation of the**

world, but he has appeared once for all at the end of age to remove sin by his own death as a sacrifice. The Blood of Jesus carries the purity sanction through the heavens to the highest heaven in the sight of Yahweh. In the purity of the blood is transferred all the wealth that mankind needs to access ABBA, be free, live an upright, wholesome and godly lifestyle. The **Blood of Yeshua Ha Mashiach** removes the stain of guilt, indictment, incrimination, hostility, eternal separation from GOD, curses, judgment and bondage to sin and shame from the spiritual account of the worshipper's heart with due execution and releases activation. **The Bible tells us {Hebrew 9:22} In fact, the law requires that nearly everything be cleansed with blood and without the shedding of blood there is no forgiveness.** The Blood of Yeshua wipes out the dead spiritual account and replaces it with the new spiritual substances of unmerited favor, new life, position of friendship with Yahweh, justification, purification and sanctification. The Blood of Jesus releases the *Redemptive Power* to be liberated *(past, present, future)*. The Blood of Jesus releases the Supernatural Power to overcome and to walk not in the pattern or course of this world, but in the pattern of the Kingdom of Light by the Spirit. The blood satisfies the penalty *(guilty, condemned)* man deserved with ABBA and likewise satisfies the worshiper with the good treasures and promises from Yahweh. Jesus said that He shall supply all our needs according to His riches and glory. The victory is *Already* established if believer's stay the course. The blood is rich in mercies and in graces that we have not comprehended fully yet. That speaks of the worthy value of the precious blood laid out for His friends to be able to feast at the King's table. **The Bible tells us {Matthew 26:28} for this is my blood of the New Testament, which is shed for many for the remission of sins.**

Honoring the **Blood of Jesus** brings wholeness and deliverance in not only the physical body, but most importantly healing to our souls. Our circumstances and bodies have a greater chance of healing when our minds, our emotions and spirits are healed. **The Bibles cautions us {3 John 2} Beloved, I wish above all things that you may prosper and be in health, even as your soul prospers.** The believer who experiences the Lord's healing internally can stand in a dry place with hope of assurance activated and receive their blessings because of the devoted honor they show and the favor GOD bestows daily. The testimony of Shadrach, Meshach and Abednego who were bound firmly for a live execution where thrown into a blazing furnace which consumed the soldiers who took them up. Yet the King saw a fourth man boundless and in one piece in the midst and the King at once summoned the three who were not consumed in the fiery furnace because of the presence of the fourth man in the fire. Their bodies, clothes nor their hair had a stench from being in a fiery furnace, only the ropes that bound them were burnt **{Daniel 3:27}**. As believers, even though, we may find ourselves in the fiery furnace in life GOD has made provision to be there with us, preserving us, sustaining us, guiding us and shielding us as we worship and seek Him while in the midst. And when He delivers us out of the fire, because we held on to Him with a firm grip, we will not look like what we have been through. Yet, we must go through the process of being processed. All that is burnt in the fire is that which was not of His character and belonged to the degenerated *(sinful)* nature. As you face your trials and go through tribulations cover your thoughts, your minds, your heart and your will with the Blood of Jesus. Ask the Lord to condition you for the journey and go to battle in the Spirit. Declare to the enemy *(adversary, works of darkness)* that the **Blood of Yeshua** is against him and the line is drawn in the sand concerning all that concerns you; present and future in Jesus Name. Declare the Blood covering as your canopy of protection that shields your vitals and lifts up a righteous standard against that which is against you.

The Blessing Grace of Yahweh that forms the Fruit of the Spirit called peace will bypass the frail understanding of mankind when in a battle. While each person's battle may be different…some may battle with mental disorders, health disorders, death of a love one, dysfunctional relationships, job loss, culture indifference or marriage differences; however, the Supernatural Peace of Yahweh can overshadow a believer who is following Holy Spirit and trained in dry or heated places in their pathway to honor the LORD in all situations at all cost. The tears may come, but believers are to gird and mount up in the Supernatural Strength with their weapons and push back. This is the Peace of God and the Peace with God that Jesus wrapped Himself in to be the substitute Lamb who settled the peace indifference for you and me by way of the bloody Cross. There is healing provided in the Wings of the LORD in many forms to overshadow our souls. The Supernatural Power of the **Blood of Jesus** is the same Power that raised

Jesus from the dead and seated him in the place of honor and majesty. The same Power that the Blood entails is the Power that seated Yeshua at the right hand in the heavenly realms far above all rule, power, authority, dominion and every name that is named not only in this present time, but also in the future age of the millennium reign {**Ephesians 1:18-21**}. The Blood of Yeshua makes available to the believer the **antidote** for **greater deliverance and power**. The Blood is one working with the Ruach *(Spirit)* of Yahweh. This supernatural weapon soars and roars in spiritual warfare against every principality, protects and covers the warrior that wars in Christ Jesus.

As we honor the blood we are declaring all that Yahweh has for me I bow my heart, my mind and my understanding to accept all that the LORD has freely given unto me by faith. It is because of the **Blood** that demons are cast out; accusations and temptations are defeated. It is because of the **Blood** that believers can invoke the Presence of Yahweh. It is because of the **Blood** we holdfast to our testimony that we overcome through the finished work of the Cross and the resurrection of the Precious Lamb of GOD. It is because of the **Blood of Yeshua** we can stand boldly and proclaim the WORD of GOD. It is because of the **Blood of JESUS** that the gates of hell shall not prevail against those that live by faith, act and feast on the Bread of Life. It is because of the **Blood of JESUS** no weapon that may form against you shall prosper. And just because something forms *(shows its head)* does not mean it will overtake you, unless you give into the bluff of the enemy. Just as something is formed, by the forming of WORD of GOD coming out of your mouth with unwavering faith it also can form a change. However, remember this is not abracadabra. Allow the WORD to work within you too. It is because of the **Blood of Jesus** the reason why the WORD of GOD is powerfully effective in the soul that is committed and sold out to the LORD. The **Blood of Jesus** *(already done)* speaks in the eternal victory at the last day against all the enemies of Yahweh, the Father. The saints of Yahweh win because the **Blood of Jesus** is still flowing richly and the blood never looses the virtue of Power. Have you allowed yourself to be touched by Him today to experience His **Blood** flowing in your life? Release yourself to touch Him. The **Blood of Yeshua** gives no room to wickedness or evil or compromise; the bona fide healer.

Many hearts have closed doors that have been marked off limits that you have not given GOD access to. Yet, He's knocking now at the door of your heart and waits as a gentleman for you to access His blood and submit those hidden divisions that He sees and know about. We all have been guilty of holding on to some things, but He is waiting on the invitation from you to him. Things may look dim in the natural, but if you are warring in the spirit with your supernatural weaponry and listening for the leading of Holy Spirit you will not be moved by what you are seeing, but what the Sword is declaring. Remember, some things have to be commanded to break and to be loosed in Jesus Name. If ABBA has *already* command it to break through Christ, then believers have the right to make the command...alignment with the WORD...you must know what the WORD is saying. This is not the time to throw tantrums, pity parties and gather with your friends to gain carnal opinions. Comfort zone is a troublesome zone for a believer in Christ. You are in that place of discomfort for the pushing of activation for the Kingdom of Yahweh's government to be released in the midst. The work starts within us first. There is no power greater than the Power of Yahweh. GOD has commanded the oppressor to *LET THE OPPRESS GO* and for the chains of captivity to fall to the ground! There is no fortress, grip or hold that can hold a worshiper bound when GOD speaks a sober divine word of authority into that soul's hungry spirit. All chains of captivity are falling and melting at the **Power of the Spoken Word and His Presence**. All! Engage in your leap of faith! Engage! Our victory is secured in the Finished Work of the Cross**. It Is Finished! It's Already Won!** Therefore, We Are Winners In Christ!

When you are in the wilderness you must search deeply, deep within your soul to reach the place of depth, breadth and width where GOD is awaiting to touch. He's the light and the oil needed within your spirit. He has given each believer His power, virtue and grace to rise up under any form of weight that presents itself to you. The pressure however, is designed for the crushing of your will that The Yahweh's divine will begins to truly unfold and expand in your hidden life. Where there is no power, expect no results, where there is little power or ability, expects little power and little result and where there is mighty power expect mighty, powerful results. The Power Is God! How much of GOD is in you? How much of what GOD speaks is instilled in you? How much of self is in you? How much of what others say is in you? How much of what is not faith base is in you? How Much? How bad do you want GOD to move on your behalf? I ask these questions for you to honestly measure yourself by the Spoken WORD in all seasons to see where you are on the spiritual thermometer and in your faith walk. This will let you know where you need to start, what you may need to drop to the side or what pace to pick up to gain entrance into the King's Presence.

Untainted Praise and Worship is another supernatural weapon unit of ammo and Lucifer, the devil, knows it all so well. Some battles are meant to be fought directly with praise out of your heart from your lips to the heart of GOD. Even though the conflict is present, pure praise and pure worship to the LORD throws a mist overcast against darkness that brings confusion and disarray to the camp of the enemy. Just as the enemy sent mist toward you, your verbal praise is like a war cry shooting arrows into the mist demolishing his arguments, bringing them to halt against that which concerns you. The adversary cannot do anything with a worshiper's verbal praise of action in spite of what things are looking like. That is a slap in the devil's face. Yahweh inhabits genuine praise from true worshipers and fills the atmosphere with His Presence which forms against opposition as a spiritual cloud. And some battles are meant to be fought by standing on and declaring the promises of GOD until heaven moves on your behalf {**2 Corinthians 1:20**}. Now this is a place where you are telling GOD you must move because I am offering myself as a living sacrifice unto you leaning, depending, trusting in your Holy Word and aligning myself with your WORD. I have come to the end of me; **"Help Me,"** ADONAI. **"Do**

What Only You Can Do!" You are the Master of miracles, signs and wonders and deliverance; and chaos is your specialty in prevailing against the demonic affects of the unseen in the atmospheric realm of the spirit. The battle is fought also with persistence and aggression {**Matthew 11:12**} which will certainly strip you of self and its gratifications because the fight is spiritual. The Church stance is not to give up or turn back, but to press into His Presence.

The **Presence of the LORD**, the place called THERE, the Secret Place, is the place the devil does not desire souls to discover, occupy or abide in. He lost his place in heaven as Lucifer and robbed ADAM of his birthright location *(Eden)*. No one humanly can actually enter and exit in the Presence of the Lord and not be "Changes." Entering into the Most Holy of Holies is like genuine intimacy of real love. The Presence of the Lord is a life altering experience that leaves you in Awe of Him with a godly fear of obeying out of a grateful earnest heart and a love for others in spite of how they may view or treat you. The last isn't a good feeling, but overall a true filling from desiring more. A continual abiding in His Presence for the overshadowing experience of His Might to rest upon you has an endless reward. There is an extreme reverence when a soul enters into His Presence that graces you with desires to please HIM and not purposely be out of His divine will; an intimate experience that will continually call for the yearning of your spirit to meet HIM again and again and again. Oh, you can't get enough of His kind of love. **The Presence of the LORD** is like ammunition and fire to darkness that attempts to rob the believer's soul and future. Abiding in the secret place of the Most High is a rewarding habitation that souls are crying out for. This Secret Place is like an invisible supernatural inflated bubble with the worshiper on the inside in the Presence of GOD, communing with the Lord and creating by design. Abiding in the Presence of the Lord is the experience that is "to be" a habitation for the Ecclesia breathing. It is our life source. In the Lord's Presence in that Secret Place, a spiritual reassurance, melting, cleansing, renewal, divine promise, strategy, insight and a divine download and more are granted. God's Presence and Power united as one. Wherever His Presence is there also will be His Power and Glory. The same **power** that brings deliverance, the same **power** that gives us abounding faith, the same **power** that lifts us when we are sinking in sorrow, the same **power** that heals our wounds, the same **power** that will comfort you, rock you in the midnight hour when you have been striped by life issues, the same **power** that will wrap you securely in the arms of safety, married or single, male or female; the same **power** that will silence the voice of the enemy who comes to sow thoughts of suicide, destruction, discord, strife, envy, racism, division, giving up on life or marriage, business, work, family, hopelessness, the same **power** that will speak to your pain and suffering and the same **power** that will war for you in all your battles is the same **power, Yahweh's Presence,** that raised our Lord and Savior Jesus Christ from the grave. Selah! His Presence is another offense and defense weapon of power. Shout, GLORY HALLELUJAH! Everybody doesn't have legal access by choice. This Grace-Favor is the same ***Divine Holy Power*** that Yahweh has given to the His Bride of Christ, the Ecclesia, to demonstrate in battle during human weaknesses though His might and to do exploits' in the earth. There is a shift in the mind of the spirit and there is a shift in the atmosphere when we open our mouth to praise and glorify the KING of Kings, the LORD of Lords and The LORD of Hosts, all one, who knows how to war in battle as we stand our ground in divine faith and united in the Spirit of Truth. Hallelujah! Glory to ADONAI for His banner of protection is a hedge around all who belong to Him in faithfulness on this journey.

Lastly, the next few supernatural spiritual weapons for the believer are attribute weapons interweaved with holiness. These are weapons that we should ask for to be downloaded into our inner-man. They should also to be prayed over our children as well. Remember, your mouth releases vibrations into the atmosphere; speak destiny over and into your children or grandchildren, spouses, family and others lives as the Spirit leads in your prayer time. The WORD of GOD never matches the situation, but the WORD of GOD casts a light to transform the situation according to divine order. These spiritual weapons are only accessed through the Ruach Hakodesh of Yahweh in Yeshua. They help us to function properly and in power in our daily dealings with people directly or indirectly because within ourselves we will fail every time. The flesh is not qualified or equipped to birth what the Spirit births into our spirit. Therefore, these weapons help us to help others who are open to receive in their down, up or in season place. These spiritual weapons help us to walk as Christ, be in readiness to respond as Christ would have us to and keep us above defeat in challenging or heated places in our walk of faith. The weaponry is filled with the supernatural impartation of **The Spirit of the LORD** for the believer **{Isaiah 11:2}**. The **Spirit of the LORD**, like a garment, manifests all from ABBA in measurement: the Spirit of wisdom and of understanding, the Spirit of counsel and might, the Spirit of knowledge and the Spirit of the fear of the LORD. When we have these Supernatural attributes advancing gradually we will not be so quick to lose our temper, will not be quick to give a person a piece of our little minds or quick to give up in the wilderness, quick to misjudge a situation or quick to criticize, find-fault, quick to hear wrong or speak or act out of a wrong motives. But because of the impartations by the Spirit of Christ and you personally coming into **agreement** with the Ruach HaKodesh work and power will submit to judging righteously **{John 7:24; Proverbs 31:9}** with justice not vengeance, criticism or wrong motive, but with sound sober God-fearing advice. The connection is Supernatural abundantly above all that we can think, see or imagine. The **Power of Agreement** *(conformity, harmony, oneness)* is a spiritual heavy weight weapon in the realm of the natural and the spiritual realm. The opposite of agreement is disagreement, disharmony and discord. Believers have to make a choice to come in agreement with Yahweh's *(ABBA, Father)* way or agree with self which leads to destruction; each has its reward. Yet, the LORD wins every time. These weapon virtues listed in this chapter operates effective though the Fire of GOD, *SEEKING* and *DWELLING* in the Secret Place of God Most High. Ecclesia, we must make and spend intimate quality time with the LORD who has called and destined the saint for greatness in the earth. Greatness is not defined as the material things that you don't possess or what you have lost through life or what you own; things can easily go quickly. **Greatness** is defined as possessing the manifestations of the character, attributes or nature of Yahweh in Christ inwardly to serve others outwardly and by not conforming to the pattern of this world. **Greatness** is the quality of your life that is hidden in Christ which is exposed through your behavior and conversation. The same way that all the other divine ammunitions are downloaded into our spiritual account the virtues are maintained from the same divine DNA source. Church, we are in a wealthy and rich place of substance at all times. When the Church as a whole awaken spiritually to let go of the traditions of men that have been taught from generations back, to let go the unlearned in order to be taught by the Spirit of Truth and how to partake to put into service true riches, then there will be supernatural manifestations in the midst through out the spiritual mechanism called the Body of Christ.

Study To Show Thy Self Approved A Workman That Need NOT Be Ashame, But Rightly Dividing The Word of God:

Write your answers to the questions below. Then write and memorize the scripture verse Ephesians 6:10-18

1. Which piece of the armor in the scripture verse above symbolically covers our hearts and other vital organs of the warrior in battle? _____.

    a) Proverbs 4:23

    _____

    _____

    _____

    b) Corinthians 5:21

    _____

    _____

    _____

2. Which piece of the armor in the scripture verse above symbolically gives the warrior readiness to move in obedience and flee temptation in battle? _____

    a) Ephesians 6:15

    _____

    _____

    _____

b) John 14:27

_____

_____

_____

c) 1 Timothy 6:11

_____

_____

_____

3. Which piece of the armor in the scripture verse above symbolically covers and shields the warrior's mind in battle? _____.

4. Who is He who seals the believer? _____.

a) Ephesians 1:13-14

_____

_____

_____

b) 1 Corinthians 2:12-16

_____

_____

_____

5. Which piece of the armor in the scripture verse above symbolically holds all the other pieces of armor together causing the warrior's whole armor to be effective and secure in battle? _____.

a) John 8:32

_____

_____

_____

b) John 8:44

_____

_____

_____

6. Which piece of the armor in the same scripture symbolically acts as a fire extinguisher to put out flames targeted against the warrior's righteousness in battle? _____.

a) Ephesians 6:16

_____

_____

_____

b) 2 Timothy 1:12

_____

_____

_____

7. Which piece of the armor in the same scripture symbolically is the inspired infallible Word of God, the written and spoken Word, Logos and the incarnate Word of God that works actively as the offense spiritual weapon of arsenal for every steadfast warrior in battle? _____.

a) 2 Timothy 3:16

_____

_____

_____

b) Meditate and Memories Hebrews 4:12

8. List the others supernatural spiritual weapons of attire and their function in this chapter. Explain how they apply to you?

- _____
- _____
- _____
- _____

9. What is spiritual warfare and the purpose for it? Are you engaging according to the Word of GOD?

_____

_____

_____

a) 1 Peter 5:8

_____

_____

_____

b) 1 Thessalonians 3:5

_____

_____

_____

c) Matthew 13:19

_____

_____

_____

d) Revelation 12:10

_____

_____

_____

10. What does the name Yeshua means? And Christ?

_____

_____

_____

11. The phrase **to hear** in the Greek means to _____,

_____ and _____.

12. What is the Hebrew word for **to hear**? _____.

13. Write Ephesians 6:10-18

_____

_____

_____

_____

_____

NOTES:

CHAPTER NINE

POWER OF FORGIVENESS

It is a choice to live by the **Law of Forgivenesss,** but it is a commandment rooted in love by the LORD to abide by. Many times when we come face to face with the confrontations and adversities even calamities in life, we have in our human genetic makeup the old inheritance *(sin nature)* that dictates not to forgive. It can lay dormant so easily without detection until the right button is pushed at the wrong time; when the offense becomes overbearing. When we have taken all we can take and feel we cannot take anymore. The weakness of our soul is literally crying out for help when it begins to step into retaliation or resentment or revenge. There are many souls that hold others and self locked up due to the lack of truly learning how to activate this force of power that will tear down any fortress or high tower in the sphere of the **psuche and nous** *(chapter 1).* We are to respond by the Holy Spirit and The WORD to counteract the darts the enemy throws below the belt that will cause the flesh to rise for payback. When we counterattack in the Ruach, it is the Spirit rising to battle what is spiritual with a physical manifestation. Remember, the storm is allowed also for you to see and to humble yourself. Allow the Ruach of Yahweh GOD to perfect those emotional areas that are easily offended.

The **Power of Forgiveness** is a SUPERNATURAL Mighty Force. During the time of my father's premature death, when his life was snatched, stolen from him through a demonic revenge; an act of violence that is breathed by hatred, vengeance and a callous heart- mind. However, my testimony is for the revealing of the Power and the Glory of the Kingdom of GOD in times that many may have thought to take revenge. Thoughts aren't easily handled or switched off when it comes to family. But The POWER Of YAHWEH SUPERCEDES, OVERTHROWS THE PLANS OF SATAN, EVEN IN THE SEAT OF THOUGHT, EVERY TIME WHEN WE PUT OUR TOTAL TRUST IN THE LORD ALONE AND LEAN ON HIM EVEN ON BEHALF OF THE CRIMINAL EVEN AS CHRIST HUNG ON THAT CROSS FOR ALL OF US WHO WERE CRIMINALS INDICTED TO ETERNAL HELL BEFORE BEING BORN AGAIN, THE NEW BIRTH. Yes, all sin, evil, wickedness, rebellion, iniquity and transgression are sins of incrimination in the Heavenly King's Court room with the penalty of execution, eternal separation from GOD; eternity's death penalty.

My brother, James *(retired veteran)* and I father was murdered in 2010. Dad's life was taken on the streets of Whitehaven, Memphis, TN. When the police arrived on the scene of the crime there wasn't a witness to tell how or who had done such a horrific act of hatred and cruelty. But I believe because of all the prayers that had been prayed prior to the tragedy on dad's behalf were at the heavenly altar stored in the bowls of incense which were released to the earth to resolve and bring closure by catching the criminal. I have always interceded for my dad and other souls. The police reported, that over in the am hour a man driving by who lived on the next block notice the street area taped off due to a crime, he approached the office to asked questions and when he arrived home, he went to his son's room being unsettled by the activity he overheard from his son's bedroom. There in the bedroom before this man's eyes stood his son in bloody clothing attempting to hide the weapon of evidence. The Father whom happened to be a pastor without hesitation that night reported

that his son was the one the police were looking for. Now this was the move of Power of Holy Spirit exposing the work of evil on behalf of daddy's blood which I believe was calling out from the land to the Lord for justice; just as Abel's blood dropped to the ground by the hand of his brother Cain, spoke; the good prevailing against the works of evil. Now this wouldn't bring dad back or even justify the means of the crime committed by this heathen. It's in the time of a crisis that we must **allow** the LORD to handle what we have no control over; in addition to our soul that's possibly in a vulnerable and open state of having a charge brought upon itself. When things of this magnitude happens in one's family, it will and can destroy love ones inside out if they do not turn their questions, complaints, bitterness and deep, painful, emotional hurts over to the LORD who is a restorer of all things; even in such horrific scenes. Such crisis can even bring inner division and in few cases unity, very few *[Unity is another powerful purpose that can rise from the residue of a crisis…good or bad]*. Yes, we bruise and bleed inwardly, out of the soul, but God still heals inner wounds. Yes, **The LORD Is Still Healing Inner Open Wounds** of the Bleeding Soul that held on and don't know how to let go. Now, I could've questioned or doubted the Lord as I did with the devastation I experienced with the sickness and death of our baby boy Isaac, but the Lord had done something extremely great within me that I completely trusted Him in this season of grief and sorrow, with no developed bitterness. The time between my firstborn's premature death and my dad's premature death was close to twelve years. The number twelve biblical symbolizes government. The revelation revealed to me during that time and the same revelation at the age of sixteen *(chapter 2)* was the same: ***"The Gates of Hell Shall Not Prevail Against the KINGDOM OF YAHWEH IN CHRIST."*** And that is "to be" the believer's attitude and mind in everything we face; with GOD we shall not crumble under the pressure. The road will not be a clear travel right off hand, but it is the road that is before you for the transitioning of your life and heart matters to be released to the Just Judge. The divine Fire of GOD is empowering warriors under the Power of Holy Spirit's anointing in these seasons to stand on the frontline for others that are coming through fiery trials of devastation that He has saw us through. When He sees us through, deliver and heal us, then it's our turn to reach back for other wounded souls. That is the heart, mind and Will of GOD and the ministry of the Ecclesia. I stayed before the LORD in prayer, groaning and moaning filled with hurt, pain and sadness, but to my amazement it baffled me that I had pity on the empty soul that committed the crime; to my amazement. This pity was a GOD urgency that caused me to pray for him in spite of the very cold act that he had committed. My dad was gone from our lives; yet, GOD filled me with Himself to pray for this criminal; although, I was the victim. This is how we release someone from guilt and in return GOD releases us that we may live anew beyond the heat of the fire that will blaze with flames that will spread to kill your life that remains. When the word I is removed from the front of the equation and replaced with JESUS that will begin a SHIFT forward into spiritual awareness that promotes and transcends the current emotional state…Just JESUS…you have to get caught up in Him; another atmosphere that breathes life and not death for your existence. This was the very act of love and forgiveness JESUS exemplified on the Cross between the two thieves. What is divine and spiritual will not make sense or agree with the flesh or the circumstance. **Forgiveness Is A Supernatural Act Of Grace!** These are spiritual weighty matters with manifested evidence. Many others were deeply hurt and disturbed due to this crime along with other related crimes that haven't received full closure. And the ancient questions we all ask arise in anger. WHY? Why Did He Do It?

When GOD reveals things and speaks to us, you must listen, whether it makes you uneasy or uncomfortable or don't make sense at the time. Whatever He shares with you I encourage you to begin a Holy Spirit revelation journal and write it down. It should go wherever you go. This is very important because it may relate to you now or seven years later. Our moments of sufferings are to transition us to what He has already appointed, but you got to transcend; His Wind is blowing now. When Holy Spirit revealed His WORD, revealed the heart conditions and His instructions to go forth to break chains of unforgiveness, release the captives, to healed open wounds of deep hurt and resentment because many in families all around are reliving past tragedies each time another related crisis occur. And when the heart and mind are not healed or not restored animosity, anger, rage, etc. will lay until another emotional pain regurgitate itself openly. Therefore, the **WORD of GOD** was sent to prevail against the Kingdom of darkness that rises in our lives. Darkness creates and acts in circumstances to imprisonment and brings on mental bondage to a soul. Remember, the **WORD of the LORD** *(not our words or opinions)* prevails not sometimes, but every time; Every Time! The Holy Spirit spoke to me, revealed the Word for me, as well as, for the extended family. He told me what He wanted done. And in the moment, I did not understand fully; nevertheless, I obeyed the voice and the leading of Holy Spirit. And with no hesitation but tears, I willingly said, "Yes,

LORD!" Holy Spirit broke up hard hearts in the ones that met during the sentencing process through repeating to the family each time **"We Must Forgive!"** Yet it was a seed planted for the start of the healing process. Holy Spirit saturates, tills and plows hearts to reply to ABBA through any means necessary. This took place over a period of two years and there was a breakthrough, like piercing as fire; first there were bitter cold spirits likes ice or brass. GOD was dealing with our hearts and minds. Glory to GOD!!! The WORD is Seed and it has authority to terminate; only if received for activation. That was a powerful revelatory action in what we would consider an untimely or fitting manner. But remember, The Lord is not time bound neither bound by emotions. He is ***LOGOS-WORD*** bound; and able to relate to our infirmities. Released the boarders, the walls and let the barriers down, He wants His people *(you)* liberated in mind, spirit, body and soul; your total being. ***"THE JUDGE RULING: GOD SAID, WE MUST FORGIVE OR HE WILL NOT FORGIVE US!"*** Holy Spirit revealed the message for the souls attending the funeral service along with the caution and assurance; *forgive*, **"MY GRACE IS SUFFICIENT AND MY STRENGTH MADE PERFECT IN WEAKNESS" {2 Corinthians 12:9}.** No matter what you hold against yourself, what somebody does or has done to you, there is strength, healing, grace and truth available through Ruach Hakodesh *(Holy Spirit)* for you to walk in the **Power of Forgiveness** with no strings attached and praying for the salvation of the weak in faith and for all our enemies **{Matthew 5:44-48}.** Praying for our enemies in love sincerely releases a **supernatural** exchange of healing into your soul. Deliverance is the children's bread and that is deliverance manifested. Under the New Covenant Law as a citizen of the kingdom of Yahweh in Christ it's our right to be set free from all repression, confusion, nets, hooks and chains that will keep us locked up in the spirit of our mind. Do not allow darkness to steal light from you, freedom from you or mercy from you. Don't allow darkness to shut you down from liberty in Christ; developing a cold unresponsive heart. ***BE SET FREE! NO MORE CHAINS, NO MORE SPIRITUAL INCARCERATION! DECLARE IT DAILY, I AM FREE IN JESUS!***

The Greek words for the English term Forgive
Aphesis: to send away, dismiss, release,
letting go, pardon and deliverance
Charizomai: the act of exercising grace from the heart
outwardly toward one who may be guilty in spite of
the crime done against another, show kindness, favor

Now demons have a legal right or legal grounds into a believer's life through the open door of the past, unconfessed sins or generational curses passed from generation to generation *(ancestor line)* rooted in sins and iniquities or through **open doors-gateways**. *(Purchase second book: <u>Bloodline Spiritual DNA</u>)*. For a believer, spiritual gates where sin may have entered and are not confessed *(not covered-washed in the blood)* the devil legally have a right to enter that gate until those gates are closed by way of **repentance and forgiving**. That legal right of entrance is broken under the New Covenant through the Life and Blood of YESHUA, rendered non-effective. When a soul is not saved they are under the authority and dominion of Satan, but when a soul is regenerated they are no longer under that dominion *(rule)* or authority *(power)*. Therefore, the devil has no authority or power over the believer unless one is living in doubt, habitual, willful sin, rebellion or compromise which will open doors; giving legal entry. Recognize, identify and close the gate(s) in YESHUA's majestic, holy and powerful name. We have the Power of God within to shut the devil down by the Authority and Power of the Spirit of GOD.

Isaiah 53:5-6

But He was wounded for our transgressions; he was bruised for our iniquities: the chastisement of our peace was upon him; and with his strips we are healed. All we like sheep have gone astray; we have turned, every one to his own way; and the LORD has laid on Him (Jesus) the iniquity of us all.

The **Power-Grace of Forgiving** and truly walking in **forgiveness** toward others is a **Law of the Kingdom of Yahweh**. Ecclesia, called out ones, caution: if you do not forgive others of their offenses against you, ABBA will **not** forgive you of your sins, which are offenses against His Holiness and Justice. You are in violation when you hold someone in prison because you have been offended by their actions in word, deed, looks, deposition or behavior. When we can't seem to step into that forgiving court room door, we must take the matter to God…you are wrestling with your flesh and your flesh mind will take you further way from the Truth of God. The Presence of God consumes such defections in our spirit by His Fire. Denying the Fire of God is the same as denying His Power and the work of Ruach Hakodesh *(Holy Spirit)*. Yahweh Jireh has provided provision for the Body of Christ and any other soul to overcome this deadly spiritual attack of offense. But we must be willing and submissive to involve ourselves in the **Power-Grace** provided for obtaining victory in the face of offenses. Those that **refuse** to eat this grace fruit from the **Tree of Life** which gives everlasting life will suffer eternity loss. We can't say we love GOD whom we have never laid eyes upon and with the same tongue we hate others whom we see daily due to heart issues, complaints, malice, ill-tempered and vain imaginations which cluster together against our greater good of overcoming. Such violations by the person who is offended conscience must be purged by the Blood of Yeshua. The demonic spirit of denial, rejection works with bitter emotional feelings of regret, resentment, anguish and pride. Souls that say they belonged to the LORD, yet divine-faith virtues aren't found in the inward parts. We don't want to stand before Yahweh who is *HOLY* with this unlawful violation in the chambers of our soul-heart *(Greek **psuche**)* reflecting darkness instead of light. Yahweh must see the blood covering banner of Yeshua sprinkled in the heart, not see your flesh; which will unveil the wrath of GOD toward rebellious souls that stubbornly don't consider their ways, repent and receive forgiveness which is the beginning of the healing process toward others and yourself and removes the guilt garment. **The Bible tells us {Haggai 1:5} now therefore, saith the Lord of hosts, Consider thy ways.** That is a spiritual warning followed by natural and eternal consequences. The Power of Forgiving is very important for every child of GOD, just as the breath you breathe is important to your life. Forgiving is an ongoing characteristic trait that is to be reflected in the heart of the saint in this world by the might, Power of the Lord. We cannot do it alone. We are known by our fruit and we are not our own. We are His prized possession and the apple of His eye. Yeshua HaMashiach said, I AM the True Vine and My Father is the vine dresser **{John 15:1}**. Forgiveness is an act of discipline, unconditional love and obedience.

⌐⌐

John 15:2-5

Every branch in me that does not bear fruit he takes away, and every branch that does bear fruit he prunes, that it may bear more fruit. Already you are clean because of the word that I have spoken to you. Abide in me, and I in you. As the branch cannot bear fruit by itself, unless it abides in the vine, neither can you, unless you abide in me. I Am the Vine; you are the branches. Whoever abides in me and I in him, bears much fruit, for apart from me you can do nothing.

The **Power of Forgiveness** cancels and removes **All Guilt, Curses, Debts, Violations and Penalties** toward the soul that may be guilty in the eyes of Yahweh *(Jehovah)* to be condemned to eternal separation from the Lord GOD. Forgiving cancels the charge against an individual and remembers that offense no longer from the heart of a true worshiper *(does not keep it fresh to bring up)*. That shame, act of guilt, stemming from the heart is erased. The only person that can continue to bring it up is the individual that chooses to return back to their vomit and rehearse it or refuses not to **Let Go** the offense done to them or others used by the devil to nail them repeatedly to the cross concerning their past. There is no past in forgiven. Selah! Forgiving rooted in agape is a healer to the spirit which brings healthiness and harmony to the body and to relationships far or near. The **Power of Forgiveness** reconciles family members, friends, people back together, unify and removes hatred out of the heart and reverses the curse. Forgiving removes the hostility between mankind and the LORD, turning one's heart back to Yahweh through the Blood of Yeshua by the work of the Holy Spirit. Yahweh requires His chosen children to exercise-walk in forgiveness which shows the fruitful evidence of His divine love living in their heart followed through with obedience. Just as the **Power of Forgiveness** removes the hostility barrier between GOD and us; is the same grace virtue works for us when we truly forgive our enemies or those that have wronged us ungratefully. The LORD knows it cannot be done without His **Power-Grace** working effectively in the heart of those who will lean on Him for this favor to become a manifested reality within the heart, mind and soul. The Will of the

LORD concerns our total being. Just as GOD the Father, GOD the Son and GOD the Holy Spirit are one; we are tripartite after the Creator…spirit, soul and body, but one.

3 John 1:2

Beloved, I wish above all things that thou may prosper and be in health and that all may go well with you even as your soul is healthy.

Talking about forgiveness and **living** in the active **Power of Forgiveness** are two different radar frequencies. Anyone can say they have forgiven *(released)* there offender. But is there any fruitfulness proof of this saying? As the saying goes talk is cheap it has no value, but action speaks much louder than mere talk. What are your actions when you're in the presence of the person being held guilty? What is the thought while in the same room, breathing the same air or conversing as if there is no harm from the past at heart? Are there any sarcastic remarks, heart palpitations, irregular heart beats, teary eyes, rolling or batting eyes, lack of eye or face contact, purposely over talking the other, short words, short breaths or deep breathing or sharp tones? These are a few signs of the residue of what is really underneath the surface in the heart that is lingering and if it is not dealt with the devil will assign demonic spirits to this swinging spiritual door for increase tension, mind imprisonment and destruction that will intertwine unclean spirits to that open soul that is swinging on loose hinges. Kill the seed. However, it rolls out, know that satan doesn't play for fairness or justice on his playground, his motto is to insult, lay blame on and destroy at whatever cost. The adversary will steal it and kill it. That cost may possibly be stealing your peace, marriage, understanding, sisters-brothers-parents relationships, church members trust, home matters, self esteem theft, identity theft, sex issues, health, insecurity, income or job related matters. Whatever has been promised in the WORD of GOD to you the devil wants to steal it. He is a thief, accuser of the brethren and a counterfeiter; he wants his own family.

Love and the Power of Forgiveness works unified to promote the Kingdom of Yahweh in the earth as one body and one spirit and one thought. You cannot truly love your enemy without forgiving him or you cannot forgive your enemies without truly loving them at the same time. It comes from God. It is in possible because Jesus life, talk and walk demonstrated the love of ABBA for wrenched mankind, yet despising the shame and endured the ransom through the Cross; the sacrifice to rectify the Power Source connection between man and GOD through forgiving sins. **The Bible tells us {John 13:35} by this all men shall know that you are the Lord's disciples that you have love *(unconditional kingdom)* toward one another.** What greater love has no man than Yeshua HaMashiach, to lay down His life for His friends {John 15:13}. The **Power of Forgiveness** is a judicial law inseparable of Jehovah's unconditional love. Forgiving is a never ending process in the life of a true Christian who fears of the LORD and dwells in the secret place of the Most High. Yes, it takes all of God working within the heart for the manifestation of this act of mercy to be practical. When we are walking in forgiveness it shows obedience and submission to GOD; dying of the flesh and the love of GOD in the heart of those that fear Him *(Fear of the LORD)*. This power and love does not come from the carnal heart, but out of a genuine heart that is being melted by the Fire of GOD Spirit and live a life of developing godly characteristics through the Spirit of GOD in obedience.

Living with an unforgiving heart condition is a curse not a blessing. Curses are like a swinging door. This demonic spirit closes and opens doors to other demonic influence and will block and blind those walking in an unforgiving spirit from Truth and from the Kingdom of GOD. Unforgiving hearts tie the Hand of GOD from releasing blessings of complete healing; obedience rewards blessings and disobedience reward a curse **{Deuteronomy 11:26-28}.** A curse injures and brings harm to the soul, mind, heart, body, destiny and attempt to do harm to others. Remember, it generates from an unholy seed. People can have all types of forms of godliness yet denying the power that sanctifies them to walk in the holiness of the Truth of GOD. Knowing intellectually *(head-strong knowledge, another source)*, which is a spirit of gnosticism, this puts a portion of *church folk* in danger of the wrath of the LORD. **The Bible tells us {2 Timothy 3:15} they will act religion, but they will reject the power that could make them godly. Avoid such people.** The LORD is requiring a heart knowledge experience which displays a fruitful action in thought and behavior out of a legitimate-pure heart. He wants a covenant *(inseparable- binding)* spiritual espousal. He is the circumcision of the heart. All that does not apply to the believer must be dealt with on this side before judgment day by the cutting away of all that opposes the *Blood of the Lamb of GOD*. The Word of the LORD is like a two–edged sword with a dual function that permeates the soul, marrow, joints and is a discerner of the attitudes of the heart and spirit of man **{Hebrew 4:12}**. Many blessings of healing, unity, deliverance and reconciliation are held up through captivity of minds and hearts that are in bondage to a demonic or stronghold which has set up a fortress causing cancer-like growth in their heart which will not allow them to freely forgive, even when they try in their own strength. This strongman conducts itself just like the cancer cell; spreading to gain territory and dominance. Our natural strength is no match for demonic activity. GOD adds His supernatural to your submission along with faith to make the spiritual transaction valid.

Greek word for the English term Offense
Skandalon: to trap, trip up, stumbling
block, strike against, to do harm to

Offense is a strongman. This demonic spirit is a gate-keeper, controlling what will enter or exit in the soul in favor of the deep hurt, revenge and retaliation. And when we go through suffering, we can become offensive and defensive and reckless. This strongman will bow guard the forgiving of baby mama or daddy drama, what the boss or co-worker on the job said, did or didn't do, death's of love ones, losing babies to premature deaths or syndromes, divorce matters, sibling rivalry, how mom or dad may have ill-treated you and or maybe mom or dad wasn't there in your childhood age so in return what they done is a repeated parenting cycle, when the spouse lied or cheated or spouse spent the bill money or when the pastor didn't return your important telephone call and the biggest one of all mad at the Lord for not prevented certain things from happening in or around your life. These are some dramatic issues which open doors for offense to come in and set up camp, planting the unfruitful seed of unforgiveness along with other demonic spirits in the heart causes a heart to be filled with tumors of darken, evil, ruthless, faintness, unkind, uncompassionate, revengeful and hardness; all detestable in the sight of the LORD toward others. These are some acts of the flesh acting out when holding a charge in the heart against another who has offended them whether intentionally or unintentionally: division, strife, resentment, grudges, spite, harassment, quarries, rage, hatred, cold love, false love, animosity, ruling and domineering. The seed of offense is sown before the very act is committed. When the seed is exposed or identified the root can be destroyed by the Word of God.

BUT THE DEVIL AND HIS CHILDREN ARE ALL LIARS AND DEFEATED BY CHRIST JESUS…DISARMING THEM IN HELL AND TAKING THE KEYS AWAY FROM SATAN OVER THE SAINTS {Colossians 2:15}.

The adversary is a trickster, he dictates through the thoughts of people to form allegations of lies. That's the bait he dangles in the mind behind his hook. The devil will make you think he has keys, but his authority doesn't have NO dominion over the blood bought born again believers. When you know who you are and that you belong to King Jesus you will be a threat to the kingdom of darkness. If any type of offense has crept up into your heart to take you into captivity or have you captive, according to the written Logos; the Eternal Word, Yeshua, Has Commanded That Devil *(evil force)* To Be Gone. Acknowledge! Renounce It! Repent! And Be Healed In JESUS Name by Faith!

James 1:13-16

Let no one say when he is tempted, I am being tempted by God [for temptation does not originate from God, but from our own flaws]; for God cannot be tempted by [what is] evil, and He Himself tempts no one. But each one is tempted when he is dragged away, enticed and baited [to commit sin] by his own [worldly] desire (lust, passion). Then when the illicit desire has conceived, it gives birth to sin; and when sin has run its course, it gives birth to death.

Hebrew word for the English term Forgive
Salach: to pardon (like the word "bara"
to create, authorized by God)

As you already understand the opposite of a forgiving heart is a grudging heart. Unforgiving comes through an offense which is a scandal, a diabolic set up waiting to get a grip on any available soul. Because Yahweh is holy and just, nothing profane can stand expecting grace without humbly receiving His **Power of Forgiveness** to restore the spiritual state according to the His governing law. He is the one who has been offended by the stench of sin. He never said it would be easy, but said His grace is sufficient. Who are we not to release others and not let go the bitterness caused by pain. After all, we cannot heal ourselves, deliver or make ourselves righteous or create the next breath to inhale or exhale. When one offends another they are also offending Yahweh who sent Christ to be the propitiation for all souls. **The Bible tells us as believers {Matthew 7:12} so in everything do unto others what you would have them do to you,** not what they are doing or did to you or what they deserve. That would be an evil act called retaliation, but by the Power of Ruach

Hakodesh treat them as you would have them to treat you regardless of there actions toward you. GOD will repay; don't sit in the seat as judge. This will call for seeking the wisdom of the LORD wholeheartedly. This act will destroy you without the protection and wisdom of GOD demonstrating His strength through a soul. This is a divine KINGDOM work to be mastered in living by the guidance of Holy Spirit. This act takes the **Power of Forgiveness** residing in you with no restraints; but discipline. Many tears may be shed to get to this point, but your arrival will be a portion of the reward and victory crown. Say yes Lord; give me more of you in JESUS Powerful Name. Remember, it is a Supernatural influence on top of your natural which means your flesh and mind with its inclinations must bow-down in submission to the LORD God Almighty who ***"Declares Vengeance Is Mine, I Will Repay"{Deuteronomy 32:35; Romans 12:19}***. JESUS *(Elohim-Godhead)* the creator is willing to create freshness in the heart of the sinner, backslider and the believer ***creating*** *(Hebraic **Bara:** to create, make by YHWH)* a new heart and a genuine spirit. This is priceless and far above rubies.

When I lost Isaac my bitterness caused me to be offended, mad at GOD. Yes, I was mad at the pastor and others indirectly. That's how the spirit of deception works when you don't know what it looks like. When my father was murdered ten plus years later the instruction from Holy Spirit was to forgive quickly. This was received through tears and heartache and much praying, but I obeyed and received the Supernatural release in my spirit. When all manner of evil is spoken directly or indirectly against me, evil plots, schemes and conspiracies working for the destruction of my marriage; in tears I sowed, yet I forgave in heart and deed and in prayer I receive Kingdom strategy and comfort and victory. **The Bible tells us {Psalms 56:8} God collects and records the tears of your sorrows.** It is Holy Spirit at work on behalf of the yielded heart. Getting angry, sarcastic or giving a piece of your mind will add coals to the fire and expand your situation further than you anticipated. The way of the LORD will always make the devil that works through people shut up and bow-down to His Spoken Word of Authority through a faithful child of GOD. What that means is the faithful will win. When I had to face the one who supposed to have been a best-friend during my early young adulthood; yet was sleeping with my boyfriend, I had to forgive in order to move on and not hold or carry that offense in my heart against men. **I Said Move On!** Some of You Who Are Reading This Must Let Go of The Mess In Order To Move On To Partake of Better. **Your Past Don't Hold Your Future It Suffocates and Kills It**: God Knows What You Need. Receive the prophetic utterances of the Lord. **Closure** will close doors to mental distress, anguish, chronic body pains and lies and bring long term emotional and spiritual healing to the life of a soul.

I took heed in prayer early in life how to **LET IT GO-** forgive and I am still learning because the enemy will increase his plots tension as GOD increase Himself in you called the anointing weight of graces; as you die to the carnal mindset *(old nature)* and live in the Spirit *(new nature)*. You have the upper hand of divine knowledge, divine power and divine wisdom that will outwit the evil schemes right in the enemies' face. Don't fulfill the deeds of the flesh, brethren in Christ; we have to walk it out in the Spirit, yielding to the leading of Holy Spirit. Walking it out in the Spirit in simple terms is responding as Christ would to our situations; when you fall go back to the altar. This is the act of taking up your cross and following Jesus at all cost. It is worth it because you are on the winning side that never loses a battle. Remember, it will be a process, but not over night. However, get involved in the process that is processing you to become new wine skin fit for New Wine. Glory! Glory Hallelujah to the King! **There Is Nothing To Hard For Yahweh GOD, NOTHING!** My experiences led me *(and should lead you)* into seeking the Lord and through seeking *(a form of worship)* He revealed His nature as Jehovah *(LORD)* Raphe. *I Am Healer. I Am That Heals* wounds, emotions, hearts, thoughts and tame the tongue. I Am Jehovah Shalom: *I Am He That Gives You Peace* in the midst or when all hell rises around you. I learned self deliverance, purging, at home not in the church deliverance service, but deliverance can take place at church. If hell *(darkness)* is in you that demonic presence got to go in Jesus Name. Many hearts are in that condition due to blockage of an unforgiving hard heart. You have to come correct in the spirit by the Spirit. GOD is not blindsided, he sees your spirit and the faintness in your minds. When a soul hold offenses, the root of bitterness, can travel with you to your next destination holding you captive, crippling and poisoning innocent relationships. The devil is like a smooth gigolo that evil seed can pass to your children and your children seed…a cycle. *LET IT GO IN JESUS NAME! I COMMAND THAT DIABOLIC PRESENCE TO LEAVE*

YOU NOW IN JESUS NAME! Come in agreement with your heavenly King. Open your mouth and cough deeply three times, sincere hearts are being delivered by the Spirit of GOD through their trust and obedience. Repent! Open your mouth and cough deeply three times. One in the name of the Father, One in the name of the Son and One in the name of the Holy Spirit. Be Made Whole In Jesus Name. Amen.

There is a lot Holy Spirit will reveal and teach you if you take the time to get before Him, in the Lord's Presence and pour out of your soul. He sees the bleeding and wants to stop the issue of blood from flowing. Bless the Lord for All of His benefits toward the born again blood redeem believer in Christ Jesus. Hallelujah! May The LORD heal all of your internal bleeding that you may walk in soundness of mind, health and wholeness. Any type of spiritual blockage due to open wounds will cause spiritual bleeding from within. Spiritual bleeding is when there have been pressures in the past that the soul has not been healed or restored in those areas that go unseen by the naked eye, because it is a spiritual matter of the heart. And because the spiritual matter is not spiritually discerned, it will increase or lie dormant until another crisis appears and then it intensifies. And instead of healing, break outs or plaques, as the scripture call them, may develop in the body. Majority of the time, a person believe it to be a health related issue only, but the revelation Holy Spirit shared is that most of it is due to spiritual matters of the heart. Offenses deep roots are like death cells to the human body that have been packed down, sweep to the side and not handled by the counsel of Holy Spirit.

The Devil Is A Liar! HOLY SPIRIT HAS EXPOSED THE WORKS OF THE EVIL ONE. REPENT NOW!

Prophesy Life Confessions of the Word Over Your Health, Your Being In Yeshua's Name.

Psalm 51: 1-8

Have mercy upon me, O God, According to Your lovingkindness; According to the multitude of your tender mercies, Blot out my transgressions. Wash me thoroughly from my iniquity, and cleanse me from my sin. For I acknowledge my transgressions, and my sin is always before me. Against You, You only, have I sinned, and done this evil in Your sight—That you may be found just when you speak, and blameless when You judge. Behold, I was brought forth in iniquity, and in sin my mother conceived me. Behold, you desire truth in the inward hidden parts, and in the hidden part you will make me to know wisdom. Purge me with hyssop, and I shall be clean; Wash me, and I shall be whiter than snow. Make me hear joy and gladness, that the bones you have broken may rejoice.

Colossians 2:11-14

In him also you were circumcised with a circumcision made without hands, by putting off the body of the flesh, by the circumcision of Christ, having been buried with him in baptism, in which you were also raised with him through faith in the powerful working of God, who raised him from the dead. And you, who were dead in your trespasses and the uncircumcision of your flesh, God made alive together with him, having forgiven us all our trespasses, by canceling the record of debt that stood against us with its legal demands. This he set aside, nailing it to the cross.

Matthew 6:12, 14-15

Forgive us our debts as we forgive our debtors. And lead us not into temptation, but deliver us from the evil one. For if you forgive men when they sin against you, your heavenly Father will also forgive you. But if you do not forgive others of their sins, your Father will not forgive your sins.

Just as forgiveness is fruitful, unforgiving is unfruitful. One fruit is sweet and can speak life toward others and the other fruit is wicked with bitterness springing forth from the core. **The Bible tells us {Galatians 6:7} do not be deceived GOD is not mocked, we all reap what we sow.** If good or bad seeds are sown, you will get a return on what was planted. GOD is Just. He looks at the heart of man and judges according to your deeds which are driven by the motives of the heart. **The Bible tells us {Luke 6:45} out of the abundance of the treasures of the heart, the mouth speaks and {Proverbs 23:7} tells us for as a man (mankind) think in his heart, so is he.** The LORD is the righteous judge. He judges all according to His divine justice. I encourage you to examine and search your heart and measure it not by the offense, pain and hurt, but by the Spoken WORD. The WORD is a mirror to our soul. Jesus shows us our character flaws and shows us the cleansing power of His grace code if you're willing and ready to **"Let It Go"** in word and deed. Of course, time is a healer. However, the Truth which sets you free is your key into the healing dimension at the moment you truly **"Let It Go."** Forgiveness opens the door. This is a serious phrase in a person's life, making the step forward to resist the lies that take the soul into bondage and hostility. Satan doesn't want no-one free. He will keep sending issues that will flare up offenses. As offenses come they will pile and pile and pile up until you can't see clearly or make sound judgment. Yeshua is the liberator of the spirit with power to sever all chains of bondage on the mind.

The **Law of the Kingdom of GOD** unwraps itself in the revelation of the Messiah leaving his Royal Kingdom to clothe Himself in human flesh for the purpose of pouring His royal blood out as an drink offering to bring sinful, wicked, undeserving humanity before the Holy Father by way of peace, reconciliation and the power of forgiveness all through His life, blood, death, resurrection and glorification. Forgiveness made possible through the ransom of GOD the Son becoming flesh, in the likeness of human; yet, GOD. That was a personal selfless act of unconditional love, think about that. Before the Bible was written, before the worlds were framed and before life existed on earth, Elohim *(plural form of EL)*, yet He Is Only ONE GOD, knew that He would have to come down to provide salvation for rebellious mankind.

⟵⟶

Psalm 40:6-8

Sacrifice and offering thou dost not desire; but thou has given me an open ear. Burnt offering and sin offering thou has not required. Then I said, Lo I come; in the roll of the book It Is Written of Me. I delight to do thy will, O my GOD; thy law is within my heart.

⟵⟶

When Yahweh made covenant with man in Genesis instituted from the beginning of time the pardon of mankind for the peace offering of Himself with his creation. Elohim *(title revealing his multifaceted nature in Strength, Power and Justice)* demonstrated the power to forgive when He said, Let Us Make Man In Our Image, creating Adam on the outside of the garden, then placing him in the Garden of Eden. No man had rebelled according to the scripture at that appointed time, but GOD who is omniscience *(all knowing)* already knew they would because they were created freewill beings with a choice in the Garden of Eden; a choice. God Election of Righteousness was predestined before anything was revealed or written under the inspiration of Ruach Hakodesh. He knew the willful, disobedience, perverted deeds that would corrode the heart, mind and soul and mar the image of mankind through the deception of the accuser of the brethren that took place after Lucifer's dethronement along with one third of the angels. But in the Lord's capacity of love and mercy beyond guilt and shame, He moved forward not backwards into His provision plan of the next phrase that was to be put into action which prophetically points to Yeshua. Whenever and whatever Yahweh Elohim thought, He spoke and that thought which was spoken became evident. What He spoke became visible to the eye. The image of His thought became material, substance or flesh. All through the Old Testament we see the people of GOD errant in their own way, but what overrides that is the escape He provided; because of mercy; because of the love for His chosen who would *turn back* to Him from their adulterous and idolatrous ways to their first love and act upon the Provision through obedience. Yahweh's provision through Moses was to inaugurate the Leviticus Priesthood for an atoning sacrifice of unblemished sacrificial animals of Yahweh's choosing for the covering of the people of Israel sins. The breaking of law is **offensive** to Yahweh. Therefore, blood had to be shed for the remission of sins, the offenses of man toward GOD {**Hebrew 9:22**}. Thank Yahweh for Yeshua who drank the Cup of Suffering and the Cup of Blessing, the provision "To See" of a better covenant {**Hebrew 8:6**}; being the guilt offering, the *ULTIMATE PERFECT SACRIFICE* for the multitudes of *SINNERS* that are coming to Him in this Age of Grace to lay their burdens upon Him, trading places by way of that Bloody Cross in **exchange** for Forgiveness, Peace, Grace, Mercy and Everlasting Eternal Life by remaining in faith and by faith… Spiritual DNA.

Psalm 85:10

Steadfast love and truth meet; righteousness and peace kiss each other.

Adonai Tov v' Salach (The Lord is good and forgiving)

Psalm 86:5

For thou, Lord, art good, and ready to forgive; and plenteous in mercy unto all them that call upon thee.

Yahweh God will not force any soul into forgiving another. He is not an overbearing, domineering forceful God. GOD is forgiving, gracious, longsuffering, compassionate and merciful giving grace to hearts that will receive what He alone is capable only of doing above human efforts. He wants the heart, soul and mind of the human race to submit willfully to His **Power of Forgiveness**, allowing His Glory to permeate the soul reflecting light. This Supernatural principle calls for the **Supernatural Power of GOD** to be infused in the spirit and mind of man as they surrender their will to Him. A person has to desire what GOD has to offer. Now the laws of the Kingdom of Light cannot be accredited to the natural strength of mere man. **That Bibles tells us {John 3:6} that which is born (birth) of flesh is flesh and that which is born (birth) of Spirit is Spirit.** The flesh cannot produce the life or power which is to be produced by the Spirit into man's heart- spirit. Therefore, we see the **Power to forgive** is birthed by Holy Spirit into the spirit- heart of man who receives in faith. Forgiveness starts with Yahweh and will end with Yahweh and it is extended to souls for peace in Christ and to reflect ABBA the Father. But mankind will have to choose to receive this powerful treasure in order to be forgiven, because without this powerful Supernatural treasure man will not be forgiven of transgressions and iniquities and will remain enemies to GOD by freewill...choice.

The Ruach Hakodesh *(Holy Spirit)* who is the life giving Spirit breathes into man's soul infusing the nature of the Father in seed form. The seed of righteousness has to grow, develop by being cultivated, watered and nourished by the WORD of GOD, faith and obedience watered in love. The seed contains all that pertains to GOD righteousness in full measure. However, the seed grows in measure within the soul of man. The Spirit of Christ now lives in the heart of believers. Now the struggle between Spirit and flesh or the carnal mind is at war with one another within the soul. You have been declared a new creation in Christ, the old way of thinking, old way of living, old way of loving, old way of talking, old way of doing and all old ways have been erased from your spiritual account before Yahweh in Christ. If you feed your new nature it will abound and conquer, if you feed your old nature it will abound and conquer; whichever you feed the most will overturn the other at will. Remember, the WORD which is Spirit wants to take on form to empower you to overcome those ways that will return to defeat and sow weeds around the WORD which is planted to choke it out. The wicked seed sown will choke out the WORD of Life to render it dormant, causing it to become non effective within your spirit. Many have the WORD, but it has become as a stillborn baby and that is what the devil wants. Remember, satan's motive is the same: to kill, to steal and to destroy. The devil, the accuser of the brethren, wants the WORD of Life to be dead within you and accuse believers of being a fraud before Yahweh.

When you prohibit the WORD from working through you, you become powerless to overcome the residue left behind from unresolved conflicts or unhealed pain. When you are not walking in alignment with what the WORD says then the residue of issues will fester and grow. Bush fires that linger will grow and get out of control. The residue will sow unseen seeds such as deep hurt, bitterness, frustration, rejection, dissension, anxiety, critical and twisting the words of others. Cut the head off of that giant that taunts you in the Name of Jesus. When **forgiveness** is activated the other problems will heal and over time vanished. No record of wrong to be established or kept in any secret chambers of the heart, only the testimony of what the LORD has done. Just has the angelic being touched Isaiah mouth with a hot coal symbolizing the Power of the Fire of Ruach Hakodesh to touch the inward or hidden parts of our spirit refining our soul as pure gold is refined for the purpose of bringing forth a continual shining light as virgin oil that never loses it's anointing fragrance to shine even brighter in dark places, dry places, heated places and in seasons that appear to be threatening.

⌒

Isaiah 6: 5-7

Woe is me, for I am undone. Because I am a man of unclean lips, and I dwell in the midst of a people of unclean lips; For my eyes have seen the King, the LORD of hosts. Then one of the seraphim flew to me, having in his hand a live coal he had taken with the tongs from the altar and he touched my mouth with it and said, behold this has touched your lips and your iniquity is taken away and your sin is forgiven, purged.

1 Corinthians 10:3-4

…and all ate the same spiritual food, and all drank from the spiritual Rock that followed them, and the Rock was Christ.

⌒

BELOVED OF GOD YOUR KEY TO YOUR SUCCESS AND YOUR VICTORY IS THROUGH THE POWER OF FORGIVING OTHERS CONTINUALLY AND FORGIVING YOURSELF!

GOD is greater and bigger than the pain or the problem. There Is Greatness In You! The option is not to give up or give in, but surrender, humble self, persevere, endure, grow in faith and learn for effectiveness by the teaching of Holy Spirit how to war properly in battle with spiritual arsenal weapons of faith.

** DELIVERANCE IS THE CHILDREN'S BREAD

PRAYER OF FAITH

Heavenly Father, in the Name that is above every name, Jesus Christ, I come before your Throne of Grace and Mercy asking you to cleanse all defilement that you see in my heart. I confess I have been walking in

_____, _____,

_____, _____,

_____ doubt, dead faith, hesitation, dishonesty, jealousy, low self-esteem, bitterness, unforgiveness, faultfinding, procrastination, manipulation, deceit, idleness, prayerlessness and compromise; I repent right now whole heartily. I ask for your forgiveness in Jesus Name. Lord I pray for strength in my relationship with you and with others. I pray that you teach me all things pertaining to godliness in this life. Heavenly Father, I seek your face, infuse me with divine humility, wisdom, knowledge, counsel, love on the inward parts and the Spirit of discernment which give power to me to make sound judgment. Fill me Lord with your Holy Spirit, increase my faith and help me to overcome my trials and tribulations, as you produce divine fruitfulness in my life, I die daily to my will. Reveal to me your divine purpose for my life hidden in you. Lord I humble myself under your hand, because I am powerless in my own strength to combat this. I trust that you will exalt and establish me in due season in the Name of Jesus Christ. Increase endurance as I go through. Sanctify my heart, eyes, ears, tongue, attitude, behavior, response, countenance, lifestyle and condition and empower me Lord to handle what may come. Restore my family, finances, job, health, children, mind, and prayer life, making me sober in your Word. I am determined to live the abundant life. I thank you Heavenly Father in Jesus Name.

Amen.

** DELIVERANCE IS THE CHILDREN'S BREAD

FAITH DECLARATION… LET'S WAR BY PROMISE

I COMMAND THE BLOCKAGE OF UNFORGIVENESS TO LOOSE ITS GRIP ON ME NOW IN JESUS NAME, BY THE AUTHORITY AND POWER OF THE RUACH HA KODESH I COMMAND EVERY ASSAULTING TORMENTING SPIRIT TO BE GONE IN JESUS NAME.

OPEN YOUR MOUTH AND DECLARE OUT LOUD…

I DENOUNCE ALL UNCLEAN SPIRITS OF RELENTLESS ACTS, RACISM, ISOLATION, BITTERNESS, ANGER, RAGE, COLDHEARTEDNESS, MEAN SPIRIT AND GRUDGES BE GONE FROM MY DWELLING IN THE NAME OF JESUS CHRIST. I DECREE THE CORDS BE SEVERED IN JESUS NAME. I COMMAND DOORS TO BE CLOSED THAT ARE RELATED TO KEEPING MY PASS ATTACHED TO ME. I TURN MY BACK TO MY PASS AND I CHOOSE LIFE AND I WILL LIVE AND NOT DIE PREMATURALLY IN THE NAME OF JESUS CHRIST. I PLEAD THE BLOOD OF JESUS OVER THE DWELLING OF MY HOME, MY BODY, MY IMAGINATION, MY TONGUE, MY DREAMS AND MY SPIRIT IN JESUS NAME AND I RECEIVE MY DELIVERANCE NOW BY FAITH IN JESUS NAME. I COMMAND MY BODY AND SPIRIT TO RESPOND TO THE WORD OF GOD. I COMMAND PAINS, TUMORS, AND ABNORMAL GROWTH TO SEIZE IN THE NAME OF JESUS CHRIST. I AM HEALED! MY MIND IS HEALED, RESTORED, I AM WHOLE AND I AM HEALTHY. I RECEIVE BY FAITH WHAT THE WORD PROMISES ME…NO WEAPON FORMED AGAINST ME SHALL PROSPER AND YOU LORD WILL SILENCE EVERY TONGUE OR VOICE AGAINST YOU IN JUDGMENT.

I DECLARE BY THE POWER AND AUTHORITY OF HOLY SPIRIT IN JESUS NAME THAT THESE CHAINS BE BROKEN OFF MY MIND. I COMMAND UNFRUITFUL SEEDS AND ROOTS TO DRY UP AND DIE; I COMMAND EVERY IDLE WORD SPOKEN TO ME OR BY ME FALL TO THE GROUND AND DIE; EVERY DIABOLIC YOKE OF THE DEVIL BE DESTROYED ON MY BEHALF IN THE NAME OF JESUS. I FORBID THE SPIRIT OF OFFENSE, UNFORGIVENESS, RESENTMENT, RETALIATION, GET BACK DEMONS TO HARASS ME ANY LONGER. I FORBID THEM AND COMMAND THEM WITH THERE RESIDUE TO GO IN JESUS NAME. I SPEAK TO EVERY DEEP HURT, ILLSPOKEN WORDS OF HURT, LINGERING PAINS, I COMMAND THEM TO LEAVE IN JESUS NAME; IN JESUS NAME.

I COMMAND EVERY UNGODLY SOUL TIE TO LOOSE ME IN JESUS NAME. I DECREE THE POWER OF FORGIVENESS TO OVERTAKE MY SPIRIT, THOUGHTS AND IMAGINATION NOW IN JESUS NAME. I SPEAK HEALING TO MY SPIRIT AND COMMAND MY SPIRIT MAN TO RISE IN JESUS NAME. I COMMAND MY THOUGHTS, HEART, BEHAVIOR AND SPEECH TO COME INTO ALIGNMENT WITH THE WORD OF GOD BY FAITH FOLLOWED BY OBEDIENCE AND LOVE IN JESUS NAME. I AM SOUND; SPIRIT, SOUL AND BODY.

Received by faith today and walk in the POWER of forgiveness.

AMEN.

Write the Scripture and Memorize Its Promise & Conditions:

1. The LORD tells us that if we are faithful and obedient… (complete the verse)

   _____

   _____

   _____

2. The children of the LORD are commanded to confess their _____.

3. What scripture of verse gives instructions for the unforgiving soul before bringing an offering to be accepted unto the Lord? Explain.

   _____

   _____

   _____

4. What has Holy Spirit revealed to you in your heart that is offensive to him?

   _____

   _____

   _____

5. If those you listed above offend Him, then what offenses in your heart has Holy Spirit revealed to you toward others that are to be actively forgiven?

   _____

_____

_____

6. What is the Greek word and meaning for the terms offense and forgive?

_____

_____

_____

7. How do you know when you are walking in forgiveness whole heartily and by the Power of Holy Spirit? What are the outward fruits?

_____

_____

_____

8. Forgiving releases who? _____.

a) How and Why?

_____

_____

_____

NOTES:

CONCLUSION

I pray that your heart is revived and illuminated through the Power of Holy Spirit's prophetic voice, revelation, knowledge, counsel and wisdom of the LORD God release through impartation for the advancement of the Rule of Christ in the sphere of your soul. This is the mystery of the Kingdom that Ruach Hakodesh has revealed unto me to impart for activation into your inner man; with great joy I digest it personally as well for excellence, increase, overflow and perfection in Christ going forward. The Lord is our eternal salvation; therefore, be still and know that He Reign with Dominion, Power, Justice and Authority Now and Forever More. The believer's victory was completed at the Cross. You are not dying; you are rising, walking as an heir of the throne of Yahweh in Yeshua. Arise out of the pit with your Sword... Declare the Promises of the Lord and Take Back What the Enemy Has Stolen. PUSH with the strength, instructions and direction of Ruach Hakodesh until Breakthrough manifest! Take it by Supernatural Holy Ghost force! Matthew 11:12 declares from the days of John the Baptist until now the kingdom of heaven suffers violence, and the violent take it by force. Ecclesia, we war from the Place of no defeat; from the Place of Victory in Yeshua HaMashiach. The Blood of Jesus has already given the Church Legal Right to Act by Faith which transcends the natural laws of time. Declare Faith Increase and the Anointing to fill you, rest in and upon you continuously. Weather the storms with the governing power and authority of the WORD and watch the Promises of Yahweh manifest!

ABOUT THE AUTHOR

Delmelodia Tipton is an author, intercessor, woman of God and the wife of David Tipton. They reside in Desoto County Mississippi...have two beautiful, lovely daughters who where born after Isaac DeShaun Tipton. Delmelodia Tipton accepted the higher calling of Yahweh on her life in 2004 under the leadership of Apostle Larry and Iliana Pratcher. Preaching the gospel was never a desire for her or even in her plans, but something happened to and within her that ignited a fire from the Supernatural Power of God. She has always loved God, but in Him loving her unconditionally He ordained an encounter to take place which took her on a journey for transforming her mind, thoughts, life, path and living. The encounter was established for the purpose of ordaining her for the mantle that was already upon her life before she was formed in her mother's womb. She believes that many believers who suffer during any type of crisis can experience the opportunity of a Supernatural encounter with the LORD which will be an awakening of the soul and life changing when one truly activates their trust in the LORD, wait upon the LORD and seek the LORD in trying moments that seem to be hopeless. When she thought her life was ending from the overbearing pressure of pain, bitterness and sadness along with suicidal thoughts, it was really in that dark place that Holy Spirit revealed to her later that the place was an altar for the dying of self in order to receive healing, restoration, a spiritual awaking and even double for the trouble. God has revealed to her over time through his revelation in portions of what is meant in becoming an offering and a living sacrifice unto the LORD in which she will give more insight concerning believers in the book. Seven years prior to humbling herself to the high calling, she had a meeting with Pastor Joyce S. Ray (deceased) months after the burial of her and her husband's first born baby, Isaac DeShaun Tipton. In the meeting she disclosed vividvis ions and revelation to Pastor Joyce Ray concerning what she heard in the spirit realm at the hospital after baby Isaac had passed. She disclosed detailed information only to Pastor Joyce Ray because she thought she was going out of her natural born mind. She was hearing and responding to what others in the room did not hear as baby Isaac body lay there still warm and blush in tone after his spirit had left his body. She also thought Pastor Ray would give her answers that would release her yoke of strain concerning the loss of baby Isaac; however the Lord did not release the answers for the Pastor to give. Yet, the Pastor's undivided attention was given as she listened attentively. The Pastor's immediate response to her was, "Have you missed the calling of GOD?" At that questioned she had no response yet quiet and emotionally upset. It was approximately six years later that Delmelodia Tipton willingly and humbly accepted the calling and mantle upon her life in 2004 after visual and verbal signs God sent directly to her during those six years. God put her in a place where the no response would not be an option for all the things He had done and how He had proven himself faithful to her during her distresses. Delmelodia Tipton has been actively engaged and serving faithfully in local outreach ministry and in the marketplace. Some of the mission ministries entailed teaching and training work in the mission field, street witnessing to the homeless, preaching in homeless shelters, feeding the homeless, preaching in the women's prison and preaching in the nursing home for several years. When that season of training was over the Lord gave her direct instructions for the foundation of the youth ministry (Warriors In Christ Youth Ministry). She directed the youth ministry with other leaders laboring for six years. While ministering in that capacity she established and trained the Unity of Praised Dance Ministry for three years. After time had passed, GOD released her from those ministries which also equipped her for future Kingdom purposes. Holy Spirit gave a Rhema Word in May 2011, during her prayer and worship time to start teaching on the airways, released in May 2013; she's the host and founder of AMBASSADORS 4CHRIST APOSTOLIC BROADCAST MINISTRY. Delmelodia Tipton has been engaged faithfully in Kingdom work with her hands to the plow spreading the gospel of Jesus Christ as GOD manifest provision for each assignment.

"To God Be All the Glory, All the
Honor and All the Praise"

Printed in the United States
By Bookmasters